staatskapelle berlin

*discography
1916-1962*

*compiled by
john hunt*

Staatskapelle Berlin

The shellac era 1916-1962

John Hunt

© John Hunt 2013

ISBN 978-1-901395-28-0

Travis & Emery Music Bookshop
17 Cecil Court
London
WC2N 4EZ
United Kingdom.
Tel. (+44) (0) 20 7240 2129.
newpublications@travis-and-emery.com

Contents

Introduction/*page 6*

Summary of prefixes/numbers/*page 8*

Discography 1916-1925/*page 9*

Discography 1926-1930/*page 48*

Discography 1931-1935/*page 139*

Discography 1936-1945/*page 157*

Discography 1946-1955/*page 181*

Discography 1956-1962/*page 195*

Index of conductors/*page 205*

Late additions/*page 211*

List of subscribers/*page 218*

Staatskapelle Berlin: the shellac era and a little beyond

The orchestra takes as its foundation date the year 1570. From 1916 it made gramophone recordings for the labels Grammophon (Polydor), Electrola (HMV), Parlophone and Odeon (these two labels often sharing rescources), Columbia, Telefunken, Homochord, Vox, Clangor, Reichsrundfunk (1933-1945) and Eterna (1951 onwards).

Even aside from musical considerations, to survey the recording activities of the world's third oldest orchestral ensemble is to make a journey starting in the final years of the German Kaiser, then through two artistically very fruitful eras of Weimar Republic and Third Reich, to a new beginning from 1945 and on to the early years of the German Democratic Republic.

By 1957-1960 the shellac 78rpm disc had outlived its usefulness as a means of classical music reproduction in the home: its forty years of important achievement is therefore the subject of this survey, aiming to chronicle the recordings made by the orchestra under its various names, principally Staatskapelle Berlin but also Orchester der Hofoper, Königliche Kapelle Berlin, Kapelle der Nationaloper Berlin, Kapelle der Staatsoper, Mitglieder der Kapelle der Staatsoper, Kapelle des Staatstheaters Opernhaus, Kapelle der Reichsoper, Preussische Staatskapelle, Orchester der Deutschen Staatsoper as well as the English title Berlin State Opera Orchestra; however, it should be noted that the description Berlin State Orchestra is frequently a mistranslation for Orchester der Städtischen Oper, or Civic Opera, which is of course today's Deutsche Oper.

Not included in the discography are those recordings made by the orchestra members when they were working outside their main contracts and simply appearing anonymously: with or without such extra duties, it almost beggars belief that a full-time opera orchestra, with daily commitments in the pit, could still chalk up such an impressive discography between the wars. In this respect, however, a slightly different situation applied in the 1950s, prior to the division of Berlin by the notorious Wall: the Electrola company continued to use orchestra, choirs and ensemble members (many of whom up to 1961 had been able to reside in the western sector of the city), but it could not be seen for a western-based organisation, amid the general paranoia about Communist infiltration, to be employing the state-owned Deutsche Staatsoper forces, resulting in the frequent use of the pseudonym "Berliner Symphoniker". The arrangement petered out around 1961-1962, although another recording company, Ariola-Eurodisc, continued to use the same description for its own extensive recording programme.

Recordings were made by the acoustic method during the earliest years, but around 1926 came the breakthrough of electrical recording and a far greater fidelity as far as sound quality was concerned (although the domestic reproduction of the discs still left much to be desired). It is an irony of our digital age that re-issues on CD and other computer-related formats can now recapture far more from those original 4-minute segments than was ever possible in the performers' lifetimes.

Competition between the various recording companies, who in Berlin had at their disposal not only the Staatskapelle but also the equally eminent Philharmonisches Orchester, was fierce. We find the same popular operatic selections and orchestral pieces being repeated time and time again by favourite singers and conductors, some of these evidently able to "commute" between record companies in spite of their contracts. Orchestral conductors had at the outset remained anonymous, and most of the first names to emerge were dependable house maestri, very often of Jewish origin, such as Leo Blech, Frieder Weissmann and Hermann Weigert. With the exception of Richard Strauss, it took another decade before real podium stars like Otto Klemperer or Bruno Walter (and Wilhelm Furtwängler with his Philharmonisches Orchester) would overcome their scepticism about the mechanical reproduction of music.

The recordings are grouped into sessions chronologically as far as can be ascertained, with matrix numbers (two such numbers for the two sides of each 78rpm disc) often acting as a guide to chronology. However, this transpires not to be the case for Grammophon (Polydor), in addition to which that company's documentation was largely lost during World War II, so that all we have is a recording year and nothing more. In the listing, these are placed at the beginning of each year. Polydor's catalogue numbers, in turn, reflect the price categories into which the records were placed, rather than any logical chronology. When only one matrix number appears, there will be reference to another date when the coupling was set down: in the absence of this, it can be assumed that the other side involved an orchestra other than the Staatskapelle.

Across from the matrix numbers you will find the original German catalogue number for each disc, as well as corresponding British and American numbers wherever possible. I have held back from entering the labyrinth of LP re-issues in favour of at least one CD re-issue, where this could be ascertained. Today's collector must surely feel debts of gratitude to the CD re-issue companies, not just the majors EMI and Deutsche Grammophon but even more those like Berlin Classics, Preiser, Pearl, Music and Arts, Pristine, Naxos, Walhall, Archipel and so on, who have enterprisingly continued to promote such a significant back catalogue.

Titles of the many German, Italian and French operatic arias are given in their original language (standard English desriptions being used for works of Slavic origin), but it should be remembered that virtually all recorded selections were, right up until the 1960s, sung in German translation as standard practice.

Although most recording companies active in the German capital originally had their own purpose-built studios, advancing techniques quickly meant that the facility to record ever larger orchestral ensembles necessitated the use of bigger halls such as the Philharmonie (Beethovensaal), Singakademie, Hochschule (not to be confused with today's Hochschule für Musik), Studio Wilhelmsaue (Telefunken-Ultraphon), Hinterbühne der Staatsoper (rehearsal stage), Haus des Rundfunks, Studio Alte Jakobstrasse (Grammophon), Aufnahmeraum der Carl-Lindström-Werke (Odeon-Parlophone) and after 1945 the Zwölf-Apostel-Kirche, Evangelisches Gemeindehaus in Berlin-Zehlendorf and, ultimately, Grunewaldkirche.

The Staatskapelle's finest recorded achievements during this era of reproduction on shellac disc must surely include the sessions with Richard Strauss (1916-1933) conducting both his own works and symphonies by Mozart and Beethoven, Oskar Fried's pioneering work with Mahler's Resurrection Symphony, Berlioz Symphonie Fantastique and Strauss Alpensinfonie, the Wagner selections recorded by Karl Muck, operatic scenes and arias captured with the legendary soprano Meta Seinemeyer and the complete operas (mainly Wagner) taken down by the Reichsrundfunk during the Second War (though these were of course made on the new magnetic tape).

My principal sources of reference for the work have been the series of discographies published by the City of London Phonograph and Gramophone Society (HMV Complete "B" and "C" series and Black and Red Label 10" and 12" 78rpm recordings; Columbia Celebrity series); publications by Greenwood Press (The Orchestra on Record 1896-1926; Die Stimme seines Herrn); Walter Legge: a discography by Alan Sanders; Parsifal and Tristan und Isolde on Record, both by Jonathan Brown); Polydor Disc Records Catalogue 1926-1927; Columbia 12" Records UK 1906-1930 by Ronald Taylor; Great Wagner Conductors by Jonathan Brown 2012; Richard Strauss: a complete discography by Peter Morse; Eterna 1958 Hauptkatalog; Stimmen die um die Welt gingen (the series of singer discographies published by Günter Walter); and my own series of discographies (Teachers and pupils; Gramophone stalwarts; Singers of the Third Reich; More twentieth-century conductors).

Information, advice and stimulation also came from John Baker, Michael H. Gray, John Hancock, Klaus Heinze, Roderick Krüsemann and Neville Sumpter.

<u>John Hunt 2012</u>

Summary of the main 78rpm prefixes/numbers occurring in this discography

Electrola
12-inch (30cm) discs: prefices EH, EJ and DB
(HMV equivalents C, D and DB)
10-inch (25cm) discs: prefixes EG, EW and DA
(HMV equivalents B, E and DA)

Grammophon
Known internationally as Polydor and later as Deutsche Grammophon
12-inch (30cm) discs in the series: 15000, 19000, 27000, 35000, 57000, 65000, 66000, 67000, 68000, 69000, 73000, 85000 and 95000
10-inch (25cm) discs in the series: 10000, 12000, 20000, 25000, 30000, 47000, 48000, 62000, 70000, 80000 and 90000
It is likely that these numbered categories reflected the purchase price categories for the discs

Columbia
12-inch (30cm) discs: prefixes LWX, LX (UK), L (UK), DWX and DX (UK)
10-inch (25cm) discs: prefixes LW, LB (UK), DW and DB (UK)

Parlophone
12-inch (30cm) discs: prefixes P, E, R (UK) and RO (UK)

Odeon
12-inch (30cm) and 10-inch (25cm) discs: prefix O
Four and five digit numbers

0001/1916/grammophon sessions/**leo blech**
bizet carmen: acts 3 and 4 preludes (entr'actes)
997m   65826/69513
1045 ¾ LC
beethoven leonore no 3 overture, parts one and two
998m   65837/69536
999m
unidentified and unpublished title
1000m
1001m
meyerbeer l'africaine: marche indienne
1002m   65822/69509
1003m
wagner die meistersinger von nürnberg overture
1004m   65823/69510/electrola ES 64
1005m
wagner kaisermarsch and lohengrin procession to the minster
1006m   65827/69514
1007m
1008m   65828/69515
1042LC
johann strauss die fledermaus overture
1010m   65824/69511
1011m
wagner tannhäuser overture and lohengrin act 3 prelude
1012m   65829/69516
1039LC
1040LC   65830/69517
1041LC
beethoven die ruinen von athen overture
1043LC   65838/69537
mozart le nozze di figaro overture and deutsche tänze
1009m   65825/69512
1044LC

0002/5, 6, 13, 15 and 20 december 1916/grammophon sessions/
richard strauss
strauss der bürger als edelmann: suite from the incidental music (including prelude to the opera ariadne auf naxos)
1047LC   65853/69522
1054 ½ LC
1048 ½ LC   65854/69523
1051 ½ LC
1049LC   65855/69524
1050LC
strauss don juan
1057LC   65856/69525
1058LC
1059LC   65857/69526
1060LC
1057 and 1058 were conducted by george szell due to the late arrival of richard strauss for the session

december 1916/grammophon sessions/richard strauss/concluded
strauss till eulenspiegels lustige streiche
1061   65858/69527
1062 ½
1063   65859/69528
1064LC
strauss der rosenkavalier: waltz sequence
1065LC   65860/69529
1066LC

0003/1917/odeon session/unnamed conductor
maria ivogün, soprano
verdi la traviata: e strano…..sempre libera!
XXB 6324   O-76982-76983/O-9009
     6325
cd issues: nimbus NI 7832 and preiser 89237
according to preiser 6324 was not published:

0004/1917-1918/grammophon sessions/**leo blech**
bizet carmen: ballet music and act 4 prelude (entr'acte)
18654L   62453/68502
18655L
blech liebesstück and ländler from the opera "versiegelt"
18657L   62454/68503
18658L
offenbach les contes d'hoffmann: barcarolle and minuet
18659L   62452/68501
18660L
smetana the bartered bride overture
18889LB   62455/68504
18890LB
mozart don giovanni overture
18997LB   62458/68507
18998LB
johann strauss an der schönen blauen donau
18999LB   62459/68508
19000LB
johann strauss du und du walzer
19001LB   62457/68506
19002LB
wagner tannhäuser: entry of the guests
19144L   62456/68505
19145L

1917-1918/grammophon sessions/leo blech/concluded
beethoven symphony no 3 "eroica": second movement
19148L 68509
19149L
19150L 68510
19151L
unidentified and unpublished title
19152L
19153L
bizet l'arlesienne suite no 1
19154L 62460/68511
19155L
19156L 62461/68512
19157L
lortzing zar und zimmermann: waltz and clog dance
62462/68513

0005/1919/grammophon sessions/**leo blech**
bizet carmen preludes acts 1 & 2 and carillon from l'arlesienne
1067LC 65832/69531
1068LC
smetana the bartered bride: polka and furiant
1069LC 65840/69541
1070LC
beethoven leonore no 3 overture, parts two and three
1072LC 65838/69537
1073LC
johann strauss g'schichten aus dem wienerwald
1074LC 65831/69530
1075LC
liszt les preludes
1153m 69550
1154m
1155m 69551
1156m
blech introduction and duet from the opera "rappelkopf"
1157m 65833/69532
1158m
wagner rienzi overture and tristan liebestod
1159m 65849/69552
1160m
1161m 65850/69553
1167m
schubert-liszt marche militaire
1165m 65851/69554
1166m

1919/grammophon sessions/leo blech/concluded
verdi aida: hymn and triumphal march
1168m   65839/69539
1169m
unidentified and unpublished title
1170m
1171m
thomas mignon overture
1172m   65852/69555
1173m
smetana vltava: the moldau
1174m   65845/69546
1175m
1176m   65846/69547
schubert rosamunde overture
1177m   65847/69548
1178m
1179m   65848/69549

0006/20 march 1919/parlophone session/**eduard mörike**
wagner lohengrin act three prelude
XXB 2422   E 10107/P 1108

0007/5 may 1919/parlophone session/**eduard mörike**
wagner tannhäuser: rome narration, arranged for orchestra
XXB 2439   E 10123/P 1017
    2440
wagner der fliegende holländer overture
XXB 2441   E 10124/P 1018
    2442   E 10125/P 1019
    2443

0008/12 and 19 may 1919/parlophone sessions/**eduard mörike**
wagner tristan und isolde prelude and shepherd's lament
XXB 2444   E 10390/P 1020
    2451
    2446   E 10391/P 1021
    2448
wagner tristan und isolde liebestod
XXB 2449   E 10171
    2450
wagner der fliegende holländer: act two introduction
XXB 2453   E 10124/P 1018

0009/26 may 1919/parlophone session/**eduard mörike**
wagner die meistersinger von nürnberg overture
XXB 2468　　　　　　　　　　　　　E 10343
　　　2469
wagner die meistersinger von nürnberg act three prelude and dance of the apprentices
XXB 2470　　　　　　　　　　　　　E 10344
　　　2471
these meistersinger pieces were re-recorded by mörike and the staatskapelle on 10 january 1925
wagner parsifal prelude and good friday music
XXB 2473　　　　　　　　　　　　　E 10183/P 1029
　　　2474
　　　2475　　　　　　　　　　　　　E 10184/P 1030
　　　2476
　　　2477　　　　　　　　　　　　　E 10185/P 1031
　　　2478

0010/23 june 1919/parlophone session/**eduard mörike**
wagner die walküre: wotan's farewell and magic fire music
XXB 2479　　　　　　　　　　　　　E 10128/P 1027
　　　2481
　　　2480　　　　　　　　　　　　　E 10129/P 1028
　　　2482

0011/19 and 25 august 1919/parlophone sessions/**eduard mörike**
wagner siegfried: forest murmurs
XXB 2487　　　　　　　　　　　　　E 10158/P 1041
　　　2488
wagner das rheingold: entry of the gods into valhalla
XXB 2489　　　　　　　　　　　　　E 10110/P 1052
　　　2490
wagner götterdämmerung: siegfried's rhine journey
XXB 2495　　　　　　　　　　　　　E 10157/P 1053
　　　2496
wagner götterdämmerung: siegfried's funeral march
XXB 2497　　　　　　　　　　　　　E 10158/P 1054
　　　2498
wagner lohengrin prelude
XXB 2499　　　　　　　　　　　　　E 10117/P 1044
　　　2500

0012/6 october 1919/parlophone session/**eduard mörike**
wagner lohengrin: bridal chorus, arranged for orchestra
XXB 2526　　　　　　　　　　　　　E 10107/P 1108

0013/ 1920/grammophon sessions/**leo blech**
weber der freischütz overture
1076LC   65835/69534
1077LC
humperdinck hänsel und gretel overture
1079LC   65836/69535
1080LC
weber oberon overture
1082LC   65844/69545
1083LC
mendelssohn a midsummer night's dream overture and scherzo
1086LC   65842/69543
1087LC
1088LC   65843/69544
1081LC
wagner parsifal: good friday music
1188m   65834/69533
1189m
berlioz la damnation de faust: hungarian march
1190m   65846/69547
berlioz la damnation de faust: dance of the will o' the wisps
1191m   65848/69549
weber-berlioz aufforderung zum tanz
1195m   69538
1196m
beethoven symphony no 5, final movement
1197m   65841/69542
1198m

0014/ 4 november 1920/parlophone session/**eduard mörike**
mendelssohn hebrides overture
XXB 2707   E 10013/P 1121
    2708
    2709   E 10014/P 1122
bizet l'arlesienne: pastorale
XXB 2712   E 10014/P 1145

0015/ 15 december 1920/parlophone session/**eduard mörike**
dvorak slavonic dances op 48 numbers 5 and 6
XXB 2737   E 10018/P 1102
    2738
saint-saens le rouet d'omphale
XXB 2739   E 10356/P 1154
    2740

0016/1921/odeon session/**max von schillings**
barbara kemp, soprano; josef mann, tenor
schillings mona lisa: duet for mona lisa and giovanni de salviati
XXB 6693 LXX 80927-8
    6694
cd issue: preiser 90294

0017/28 february 1921/parlophone session/**eduard mörike**
mozart die zauberflöte overture
XXB 2811 E 10012/P 1171/odeon O-5017
    2812
mozart die zauberflöte: march of the priests
XXB 2813 P 1170
offenbach les contes d'hoffmann, introduction and minuet
XXB 2815 P 1367/odeon O-5013

0018/3 march 1921/parlophone session/**bruno weyersberg**
lortzing alessandro stradella overture
XXB 2822 P 1172/odeon O-6241
    2823

0019/7 april 1921/parlophone session/**eduard mörike**
smetana the bartered bride overture
XXB 2856 E 10355/P 1236
    2857

0020/7 june 1921/parlophone session/**bruno weyersberg**
gounod faust, prelude and waltz
XXB 2908 P 1218
    2909

0021/25 june 1921/parlophone session/**eduard mörike**
wagner rienzi overture and march
XXB 2944 E 10146/P 1201/odeon O-5032
    2945
    2946 E 10147/P 1202/odeon O-5033
    2947

0022/19 september 1921/parlophone session/**eduard mörike**
mendelssohn a midsummer night's dream overture
XXB 5500 E 10015/P 1255
    5501
    5502 E 10016/P 1256

0023/8 and 11 october 1921/parlophone session/**eduard mörike**
emmy bettendorf, soprano; werner engel, baritone
wagner der fliegende holländer: wie aus der ferne längst vegang'ner zeiten
XXB 5538   E 10182/P 1261
    5540
    5539   E 10478/P 1262
wagner tannhäuser: o du mein holder abendstern
XXB 5542   E 10452/P 1337

0024/22 october 1921/parlophone session/**frieder weissmann**
emmy bettendorf, soprano
offenbach les contes d'hoffmann: ella a fui la tourturelle
XXB 5555   E 10474
wagner träume/wesendonk-lieder
XXB 5557   E 10495

0025/22 november 1921/parlophone session/**eduard mörike**
schubert symphony no 8 in b minor d759 "unfinished"
XXB 5593   E 10052/P 1265
    5594
    5595   E 10053/P 1266
    5590
    5591   E 10054/P 1267
    5592

0026/23 december 1921/parlophone session/**eduard mörike**
mozart le nozze di figaro overture
XXB 5640   E 10111/P 1320

0027/january 1922/parlophone sessions/**frieder weissmann**
gertrud bindernagel, soprano
verdi aida: ritorna vincitor
XXB 5681   P 1314
    5682
nicolai die lustigen weiber von windsor overture
XXB 5686   E 10051/P 1282
    5687

0028/10 january 1922/parlophone session/**eduard mörike**
verdi aida prelude
XXB 5685   E 10288/P 1316

0029/14 january 1922/parlophone session/**eduard mörike**
liszt les preludes
XXB 5698   E 10159/P 1420
    5699
    5700   E 10160/P 1421
    5701
    5702   E 10161/P 1422

0030/23 january 1922/parlophone session/**eduard mörike**
tchaikovsky casse noisette: waltz of the flowers
XXB 5709   E 10055/P 1295
wagner tannhäuser: pilgrims' chorus, arranged for orchestra
XXB 5711   E 10451/P 1336

0031/16 and 22 february 1922/parlophone sessions/**eduard mörike**
leoncavallo i pagliacci, orchestral selection
XXB 5738   E 10011/P 1305
    5739

0032/17 march 1922/parlophone session/**eduard mörike**
verdi aida ballet music
XXB 5774   E 10055/P 1316

0033/8 april 1922/parlophone session/**frieder weissmann**
mozart der schauspieldirektor overture
XXB 5844   E 10232/P 1742

0034/27 april 1922/parlophone session/**fritz stiedry**
cornelius der barbier von bagdad overture
XXB 5864   P 1368
    5865

0035/11 may 1922/parlophone session/**fritz stiedry**
cornelius der barbier von bagdad overture, alternative version
XXB 5887   P 1369
    5888

0036/20 october 1922/parlophone session/**frieder weissmann**
humperdinck hänsel und gretel, orchestral selection
XXB 6053   E 10019/P 1401
    6054
    6050   E 10020/P 1402
    6051

0037/26 october 1922/parlophone session/**eduard mörike**
weber oberon overture
XXB 6067   E 10089/P 1437
    6068
    6069   E 10090/P 1438

0038/26 october 1922/parlophone session/**frieder weissmann**
beethoven symphony no 6 "pastoral", first movement
XXB 6070   E 10148/P 1451
    6071

0039/13 and 18 november 1922/parlophone sessions/**eduard mörike**
elsa alsen, soprano
wagner die walküre: hojotoho !
XXB 6084 E 10253
wagner tristan und isolde: mild und leise
XXB 6085 E 10453
     6086
wagner götterdämmerung: grane mein ross !
XXB 6105 E 10253

0040/22 december 1922/parlophone session/**eduard mörike**
liszt the legend of saint elizabeth: crusade march
XXB 6133 E 10161/P 1421

0041/1923/vox session/**erich kleiber**
johann strauss an der schönen blauen donau
2365 ½ A 01896
2366 A
2367 B 01897
2368 B
cd issue: archiphon ARC 102

0042/1923/grammophon sessions/**oskar fried**
berliner domchor; gertrud bindernagel, soprano; emmi leisner, contralto
mahler symphony no 2 in c minor "resurrection"
371az 66290/6981
370az
1552as 66291/6982
372az
1554as 66292/6983
1555as
1556as 66293/6984
1557as
1558as 66294/6995
1559as
1560as 66295/6986
1567 ½ as
373az 66296/6987
1553as
1561as 66297/6988
1562as
1564as 66298/6989
1563 ½ as
322 ½ az 66299/6990
374az
375az 66300/6991
376az
cd issue: pearl GEMMCDS 9929

0043/24 january 1923/parlophone session/**frieder weissmann**
bizet carmen suite
XXB 6177	E 10245/P 1454
6178	
6179	E 10246/P 1455
6182	
6180	E 10247/P 1456
6181	

0044/6 february 1923/parlophone session/**frieder weissmann**
weber-berlioz aufforderung zum tanz
XXB 6190	E 10172/P 1484
6191	

0045/9 may 1923/parlophone session/**frieder weissmann**
mendelssohn ruy blas overture
XXB 6329	E 10109/P 1578
6330	

0046/16 may 1923/parlophone session/**frieder weissmann**
mozart 3 deutsche tänze
XXB 6338	E 10123/P 1542
6339	

0047/6 and 18 june 1923/parlophone sessions/**frieder weissmann**
tchaikovsky symphony no 6 in b minor "pathetique"
XXB 6604	E 10207/P 1638/odeon O-8154
6650	
6606	E 10208/P 1639/odeon O-8155
6607	
6651	E 10209/P 1640/odeon O-8156
6379	
6380	E 10210/P 1641/odeon O-8157
6392	
6394	E 10211/P 1642/odeon O-8158
6393	
6395	E 10212/P 1643/odeon O-8159
6396	

6604, 6606 and 6607 recorded on 15 december 1923; 6650 and 6651 recorded on 26 january 1924

0048/19 november and 1 december 1923/parlophone sessions/
frieder weissmann
grieg peer gynt suite no 2
XXB 6563	E 10325/P 1588
6565	
6582	E 10326/P 1589
6583	

0049/december 1923/homochord sessions/**johannes heidenreich**
beethoven coriolan overture
          B 8419

beethoven egmont overture
no data available
mendelssohn hebrides overture
no data available
schubert symphony no 8 in b minor "unfinished"
no data available
bizet l'arlesienne suite
no data available
bizet carmen prelude
no data available

0050/15 december 1923/*see 6 and 18 june 1923*

0051/1924/grammophon sessions/**oskar fried**
weber oberon overture
501az   65938
502az
cd issue: music and arts CD 1157
verdi aida, orchestral selection
493az   65940
494az
495az   65941
496az
497az   65942
498az
gounod faust ballet music
1619as   65971
1620as
1621as   65972
1622as

0052/1924/grammophon session/**max von schillings**
wagner das rheingold: entry of the gods into valhalla
1638as   65976
1639as

0053/3 january 1924/parlophone session/**frieder weissmann**
mozart don giovanni overture
XXB 2873 E 10130
    2874

0054/8 and 12 february 1924/parlophone sessions/**frieder weissmann**
rossini william tell overture
XXB 6669 E 10186/P 1667
    6670
    6671 E 10186/P 1668
    6672
grieg wedding day at troldhaugen
XXB 6676 E 10233/P 1656

0055/13 and 18 february 1924/odeon sessions/**carl besl**
lotte lehmann, soprano
thomas mignon: profitons bien de la jeunesse
XXB 6945 O-80934/O-9510
massenet manon: adieu notre petite table
XXB 6952 O-80938/O-9510
puccini tosca: vissi d'arte
XXB 6946 O-80935/O-9511
puccini la boheme: si mi chiamano mimi
XXB 6947 O-80933/O-9502
puccini manon lescaut: in quelle trine morbide
XXB 6948 O-80936/O-9503
puccini madama butterfly: un bel di vedremo
XXB 6949 O-80937/O-9503
wagner tannhäuser: dich teure halle
XXB 6953 O-80939/O-9504
wagner die walküre: du bist der lenz
XXB 6954 O-80940/O-9504
all arias issued on cd by pearl, preiser and romophone

0056/19 february 1924/odeon session/**carl besl**
wilhelm rode, bass-baritone
wagner die meistersinger von nürnberg: jerum! jerum!
XXB 6955 O-80894/O-80190/O-8510
wagner die meistersinger von nürnberg: was duftet doch der flieder
XXB 6956 O-80875/O-80191/O-8510

0057/29 february 1924/odeon session/**carl besl**
helene wildbrunn, soprano
mozart don giovanni: or sai chi l'onore
XXB 6957   O-80870/O-8502
gluck alceste: divinites du styx!
XXB 6960   O-80871/O-8502
wagner götterdämmerung: starke scheite schichtet mir dort
XXB 6958   O-80872-80873/O-8503
    6959

0058/march 1924/grammophon session/**johannes heidenreich**
mozart symphony no 41 in c "jupiter"
1535as   69655/66286
1536 ½ as
1537   69656/66287
1538as
1547as   69657/66288
1548as
1549as   69658/66289

0059/march 1924/grammophon sessions/**walter wohllebe**
wagner der fliegende holländer overture
                                          65943
wagner tannhäuser overture
                                          65944

                                          65945
wagner tristan und isolde prelude
1531as   65947
1532as
1533as   65948
beethoven symphony no 7 in a
1539as   69659/66260
1540as
1541as   69660/66261
1556as
1557as   69661/66262
1544as
1545as   69662/66263
1546as

0060/march 1924/vox session/**erich kleiber**
verdi aida prelude; rigoletto prelude
1558   01532
1559
mozart symphony no 33 in b flat k319, second and third movements
1560   01533
1561

0061/3 march 1924/odeon session/**carl besl**
trajan grosavescu, tenor
offenbach fürstin tanagra: seh' ich recht, tanagra?
XXB 6961   O-80941

0062/15 march 1924/parlophone session/**frieder weissmann**
weber preciosa overture
XXB 6738   E 10426/P 1687
    6739
mozart turkish march
XXB 6740   E 10233/P 1742

0063/17 march 1924/parlophone session/**frieder weissmann**
beethoven symphony no 3 in e flat "eroica"
XXB 6748   E 10299/P 1845/odeon O-8128
    6944
    6945   E 10300/P 1846/odeon O-8129
    6946
    7549   E 10301/P 1847/odeon O-8130
    7550
    7551   E 10302/P 1848/odeon O-8131
    7552
    7553   E 10303/P 1849/odeon O-8132
    7554
    7555   E 10304/P 1850/odeon O-8133
    7556
    7557   E 10305/P 1851/odeon O-8134
    7558
only matrix 6748 was recorded on 17 march: 6944-6946 recorded on 10 may 1924, the rest on 24 and 25 september 1924

0064/24 march 1924/odeon session/**carl besl**
lotte lehmann, soprano
wagner tannhäuser: allmächtige jungfrau; lohengrin: euch lüften die mein klagen
XXB 6972   O-9509
    6974
verdi otello: piangea cantando
XXB 6973   O-9511
arias issued on cd by pearl, preiser and romophone

0065/april 1924/homochord sessions/**johannes heidenreich**
rossini william tell overture
no data available
weber oberon overture
no data available
boieldieu le caliphe de bagdad overture
no data available
wagner die meistersinger von nürnberg overture
no data available

0066/2 april 1924/odeon session/**carl besl**
wilhelm rode, bass-baritone
wagner lohengrin: dank könig dir
XXB 6975   O-80898/O-8543
wolf der feuerreiter
XXB 6976   O-80896/O-8537
wagner die meistersinger von nürnberg: ein kind ward hier geboren
XXB 6977   O-80899/O-80195/O-8511
wagner das rheingold: abendlich strahlt der sonne auge
XXB 6978   O-80897/O-80193/O-8511

0067/12 april 1924/parlophone session/**eduard mörike**
rimsky-korsakov scheherazade
XXB 6818   E 10227/P 1730
    6819
    6820   E 10228/P 1731
    6846
    6847   E 10229/P 1732
    6821
    6822   E 10230/P 1733
    6843
    6844   E 10231/P 1734
    6845
6843-6847 recorded on 30 april 1924

0068/15 april 1924/parlophone session/**frieder weissmann**
eddy brown, violin
mendelssohn violin concerto, first and third movements
XXB 6823   E 10175/P 1719
    6824
    6825   E 10176/P 1720
    6826
    6827   E 10177/P 1721
recorded in order to complete a version of the second movement made by edith lorand and the blüthner orchestra conducted by camillo hildebrand in january 1924

0069/24 april 1924/parlophone session/**frieder weissmann**
strauss salome: dance of the seven veils
XXB 6832   E 10188/P 1700/odeon O-5093
    6833

0070/30 april 1924/*see 12 april 1924*

0071/1 may 1924/parlophone session/**frieder weissmann**
beethoven coriolan overture
XXB 6848   E 10454/P 1711/odeon O-3145
    6849
beethoven leonore no 3 overture
XXB 6850   E 10199/P 1760/odeon O-3155
    6851
    6852   E 10200/P 1761/odeon O-3156
    6853

0072/10 may 1924/*see 17 march 1924*

0073/13 may 1924/parlophone session/**eduard mörike**
wagner tannhäuser overture
XXB 6894   E 10169/P 2033
    6895
    6896   E 10170/P 2034
    6897

0074/15 may 1924/parlophone session/**eduard mörike**
beethoven symphony no 7 in a
XXB 6904   E 10222/P 1781/odeon O-8140
    6905
    6906   E 10223/P 1782/odeon O-8141
    6911
    6912   E 10224/P 1783/odeon O-8142
    6913
    6907   E 10225/P 1784/odeon O-8143
    6908
    6909   E 10226/P 1785/odeon O-8144
    6910
recording completed on 26 september 1924

0075/30 may 1924/parlophone session/**frieder weissmann**
mozart le nozze di figaro overture
XXB 6947   P 1320/odeon O-3154

0076/26 june 1924/parlophone session/**frieder weissmann**
mozart die zauberflöte overture
XXB 6998   P 1796
    6999

mozart cosi fan tutte overture
XXB 7500   E 10232/P 1742

0077/july and august 1924/grammophon sessions/**oskar fried**
brahms symphony no 1 in c minor
507az	69701/66304
508az	
509az	69702/66305
512az	
511az	69703/66306
513az	
515az	69704/66307
516az	
517az	69705/66308

beethoven symphony no 3 in e flat "eroica"
1600as	69706/66239
1601as	
1602as	69707/66240
1603as	
1604as	69708/66241
1605as	
1606as	69709/66242
1607 ½ as	
1608 ½ as	69710/66243
1609as	
1610as	69711/66244

cd issues: music and arts CD 1185 and arbiter 140

0078/august 1924/grammophon sessions/**max von schillings**
strauss also sprach zarathustra
1654as	69742/66315
1655as	
1656as	69743/66316
1666as	
1667as	69744/66317
1668as	

0079/august 1924/grammophon sessions/**hans pfitzner**
beethoven symphony no 4 in b flat
377 ½ az	69663/66245
378az	
379az	69664/66246
380az	
381az	69665/66247
382az	
385az	69666/66248
386az	
383az	69667/66249
384az	

0080/24 and 25 september 1924/*see 17 march 1924*

0081/26 september 1924/*see 15 may 1924*

0082/26 september 1924/parlophone session/**frieder weissmann**
beethoven symphony no 8 in f
XXB 7559	E 10256/P 1786/odeon O-5067
7560	
7561	E 10257/P 1787/odeon O-5068
7562	
7563	E 10258/P 1788/odeon O-5069
7564	

recording completed on 21 october 1924

0083/27 september 1924/parlophone session/**eduard mörike**
strauss tod und verklärung
XXB 7568	E 10270/P 1865/odeon O-5070
7569	
7570	E 10271/P 1866/odeon O-5071
7571	
7572	E 10272/P 1867/odeon O-5072
7573	

0084/1 and 2 october 1924/odeon sessions/**hermann weigert**
jacques urlus, tenor
massenet le cid: tout est bien fini
XXB 7046   O-124004
mehul joseph: champs paternels
XXB 7047   O-80985
ponchielli la gioconda: cielo e mar
XXB 7048   O 80977/O 80691/O 8568
leoncavallo i pagliacci: pagliaccio non son
XXB 7051   O-80975/O-80690/O-8568
wagner die walküre: winterstürme wichen dem wonnemond
XXB 7049   O-80694/O-8563
wagner die walküre: ein schwert verhiess mir der vater
XXB 7050   O-80695/O-8563

0085/7 october 1924/odeon session/**hermann weigert**
rudolf ritter, tenor
d'albert tiefland: schau her das ist ein taler
XXB 7052   O-80223/O-8001
d'albert tiefland: ich grüsse' noch einmal meine berge
XXB 7053   O-80224/O-8001
wagner tannhäuser: inbrunst im herzen
XXB 7054   O-80219-80220/O-8098
    7055

0086/10 october 1924/odeon session/**hermann weigert**
sabine kalter, contralto
saint-saens samson et dalila: printemps qui commence
XXB 7056 O-80710/O-8504
saint-saens samson et dalila: mon coeur s'ouvre a ta voix
XXB 7057 O-80711/O-8504
verdi il trovatore: stride la vampa
XXB 7058 O-80775/O-8112
verdi don carlo: o don fatale!
XXB 7059 O-80776

0087/14 october 1924/odeon session/**hermann weigert**
wilhelm rode, bass-baritone
wolf der tambour
XXB 7060 O-80767/O-8537
schumann mein wagen rollet langsam
XXB 7063 O-80766/O-8530
mozart don giovanni: deh vieni alla finestra
XXB 7061 O-80765/O-8530
wagner die meistersinger von nürnberg: euch macht ihr's leicht
XXB 7062 O-80768/O-8543

0088/17 october 1924/odeon session/**hermann weigert**
hans heinz bollmann, tenor
bizet carmen: la fleur que tu m'avais jetee
XXB 7064 unpublished recording
verdi rigoletto: la donna e mobile
XXB 7065 O-80218/O-8070

0089/21 october 1924/*see 26 september 1924*

0090/22-23 october 1924/parlophone sessions/**frieder weissmann**
beethoven symphony no 5 in c minor
XXB 7624 E 10284/P 1792/odeon O-8053
    7625
    7626 E 10285/P 1793/odeon O-8054
    7627
    7628 E 10286/P 1794/odeon O-8055
    7629
    7630 E 10287/P 1795/odeon O-8056
    7631
haydn symphony no 94 in g "surprise"
XXB 7635 E 10242/P 1821
    7636
    7689 E 10243/P 1822
    7690
    7637 E 10244/P 1823
    7691

7689, 7690 and 7691 recorded on 2 and 4 november 1924

0091/23 october 1924/odeon session/**george szell**
mozart wind serenade in c minor k388
XXB 7066	O-80769/O-8522	
7067	O-80770/O-8522	
7068	O-80771/O-8538	
7069	O-80772/O-8538	
7070	O-80773/O-8539	
7071	O-80774/O-8539	

0092/27 october 1924/parlophone session/**eduard mörike**
strauss don juan
XXB 7642	E 10254/P 1824
7643	
7644	E 10255/P 1825
7645	

berlioz la damnation de faust: danse des sylphes
XXB 7646	E 10345/P 1897

0093/november 1924/grammophon sessions/**oskar fried**
bruckner symphony no 7 in e
1716as	66318/69753
1717as	
1718as	66319/69754
1727as	
565 ½	66320/69755
566	
570 ½	66321/69756
571az	
572az	66322/69757
1703as	
1704as	66323/69758
1728as	
1735as	66324/69759
1736as	

cd issues: music and arts CD 1231 and wing WCD 61

0094/2 and 4 november 1924/*see 22-23 october 1924*

0095/7 november 1924/odeon session/**hermann weigert**
paul stieber-walter, tenor
strauss ach weh mir unglückhaftem mann
XXB 7072 O-80225/O-8105
strauss heimliche aufforderung
XXB 7073 O-80226/O-8105
gounod faust: salut demeure; adam le postillon de lonjumeau: mes amis ecoutez l'histoire!
XXB 7074 unpublished recordings
    7075

0096/11 november 1924/parlophone session/**bruno weyersberg**
johann strauss der zigeunerbaron overture
XXB 7662 E 10455
    7663

0097/20 november 1924/odeon session/**hermann weigert**
jean stern, baritone
lortzing undine: es wohnt' am seegestade
XXB 7080 O-80231/O-8002
verdi un ballo in maschera: eri tu
XXB 7081 O-80229/O-8081
leoncavallo i pagliacci: si puo?
XXB 7082 O-80230/O-8081
das goldene kreuz: wie anders war es
XXB 7083 O-80232/O-8002

0098/21 and 24 november 1924/parlophone sessions/**frieder weissmann**
beethoven symphony no 6 in f "pastoral"
XXB 7692 E 10318/P 1826/odeon O-8135
    7693
    7701 E 10319/P 1827/odeon O-8136
    7702
    7703 E 10320/P 1828/odeon O-8137
    7704
    7694 E 10321/P 1829/odeon O-8138
    7705
    7706 E 10322/P 1830/odeon O-8139
    7707
recording completed on 21 january 1925

0099/26 november 1924/parlophone session/**frieder weissmann**
fritzi jokl, soprano
mozart le nozze di figaro: deh vieni non tardar
XXB 7716　　　　　　　　　E 10373
meyerbeer les huguenots: une dame noble et sage
XXB 7719　　　　　　　　　E 10362/P 1817

0100/26 and 28 november 1924/parlophone sessions/**eduard mörike**
mozart die entführung aus dem serail overture
XXB 7718　　　　　　　　　E 10273/P 1902
johann strauss der lustige krieg overture
XXB 7736　　　　　　　　　E 10273/P 1909

0101/28 november 1924/parlophone session/**frieder weissmann**
max hirzel, tenor
wagner lohengrin: in fernem land; atmest du nicht
XXB 7733　　　　　　　　　E 10264/P 1834
　　　7734
wagner lohengrin: mein lieber schwan
XXB 7735　　　　　　　　　E 10372/P 2220
parlophone listings suggest that mein lieber schwan was conducted by paul breisach

0102/december 1924/grammophon session/**oskar fried**
leoncavallo i pagliacci, orchestral selection (potpourri)
1617as II　　　　　　　　　65939
1618as II

0103/december 1924/vox session/**erich kleiber**
mozart serenade in e flat k375
1948　　　　　　　　　　　06210
1949
1959　　　　　　　　　　　06211
1960
1961　　　　　　　　　　　06212

0104/december 1924/grammophon sessions/**otto klemperer**
beethoven symphony no 1 in c
1768as　　　　　　　　　　66231/69760
1769as
1767as　　　　　　　　　　66232/69761
1766as
1763as　　　　　　　　　　66233/69762
1764as
1756as　　　　　　　　　　66234/69763
cd issue: archiphon ARC 121-125

december 1924 / grammophon sessions / otto klemperer / concluded
bruckner symphony no 8 in c minor, third movement
1770 ½ as   66325/69764
1771as
1772as   66326/69765
1773as
1774as   66327/69766
1775as
1789as   66328/69767
cd issue: archiphon ARC 121-125

0105/3 december 1924/parlophone session/**frieder weissmann**
lauritz melchior, tenor
wagner die walküre: winterstürme; parsifal: nur eine waffe taugt
XXB 7742   E 10352/P 1903
    7743

0106/9-10 december 1924/odeon sessions/**hermann weigert**
jacques urlus, tenor
strauss traum durch die dämmerung
XXB 7095   O-80714/O-8532
wagner rienzi: allmächtiger vater!
XXB 7096   O-80981
strauss heimliche aufforderung
XXB 7097   O-80715/O-8532
wagner lohengrin: in fernem land
XXB 7098   O-124005
wagner götterdämmerung: brünnhilde heilige braut!
XXB 7099   O-80692/O-80983/O-8571
wagner lohengrin: höchstes vertrauen
XXB 7100   O-80693/O-80984/O-8571

0107/11 december 1924/odeon session/**hermann weigert**
mafalda salvatini, soprano
strauss ständchen
XXB 7101   unpublished recording
dvorak rusalka: song to the moon
XXB 7102   O-80746/O-8501
pacini saffo: l'ama ognor qual io
XXB 7103   O-80747/O-8501

0108/12 december 1924/odeon session/**hermann weigert**
sabine kalter, contralto
handel semele: o holder süsser schlaf
XXB 7104　　　　　　　　　　　　O-80726
mussorgsky boris godunov: marina is bored
XXB 7105　　　　　　　　　　　　O-80727
wagner träume/wesendonk-lieder
XXB 7106　　　　　　　　　　　　O-80718/O-8101
wagner schmerzen/wesendonk-lieder
XXB 7107　　　　　　　　　　　　O-80721/O-8101
thomas mignon: connais-tu le pays?
XXB 7108　　　　　　　　　　　　O-80734

0109/22 december 1924/parlophone session/**eduard mörike**
strauss ein heldenleben
XXB 7786　　　　　　　　　　　　E 11306/P 1915/odeon O-5108
　　　7787
　　　7788　　　　　　　　　　　　E 11307/P 1916/odeon O-5109
　　　7789
　　　7790　　　　　　　　　　　　E 11308/P 1917/odeon O-5110
　　　7795
　　　7796　　　　　　　　　　　　E 11309/P 1918/odeon O-5111
　　　7797
　　　7836　　　　　　　　　　　　E 11310/P 1919/odeon O-5112
　　　7837
7836 and 7837 recorded on 10 january 1925

0110/26, 29, 30 and 31 december 1924/parlophone sessions/
frieder weissmann
beethoven symphony no 4 in b flat
XXB 7802　　　　　　　　　　　　E 10280/P 1861/odeon O-5073
　　　7803
　　　7804　　　　　　　　　　　　E 10281/P 1862/odeon O-5074
　　　7805
　　　7806　　　　　　　　　　　　E 10282/P 1863/odeon O-5075
　　　7807
　　　7808　　　　　　　　　　　　E 10283/P 1864/odeon O-5076
　　　7809
beethoven die weihe des hauses overture
XXB 7812　　　　　　　　　　　　E 10354/P 1972
　　　7813
beethoven namensfeier overture
XXB 7814　　　　　　　　　　　　E 10337/P 2084
　　　7815
mozart idomeneo and die entführung aus dem serail overtures
XXB 7816　　　　　　　　　　　　E 10346/P 1902
　　　7817

0111/january 1925/homochord session/**johannes heidenreich**
wagner parsifal: good friday music
MS 1767　　　　　　　　　　　　8613
　　　1768

0112/3 and 5 january 1925/parlophone sessions/**paul breisach**
emmy bettendorf, soprano; lauritz melchior, tenor
wagner parsifal: amfortas die wunde!
XXB 7821   E 10298/P 1883
    7822
wagner tannhäuser: dich teure halle
XXB 7823   E 10372/P 2220
wagner tannhäuser: o fürstin!
XXB 7824   E 10332/P 1927
    7825

0113/10 january 1925/*see 26 may 1919 and 22 december 1924*

0114/14 january 1925/parlophone session/**bruno weyersberg**
emmy bettendorf, soprano
strauss der rosenkavalier: kann mich auch an ein mädel erinnern…..
quinquin er soll jetzt geh'n!
XXB 7855   E 10341/P 1899
    7856
bizet carmen: en vain pour eviter les reponses ameres
XXB 7857   E 10441/P 1960

0115/20 january 1925/parlophone session/**frieder weissmann**
emmy bettendorf, soprano
XXB 7889   E 10441/P 1960

0116/21 january 1925/*see 21 november 1924*

0117/21 january 1925/parlophone session/**frieder weissmann**
beethoven symphony no 2 in d
XXB 7891   E 10314/P 1889/odeon O-8124
    7919
    7920   E 10315/P 1890/odeon O-8125
    7892
    7893   E 10316/P 1891/odeon O-8126
    7894
    7921   E 10317/P 1892/odeon O-8127
    7922
7919, 7920, 7921 and 7922 recorded on 10 february 1925

0118/31 january 1925/parlophone session/**eduard mörike**
chorvereinigung arnold ebels; lotte leonard, soprano; hilde ellger, contralto; paul stieber-walter, tenor; albert fischer, bass
beethoven symphony no 9 in d minor, choral finale

XXB 7902	P 1858/odeon O-8151
7903	
7904	P 1859/odeon O-8152
7905	
7906	P 1860/odeon O-8153
7907	

recorded in order to complete a version of the first three movements made by the blüthner orchestra conducted by frieder weissmann

0119/february 1925/grammophon session/**franz schreker**
schreker der geburtstag der infantin, suite

591az	66329/69768
592az	
593az	66330/69769
594az	
595az	66331/69770
596az	

0120/10 february 1925/*see 21 january 1925*

0120a/10 february 1925/parlophone session/**siegfried wagner**
staatsopernchor; genia guszalewicz, contralto; max lorenz, tenor
wagner parsifal: hier war das tosen (blumenmädchenszene)

XXB 8576	E 10477
8577	
8578	E 10478

0121/11 february 1925/parlophone session/**frieder weissmann**
beethoven symphony ni 1 in c

XXB 7923	E 10311/P 1886/odeon O-8121
7924	
7925	E 10312/P 1887/odeon O-8122
7926	
7927	E 10313/P 1888/odeon O-8123
7928	

0122/13 and 18 february 1925/parlophone sessions/**bruno weyersberg**
suppe dichter und bauer overture

XXB 7939	E 10346/P 1921
7940	

heuberger der opernball overture

XXB 7941	P 1908
7942	

0123/24 february 1925/parlophone session/**siegfried wagner**
siegfried wagner der bärenhäuter overture
XXB 7955 E 10353/P 1952
    7956
wagner siegfried idyll
XXB 7957 E 10323/P 1953
    7958
    7959 E 10324/P 1954
    7960

0124/26-27 february 1925/parlophone sessions/**frieder weissmann**
berlioz la damnation de faust: marche hongroise
XXB 7971 E 10345/P 1897
berlioz carnaval romain overture
XXB 7972 E 10336/P 1920
    7973
weber der freischütz overture
XXB 7974 E 10444/P 1993
    7975
weber der freischütz: act three intermezzo
XXB 7976 E 10445/P 1994
    7977
thomas mignon overture
XXB 7978 E 10375/P 1974
    7979
brahms academic festival overture
XXB 7980 E 10378/P 1940
    7981

0125/march 1925/grammophon session/**otto klemperer**
schubert symphony no 8 in b minor "unfinished"
1912as 66339/69778
1915as
1916as 66340/69779
1910as
1911as 66341/69780
1913as
cd issue: archiphon ARC 121-125

0126/march 1925/grammophon session/**hans knappertsbusch**
franckenstein variations on a theme of meyerbeer
1944as 66120
1945as
1946as 66121
cd issue: preiser 90389
haydn symphony no 92 in g "oxford"
1948as 66344/69783
1949as
1941as 66345/69784
1942as
1943as 66346/69785
1947as II
cd issue: preiser 90389

0127/march 1925/grammophon session/**max von schillings**
wagner die meistersinger von nürnberg: dance of the apprentices and entry of the masters
1640as 66076

0128/march 1925/grammophon sessions/**bruno walter**
mozart cosi fan tutte overture; idomeneo overture
646az 66072
649az
cherubini les deux journees overture
647az 66073
648az
schumann manfred overture
1836 ½ as 66074
1837as
berlioz benvenuto cellini overture
621 ½ az 66075
622az
623az 66076
tchaikovsky symphony no 6 in b minor "pathetique"
1634as 66332/69771
1641 ½ as
1142as 66333/69772
1750as
1751as 66334/69773
1913as
1919as 66335/69775
1920as
1921as 66336/69776

cd issues: polygram (japan) POCG 6067, wing WCD 29 and grand slam GS 2073

0129/march 1925/grammophon sessions/**oskar fried**
stravinsky firebird suite
1917 ½ as   66337/69776
1930 ½ as
1931 ½ as   66338/69777
1932 ½ as
cd issue: music and arts CD 1198
fried recorded the suite again in 1928 with the berliner philharmoniker
weber oberon overture
                                   65938

cd issue: music and arts CD 1167
liszt mazeppa
2000as   66117
2001as
2002as   66118
2003as
cd issue: music and arts CD 1185
fried recorded the work again in 1928 with the berliner philharmoniker
beethoven könig stephan overture
1979 ½ as   66119
1980as
boieldieu le caliphe de bagdad overture
1981as   66211
1982as
strauss eine alpensinfonie
2138 ½ as   66351/69803
2139as
2140as   66352/69804
2141as
2142as   66353/69805
2143as
2145 ¾ as   66354/69806
2163as
2164as   66355/69807
cd issue: music and arts CD 1167

0130/19 march 1925/parlophone session/**frieder weissmann**
flotow martha overture
XXB 8004   E 10437/P 1959
    8005

0131/19 march 1925/parlophone session/**bruno weyersberg**
rossini la gazza ladra overture
XXB 8006   E 10357/P 1946
    8007

0132/23 march 1925/parlophone session/**frieder weissmann**
emmy bettendorf, soprano
wagner lohengrin: einsam in trüben tagen; euch lüften die mein klagen
XXB 8014   E 10351/P 1965
    8015

0133/25 march 1925/parlophone session/**frieder weissmann**
berlioz symphonie fantastique

XXB 8024	P 1934
8025	
8026	P 1935
8112	
8113	P 1936
8121	
8122	P 1937
8123	
8027	P 1938
8114	
8115	P 1939
8116	

8112-8116 and 8121-8123 recorded on 28 and 30 april 1925

0134/26 march 1925/parlophone session/**frieder weissmann**
fritzi jokl, soprano
mozart die zauberflöte: der hölle rache
XXB 8028   E 10373
thomas mignon: je suis titania
XXB 8029   E 10410/P 2001
verdi un ballo in maschera: saper vorreste
XXB 8030   E 10410/P 2001

0135/26 march 1925/parlophone session/**eduard mörike**
emmy bettendorf, soprano
strauss morgen
XXB 8034   E 10425

0136/28 march 1925/parlophone session/**eduard mörike**
strauss macbeth

XXB 8036	E 10423/P 2022
8037	
8038	E 10424/P 2023
8039	
8040	E 10425/P 2024

0137/april 1925/grammophon sessions/**georg hoeberg**
bach brandenburg concerto no 3

1629 ½ as	66014
1630 ½ as	
1631 ½ as	66015

rimsky-korsakov le coq d'or: bridal march

1637as	66015

beethoven leonore no 3 overture

	66070
	66071

grieg peer gynt: death of aase

	66071

0138/april 1925/grammophon session/**frederik schnedler-petersen**
alfven swedish rhapsody no 1 (midsummer vigil)
408az	66077
409az	
410az	66078

nielsen maskerade: dance of the cockerels
407az	66078

halvorsen suite ancienne: aria con variazioni
	66079

0139/4 april 1925/parlophone session/**siegfried wagner**
wagner der fliegende holländer overture and spnning chorus
XXB 8053	E 10334/P 1955
8054	
8055	E 10335/P 1956
8056	

cd issue of overture: gebhardt JGCD 0062

0140/15 april 1925/parlophone session/**michael balling**
wagner parsifal prelude and transformation music
XXB 8077	P 1957
8078	
8079	P 1958
8080	

0141/15 and 20 april 1925/parlophone sessions/**george szell**
haydn symphony no 88 in g
XXB 7163	E 10498/odeon O-8553
7164	
7171	E 10499/odeon O-8554
7165	
7172	E 10500/odeon O-8555

0142/21 and 27 april 1925/odeon sessions/**george szell**
beethoven symphony no 4 in b flat
XXB 7175	O-8544
7176	
7183	O-8545
7184	
7173	O-8546
7185	
7174	O-8547

0143/27 april 1925/parlophone session/**frieder weissmann**
robert burg, baritone
wagner tannhäuser: als du in kühnem sange; blick ich umher
XXB 8107   unpublished recordings
    8108
verdi otello: credo
XXB 8109   P 1984
gounod faust: avant de quitter ces lieux
XXB 8110   unpublished recording

0144/28-30 april 1925/*see 25 march 1925*

0145/may 1925/grammophon session/**otto klemperer**
beethoven symphony no 8 in f
1977as   66264/69786
1978as
2004as   66265/69787
1965as
2005as   66266/69788
2006as
cd issue: archiphon ARC 121-125

0146/may 1925/grammophon sessions/**helmut thierfelder**
josef wolfsthal, violin
beethoven violin concerto in d
860az   69789
845 ½ az
846 ½ az   69790
847 ½ az
861 ½ az   69791
862 ½ az
863az   69792
866 ½ az
867az   69793
868az
beethoven violin romance no 2 in f
869az   69794
870az
wolfsthal later re-recorded the concerto with the staatskapelle and manfred gurlitt (see 1929)

0147/may 1925/homochord session/**johannes heidenreich**
mozart die zauberflöte overture
                        1-8630

0148/1 may 1925/parlophone session/**frieder weissmann**
grieg sigurd jorsalfar suite
XXB 8124   E 10412
    8125
    8126   E 10413
    8127
goldmark sakuntala overture
XXB 8128   E 10401
    8129
    8130   E 10402
    8131

0149/4 may 1925/parlophone session/**frieder weissmann**
riele queling, violin
mozart violin concerto no 4 k218
XXB 8132   E 10383/P 1978
    8133
    8134   E 10384/P 1979
    8135
    8136   E 10385/P 1980
    8137

0150/4 may 1925/parlophone session/**frieder weissmann**
alexander barjanski, cello
haydn cello concerto in g
XXB 8140   E 10407
    8141
    8142   E 10408

0151/8 may 1925/parlophone session/**eduard mörike**
strauss till eulenspiegels lustige streiche
XXB 8153   E 10364/P 1970/odeon O-5113
    8154
    8155   E 10365/P 1971/odeon O-5114
    8156

0152/8 may 1925/parlophone session/**george szell**
brahms symphony no 2 in d
XXB 7186   E 10487/odeon O-8549
    7187
    7188   E 10488/odeon O-8550
    7196
    7197   E 10489/odeon O-8551
    7195
    7198   E 10490/odeon O-8552
    7216
recording completed on 19 and 29 may 1925 and 24 august 1925

0153/13 may 1925/parlophone session/**eduard mörike**
strauss aus italien
XXB 8161   P 2053
    8162
    8413   P 2054
    8414
    8157   P 2055
    8158
    8159   P 2056
    8160
    8410   P 2057
    8411
    8412   P 2058
recording completed on 31 october 1925

0154/18 may 1925/parlophone session/**paul breisach**
emmy bettendorf, soprano
strauss ariadne auf naxos: ein schönes war's....es gibt ein reich
XXB 8169   E 10421/P 2064
    8170

0155/19 may 1925/*see 8 may 1925*

0156/26 may 1925/parlophone session/**frieder weissmann**
goldmark die königin von saba: einzugsmarsch
XXB 8184   E 10377/P 1973
    8185

0157/26 may 1925/parlophone session/**frieder weissmann**
emmy bettendorf, soprano
verdi un ballo in maschera: ecco l'orrido campo
XXB 8188   E 10431/P 2098
    8189
johann strauss die fledermaus: mein herr was dächten sie?; klänge der heimat
XXB 8190   E 10411
    8191

0158/27 may 1925/parlophone session/**frieder weissmann**
beethoven 12 deutsche tänze woO8
XXB 8196   E 10446/P 1991
    8197
    8198   P 1992
    8199
recording completed on 10 june 1925

0159/29 may 1925/*see 8 may 1925*

0160/10 june 1925/parlophone session/**frieder weissmann**
mozart symphony no 41 in c k551 "jupiter"
XXB 8229	E 10433
8230	
8231	E 10434
8232	
8267	E 10435
8268	
8269	E 10436

recording completed on 24 june 1925

0161/10 june 1925/*see 27 may 1925*

0162/24 june 1925/*see 10 june 1925*

0163/24-25 june 1925/parlophone sessions/**frieder weissmann**
mozart symphony no 40 in g minor k550
XXB 8270	E 10366/P 2164
8271	
8272	E 10357/P 2165
8273	
8274	E 10368/P 2166
8275	

gluck iphigenie in aulis overture
XXB 8276	E 10376/P 2071
8277	

mozart symphony no 39 in e flat k543
XXB 8278	E 10392/P 2240
8279	
8280	E 10393/P 2241
8281	
8282	E 10394/P 2242
8283	

0164/august 1925/vox session/**erich kleiber**
beethoven deutsche tänze woO17, numbers 1, 3, 10 and 11
2277	01879
2278	

0165/24 august 1925/*see 8 may 1925*

0166/september 1925/grammophon session/**siegmund von hausegger**
liszt tasso
2117as	66361/69812
2118as	
2119as	66362/69813
2120 ½ as	
2121as	66363/69814

0167/september 1925/grammophon session/unnamed conductor
wilhelm kempff, piano
beethoven piano concerto no 1 in c
822 ½ az   69815
823 ½ az
824 ½ az   69816
825 ½ az
828az   69817
829az
830 ½ az   69818
831 ½ az
it has not been established whether kempff conducts this recording from the keyboard

0168/15 september 1925/parlophone session/**frieder weissmann**
robert burg, baritone
wagner das rheingold: abendlich strahlt der sonne auge
XXB 8303   E 10422/P 2075
wagner tannhäuser: als du in kühnem sange
XXB 8304   E 10721/P 9200
wagner die walküre: leb wohl du kühnes herrliches kind
XXB 8305   E 10409/P 2018
      8306

0169/october 1925/grammophon sessions/**hans pfitzner**
schumann symphony no 1 in b flat "spring"
2013as   66347/69795
2014 ½ as
2015as   66348/69796
2016as
2038as   66349/69797
2039as
2040as   66350/69798
2041as

0170/october 1925/grammophon sessions/**oskar fried**
berlioz symphonie fantastique
2030 ½ as   69808
2031 ½ as
2033as   69809
838 ½ az
2009as   69810
836az
2032as   69811
this recording omitted the fourth movement (marche au supplice); complete symphony was re-recorded by fried and the staatskapelle ie july 1926
boieldieu le caliphe de bagdad overture
1981as   66211
1982as

0171/21 october 1925/odeon session/**hermann weigert**
carlotta vanconti, soprano; richard tauber, tenor
lehar paganini: was ich denke, was ich fühle
XXB 7247 O-80387/O-8162
lehar paganini: einmal möcht' ich was närrisches tun
XXB 7248 O-80388/O-8163

0172/31 october 1925/*see 13 may 1925*

0173/november 1925/odeon session/**hermann weigert**
beethoven könig stephan overture
XXB 8411 O-6050
    8412

0174/november 1925/grammophon session/**oskar fried**
beethoven symphony no 2 in d
2048 ½ 66235
2049 ½
2050as 66236
2051as
2052as 66237
884 ½ az
885az 66238
886az
cd issue: music and arts CD 1198

0175/november 1925/vox session/**erich kleiber**
johann strauss an der schönen blauen donau
2365 ½ A 01896
2366A
2367A 01897
2368A
cd issue: archiphon ARC 102

0176/11 november 1925/parlophone session/**frieder weissmann**
alfred jerger, bass
wagner die meistesinger von nürnberg: wahn wahn überall wahn!
XXB 8436 E 10463
    8437

0177/17 november 1925/parlophone session/**frieder weissmann**
meta seinemeyer, soprano
giordano andre chenier: la mamma morta
XXB 8439					P 2089
cd issue: preiser 89402
puccini madama butterfly: un bel di vedremo
XXB 8440					P 2089
cd issue: preiser 89402
puccini la boheme: si mi chiamano mimi
XXB 8441					unpublished recording
gounod faust: ah je ris!
XXB 8442					unpublished recording

0178/28 november 1925/parlophone session/**eduard mörike**
strauss sinfonia domestica
XXB 8471					P 2248
    8472
    8473					P 2249
    8474
    8475					P 2250
    8750
    8751					P 2251
    8752
    8753					P 2252
    8754
recording completed on 19 march 1926

0179/december 1925/vox session/**erich kleiber**
johann strauss der zigeunerbaron overture
2489A						08015
2499A

0180/3 december 1925/parlophone session/**frieder weissmann**
emmy bettendorf, soprano
massenet elegie
XXB 8484					E 10495
tosti serenade
XXB 8485					E 10474

0181/4 december 1925/parlophone session/**frieder weissmann**
max hirzel, tenor
wagner die meistersinger von nürnberg: morgenlich leuchtend; gounod faust: salut demeure
XXB 8490					E 10462
    8489

0182/15 december 1925/odeon session/**george szell**
dukas l'apprenti sorcier
XXB 7402					O-80639-80640/O-8561
    7403

0183/1926/grammophon sessions/**leo blech**
these sessions are assumed to include the first electrically made recordings by the company
nicolai die lustigen weiber von windsor overture
4bi   66381
5bi
rossini il barbiere di siviglia overture
6bi   66382
7bi
flotow martha overture
8bi   66383
9bi
weber oberon overture
10 ½ bi   66384
11bi
mascagni cavalleria rusticana prelude
18bi   66432
verdi aida hymn and triumphal march
19bi   66385
20bi
thomas mignon overture
21bi   66386
22bi
bellini norma overture
23bi   66387
24bi
auber la muette de portici overture
25bi   66388
26bi
johann strauss die fledermaus overture
30bi   66389
31 ½ bi
boieldieu la dame blanche overture
32bi   66390
33bi
cornelius der barbier von bagdad overture
34bi   66391
35bi
auber fra diavolo overture
36bi   66392
37bi
maillart les cloches de corneville overture
38bi   66393
39bi
kreutzer das nachtlager von grenada overture
32bm   66394
33bm
reznicek eine lustspiel-ouvertüre
34bm   66395
35bm

1926/grammophon sessions/leo blech/cocluded
grieg peer gynt suite no 2
36bm   66396
37bm
38bm   66397
39bm
wagner die meistersinger von nürnberg overture
41bm   66400
42bm
wagner rienzi overture
43 ½ bm   66398
44bm
45 ½ bm   66399
meyerbeer le prophete coronation march
46bm   66399/66432
weber-berlioz aufforderung zum tanz
47bm   66401
48bm
mozart die zauberflöte overture
49bm   66402
50bm

0184/1926/grammophon sessions/**oskar fried**
mozart eine kleine nachtmusik
222 ½ bg   66364/69826
223 ½ bg
229bg   66365/69827
230bg
liszt mazeppa
2000as   67117
2001as
2002as   67118
2003as
cd issue: *music and arts CD 1185*

0185/january 1926/grammophon session/**dirk fock**
rimsky-korsakov scheherazade, first and second movements
1904 ½ as   66067
1905as
1906 ½ as   66068
1907as
1908 ½ as   66069
1909as

0186/january 1926/vox session/**erich kleiber**
wagner die meistersiger von nürnberg overture
2503A   08034
2507A

0187/january 1926/parlophone session/**george szell**
schubert rosamunde overture
XXB 8792   E 10510/odeon O-7500
     8793
     8794   E 10511/odeon O-7501

0188/january 1926/grammophon sessions/**otto klemperer**
ravel alborada del gracioso
296bm   66463
297bm
cd issue: archiphon ARC 121-125
debussy fetes (trois nocturnes)
319bm   66465
320bm
cd issue: archiphon ARC 121-125
beethoven symphony no 8 in f op 93
321 ½ bm   66460
322bm
323bm   66461
324bm
325bm   66462
326bm
cd issue: archiphon ARC 121-125
debussy nuages (trois nocturnes)
331bm   66464
332bm
cd issue: archiphon ARC 121-125

0189/9 february 1926/parlophone sesssion/**siegfried wagner**
wagner lohengrin: procession to the minster
XXB 8572   E 10476
     8573

0190/ 11, 12 and 15 february 1926/parlophone sessions/**frieder weissmann**
meta seinemeyer, soprano; carl martin oehmann, tenor;
robert burg, baritone
verdi la forza del destino: son guinta; pace pace
XXB 8579 P 2168
    8580
cd issue: preiser 89402
puccini tosca: vissi d'arte
XXB 8581 P 2182
cd issue: preiser 89402
verdi la forza del destino: me pellegrina ed orfana
XXB 8582 P 2182
cd issue: preiser 89402
puccini tosca: franchigia a floria tosca!
XXB 8583 P 2219
    8584
    8585 unpublished recording
cd issue: preiser 89402
mussorgsky boris godunov: my soul is bad; i have attained the highest power
XXB 8590 E 10473/P 2172
    8591
mussorgsky boris godunov: death of boris
XXB 8592 P 2258
tchaikovsky evgeny onegin: everyone knows love on earth
XXB 8593 E 10485/P 2245
    8594
leoncavallo i pagliacci: ecco il prologo!
XXB 8595 P 2258

0191/ 17 february 1926/parlophone session/**franz schreker**
schreker ein rokoko-tanzspiel
XXB 8597 P 2195
    8598
    8599 P 2196
    8600

0192/ 24 and 26 february 1926/grammophon sessions/**richard strauss**
beethoven symphony no 7 in a op 92
339 ½ bg 69836/brunswick 25010
340bg
341bg 69837/brunswick 25011
342bg
343bg 69838/brunswick 25012
344bg
345bg 69839/brunswick 25013
346bg
cd issue: naxos 81.10926
mozart symphony no 39 in e flat k543
347bg 69833
348bg
349bg 69834
350bg
351bg 69835
352bg
cd issue koch 3-7076-2:

0193/ 28 february 1926/electrola session/**ernst viebig**
suppe dichter und bauer overture
CWR 31   EH 52/hmv C 1394
    32

0194/ february-march 1926/grammophon sessions/**hans pfitzner**
schumann symphony no 2 in c
2200as   66366/69828
2201as
2202as   66367/69829
2203as
2204as   66368/69830
2205as
2206as   66369/69831
2207as
2208as   66370/69832
2209 ½ as
pfitzner palestrina, act one prelude
2212as   66121
pfitzner palestrina, act two prelude
2010as   66122
2011as
pfitzner palestrina, act three prelude
2042as   66123
2043as

0195/ 4-5 march 1926/grammophon sessions/**richard strauss**
strauss ein heldenleben
360bg   69840/brunswick 25000
361bg
362bg   69841/brunswick 25001
363bg
364bg   69842/brunswick 25002
6bm
366bg   69843/brunswick 25003
367bg
368bg   69844/brunswick 25004
369bg

0196/ 17 march 1926/parlophone session/**frieder weissmann**
saint-saens samson et dalila: bacchanale
XXB 8742   E 10469/P 2212
    8743

0197/ 19 march 1926/*see 28 november 1925*

0198/25 march 1926/parlophone session/**michael taube**
emanuel feuermann, cello
dvorak cello concerto, adagio movement
XXB 8759   E 10482
      8760
popper hungarian rhapsody
XXB 8761   E 10505
      8762

0199/29 march 1926/odeon session/**george szell**
wagner der fliegende holländer overture
XXB 7444   O-55144-55145
      7445

0200/9 and 12 april 1926/parlophone sessions/**frieder weissmann**
meta seinemeyer, soprano
strauss cäcilie
XXB 8802   P 2218
verdi otello: piangea cantando
XXB 8803   E 10506/P 2243
offenbach les contes d'hoffmann: ella a fui la tourturelle
XXB 8804   P 2235
weber der freischütz: leise leise
XXB 8805   E 10484
      8806
weber der freischütz: und ob die wolke
XXB 8807   E 10506/P 2243
bizet carmen: je dis que rien ne m'epouvante
XXB 8808   unpublished recording
strauss morgen
XXB 8809   P 2218
cd issue of all published arias: preiser 89402

0201/april 1926/vox session/**erich kleiber**
mozart die entführung aus dem serail and le nozze di figaro overtures
                                     08129

0202/july 1926/vox session/**erich kleiber**
weber der freischütz overture and entr'acte
2731   08190
2732
2733   08198
2734

0203/july 1926/grammophon sessions/**oskar fried**
berlioz symphonie fantastique
2030 ½ as	66356
2031 ½ as	
2033as	66357
838 ½ az	
2222as	66358
2224as	
2223as	66359
2009 ½ as	
836 az	66360
2032as	

this was a second recording of the work by fried and the staatskapelle, this time complete but using the same matrix numbes (see october 1925)

0204/september 1926/vox session/**erich kleiber**
johann strauss g'schichten aus dem wienerwald
2739 ½ A	08234
2740A	
2741A	08235
2742A	

0205/6 and 24 september 1926/electrola sessions in the berliner singakademie/
leo blech
wagner die meistersinger von nürnberg overture
CWR 291	EJ 43/hmv D 1314
292	

wagner tannhäuser overture
CWR 293	EJ 51/hmv D 1318
359	
360	EJ 52/hmv D 1319

0206/23 september 1926/electrola session in the berliner singakademie/
ernst viebig
johann strauss die fledermaus overture
CWR 355	EH 17/hmv C 1414
356	

0207/29 september 1926/electrola session in the berliner singakademie/
leo blech
mozart le nozze di figaro overture
CWR 370	EJ 57//hmv D 1224

mozart die zauberflöte: march of the priests
CWR 371	unpublished recording

bizet carmen, preludes act one and two
BWR 371	EW 11/E 468
372	

0208/11 october 1926/parlophone session/**siegfried wagner**
wagner tristan und isolde prelude and liebestod
XXB 8922   E 10508/P 9012
     8923
     8924   E 10509/P 9013
     8925
cd issue: trax classique TRXCD 112

0209/11 october 1926/electrola session in the berliner singakademie/
leo blech/staatsopernchor
wagner die meistersinger von nürnberg: da zu dir der heiland kam; wach auf!
CWR 398   EJ 53/hmv D 1211/victor 9160
     399
wagner tannhäuser: pilgrims' chorus
CWR 397   EJ 44/hmv D 1292/D 1317
wagner tannhäuser: entry of the guests
CWR 400   EJ 44/hmv D 1292

0210/12 october 1926/parlophone session/**frieder weissmann**
meta seinemeyer, soprno
ponchielli la gioconda: suicidio!
XXB 8926   P 9016
verdi aida: ritorna vincitor
XXB 8927   P 9653/P 9862/odeon O-7646
     8928
puccini la boheme: si mi chiamano mimi
XXB 8929   P 9016
cd issue of all arias: preiser 89402

0211/14 october 1926/electrola session in the berliner singakademie/
leo blech/alexander kipnis, bass
wagner die walküre: leb wohl du kühnes herrliches kind
CWR 407   EJ 45/hmv D 1225
     408
     409   EJ 46/hmv D 1226

0212/14 october 1926/electrola session in the berliner singakademie/
leo blech/friedrich schorr, bass-baritone
wagner die meistersinger von nürnberg: verachtet mir die meister nicht
CWR 410   EJ 46/hmv D 1226

0213/15 october 1926/electrola session in the berliner singakademie/
leo blech
weber der freischütz overture
CWR 415   EJ 55/hmv D 1249
     416
weber oberon overture
CWR 417   EJ 54/hmv D 1316
     418

0213a/november 1926/vox session/**erich kleiber**
wagner der fliegende holländer overture
678AA   08296
679AA
680AA   08297
681AA

0214/1-2 november 1926/grammophon sessions/**richard strauss**
mozart symphony no 41 in c l551 "jupiter"
180bm   69845/brunswick 25017
181bm
182bm   69846/brunswick 25018
183bm
184bm   69847/brunswick 25019
185bm
196bm   69848/brunswick 25020
cd issues: koch 3-7076-2 and deutsche grammophon 431 8742
strauss tod und verklärung
219bm   69849/brunswick 25026
220bm
221bm   69850/brunswick 25027
222bm
223bm   69851/brunswick 25028
224bm
cd issue: deutsche grammophon 429 9252
strauss intermezzo: interlude and waltz scene
225bm   69852/brunswick 25014
226bm
229bm   69853/brunswick 25015
230bm
strauss der rosenkavalier: waltz sequence
227bm   69854/brunswick 25016
228bm

0215/2 november 1926/electrola session in the singakademie/**leo blech**
smetana the bartered bride overture
BWR 465   EW 12/hmv E 465
    466
offenbach orfee aux enfers overture
CWR 462   EJ 58/hmv D 1293
    463
mozart cosi fan tutte
CWR 464   EJ 57/hmv D 1224

0216/3 november 1926/parlophone session/**frieder weissmann**
meta seinemeyer, soprano; tino pattiera, tenor
puccini la boheme: o soave fanciulla
XXB 8940   E 10976/P 9048/odeon O-8701/O-7524
cd issue: preiser 89402
giordano andrea chenier: vicino a te
XXB 8938   E 10619/P 9028/odeon O-8700/O-7525
    8939
giordano andrea chenier: udite! sono sola!
XXB 8941   E 10976/P 9048
cd issue: preiser 89402

0217/3 november 1926/parlophone session/**frieder weissmann**
emmy bettendorf, soprano; carl martin oehmann, tenor; michael bohnen, bass; leo schützendorf, baritone
wagner die meistersinger von nürnberg: geliebter spare den zorn!; jerum! jerum!
XXB 8903 E 10541/odeon O-8708/O-7531
    8904
wagner die meistersinger von nürnberg: o ihr boshaften gesellen; den tag seh' ich erscheinen
XXB 8905 E 10542
    8906

0218/4 november 1926/electrola session in the singakademie/**leo blech**
mozart don giovanni overture
BWR 471 EW 17/hmv E 463
    472
mozart die zauberflöte overture
BWR 473 EW 13/hmv E 464
    474
rossini il barbiere di siviglia overture
CWR 475 EJ 60/hmv D 1294
    476

0219/5 november 1926/odeon session/**george szell**
richard tauber, tenor
puccini turandot: non piangere liu; nessun dorma
XXB 7508 O-9100
    7509
cd issue: emi 698 5422

0220/8 november 1926/electrola session in the singakademie/**hugo rüdel**
staatsopernchor und domchor
lotti crucifixus; corsi adoremus te
CWR 488 EH 66/hmv D 1291
    489

0221/9 november 1926/parlophone session/**george szell**
carl martin oehmann, tenor
wagner die meistersinger von nürnberg: am stillen herd; morgenlich leuchtend
XXB 8955 P 9030/odeon O-8702
    8954

0222/10 november 1926/odeon session/**george szell**
jan kiepura, tenor
puccini tosca: recondita armonia; e lucevan le stelle
XXB 7514 O-9600
    7515
verdi rigoletto: questa o quella; la donna e mobile
XXB 7516 O-9601
    7517

0223/20 and 26 november 1926/parlophone sessions/**eduard mörike**
tchaikovsky casse noisette suite
XXB 8969   E 10516/P 9024
    8970
    8971   E 10517/P 9025
    8972
    8973   E 10518/P 9037
    8974
    8975   E 10519/P 9038
    8976
smetana the bartered bride overture
XXB 8988   E 10520/P 9028
    8989
weber-berlioz aufforderung zum tanz
XXB 8985   E 10529/odeon O-6642
    8986
    8987   E 10530/odeon O-6643
wagner die meistersinger vo nürnberg: dance of the apprentices
XXB 8990   E 10530/odeon O-6643

0224/23 november 1926/parlophone session/**george szell**
beethoven leonore no 3 overture
XXB 8805   E 10545/odeon O-7503
    8806
    7534   E 10546/odeon O-7504
    7559
7559 recorded on 4 january 1927

0225/27 november 1926/parlophone session/**frieder weissmann**
meta seinemeyer, soprano; ivar andresen, bass
verdi la forza del destino: or siam soli
XXB 8995   unpublished recording
    8996
    8997   unpublished recording
    8998

0226/7-8 december 1926/parlophone sessions/**george szell**
björn talen, tenor
puccini manon lescaut: donna non vidi mai
XXB 7537   O-124007
puccini la fanciulla del west: ch'ella mi creda libero
XXB 7538   O-124006/O-6630
wagner lohengrin: in fernem land
XXB 7539   O-6576/O-8716
verdi rigoletto: la donna e mobile; parmi veder
XXB 7540   O-6570
    7541

7-8 december 1926/odeon sessions/george szell/concluded
mozart die zauberflöte: dies bildnis ist bezaubernd schön
XXB 7542   O-6589
wagner die meistersinger von nürnberg: am stillen herd
XXB 7543   O-6576/O-8716
puccini il tabarro: hai ben ragione
XXB 7544   unpublished recording
cornelius der barbier von bagdad: so leb' ich noch
XXB 7545   O-6589
verdi il trovatore: ah si ben mio
XXB 7546   O-6630
verdi la traviata: deh miei bollenti spiriti
XXB 7803   unpublished recording

0227/8 december 1926/parlophone session/**siegfried wagner**
wagner parsifal: good friday music
220011   E 10543
220012
220013   E 10544
wagner die walküre: ride of the valkyries
220014   E 10528/P 9040
220015
cd issue of both items: trax classique TRXCD 112

0228/9, 10, 14 and 15 december 1926/electrola sessions in the singakademie/**leo blech**/fritz kreisler, violin
mendelssohn violin concerto in e minor
CWR 614   hmv DB 997/victor 8080
    615
    616   hmv DB 998/victor 8081
    617
    618   hmv DB 999/victor 8082
    619
    620   hmv DB 1000/victor 8083
beethoven violin concerto in d op 61
CWR 631   hmv DB 990/victor 8074
    632
    633   hmv DB 991/victor 8075
    634
    635   hmv DB 992/victor 8076
    636
    637   hmv DB 993/victor 8077
    638
    639   hmv DB 994/victor 8078
    640
    641   hmv DB 995/victor 8079
cd issues of both concerti: biddulph LAB 049-050

0229/15 december 1926/parlophone session/**eduard mörike**
johann strauss an der schönen blauen donau
220039 E 10636/P 9181
220040

0230/21 and 23 december 1926/odeon sessions/**george szell**
emmy land, soprano; sabine kalter, contralto; tino pattiera, tenor
verdi aida: fu la sorte dell' armi
XXB 7550 unpublished recording
    7551
wagner lohengrin: entweihte götter!
XXB 7552 unpublished recording
    7553
puccini tosca: recondita armonia
XXB 7555 O-124002/O-8707/O-7534
puccini tosca: e lucevan le stelle
XXB 7556 O-124003/O-8707/O-7534
puccini la boheme: che gelida manina
XXB 7557 O-124000/O-8714/O-7526
bizet carmen: la fleur que tu m'avais jetee
XXB 7558 O-124001/O-8714/O-7526

0231/1927/grammophon session/**erich kleiber**
dvorak slavonic dance op 46 no 1
629bm 66913
cd issue: naxos 81.10907

0232/1927/grammophon session/**oskar fried**
suppe dichter und bauer overture
249be 60007/19739
250be
adam si j'etais roi overture
243be 19743
244be

0233/1927/grammophon sessions/**oskar fried**/staatsopernchor
mascagni cavalleria rusticana: regina coeli
157bi 66517
wagner tannhäuser: pilgrims' chorus
169bi 66516
weber der freischütz: huntsmens' chorus
170bi 66518
wagner lohengrin: bridal chorus
171bi 66517
wagner tannhäuser: entry of the guests
172bi 66516
wagner der fliegende holländer: spinning chorua
173bi 66518
cd issue of all choruses: music and arts CD 1231

0234/1927/grammophon session/**hans pfitzner**
weber der freischütz overture
320bi 66545
321bi
322bi 66546
weber preciosa overture
323bi 66544
324bi

0235/1927/grammophon sessions/**max von schillings**
wagner siegfried: forest murmurs
358bi 66590
359bi
wagner götterdämmerung: siegfried's rhine journey
360bi 66591
361bi
wagner tristan und isolde prelude
364bi 66589
365bi
wagner tristan und isolde liebestod
368bi 66607
wagner parsifal prelude
369bi 66592
370bi
371bi 66593
wagner parsifal: conclusion of act three
372bi 66593
wagner parsifal: good friday music
373bi 66594
374bi
wagner parsifal: flower maidens scene, orchestral arrangement
375bi 66595
376bi
wagner lohengrin prelude
379bi 66588
380bi
cd issue of all items: preiser 90080

0236/1927/grammophon sessions/**otto klemperer**
beethoven coriolan overture
387 ½ bi   66599
388bi
beethoven egmont overture
389 ½ bi   66600
390bi
beethoven leonore no 3 overture
391bi   66601
392bi
393bi   66602
wagner siegfried idyll
394bi   66604
395bi
396bi   66605
397bi
mendelssohn a midsummer night's dream overture
398bi   66602
449bm   66603
400bi
weber euryanthe overture
450bm   66629
456bm
cd issue of all items: archiphon ARC 121-125

0237/2 january 1927/parlophone session/**frieder weissmann**
mozart le nozze di figaro overture
220084   E 10621
flotow alessandro stradella overture
220088   E 10612/P 9050
220089

0238/4 january 1927/parlophone session/**george szell**
auber fra diavolo overture
XXB 7560   E 10687/odeon O-7507
    7561
nicolai die lustigen weiber von windsor overture
XXB 7562   E 10588/odeon O-7504
    7589
recording completed on 25 january 1927

0239/17 january 1927/electrola session in the singakademie/**leo blech**
wagner rienzi overture
CWR 666   EJ 90
    667
    668   EJ 91
wagner der fliegende holländer overture
CWR 669   EJ 89/hmv D 1290
    670

0240/20 january 1927/electrola session in the singakademie/**leo blech**
johann strauss der zigeunerbaron overture
CWR 679   EJ 94/hmv D 1289
     680
auber fra diavolo overture
CWR 681   EJ 92
     682

0241/20-21 january 1927/parlophone sessions/**frieder weissmann**
mozart don giovanni overture
220086   E 10568/P 9049
220087
thomas mignon overture
220098   E 10557/P 9051
220099
flotow martha overture
220100   E 10578/P 9074
220101
wagner tannhäuser: entry of the guests
220102   E 10577

0242/21 and 24 january 1927/electrola sessions in the singakademie/**leo blech**
thomas mignon overture
CWR 687   EJ 93/hmv D 1246
     688
mascagni cavalleria rusticana: prelude and siciliana
CWR 689   EJ 135
     690
beethoven fidelio overture
BWR 695   EW 19/victor 45725
     696
beethoven egmont overture
CWR 697   EJ 96/victor 45727
     698

0243/25 january 1927/parlophone session/**george szell**
herold zampa overture
XXB 7590   E 10623/odeon O-7505
     7662

0244/25-26 january 1927/parlophone sessions/**siegfried wagner**
wagner die walküre: leb wohl du kühnes herrliches kind, orchestral arrangement
220107   E 10566/P 9096/odeon O-6532
220108
220109   E 10566/P 9097/odeon O-6533
220110
wagner das rheingold: entry of the gods into valhalla, orchestral arrangement
220111   E 10554/P 9695
220112
cd issue of both items: trax classique TRXCD 112

0245/26 january 1927/electrola session in the singakademie/**leo blech**
johann strauss an der schönen blauen donau
CWR 709 EJ 95/hmv D 1295
710
johann strauss perpetuum mobile and radetzky march
BWR 711 EW 18
712

0246/28 january 1927/electrola session in the singakademie/**leo blech**
elisabeth van endert, soprano
puccini la boheme: si mi chiamano mimi; tosca: vissi d'arte
CWR 718 unpublished recordings
720
wagner lohengrin: euch lüften die mein klagen; tannhäuser: dich teure halle
CWR 719 EH 65
721

0247/2 february 1927/parlophone session/**otto dobrindt**
mussorgsky boris godunov: polonaise
220131 E 10621

0248/4 february 1927/parlophone session/**frieder weissmann**
karol szreter, piano
beethoven piano concerto no 4 in g op 58
XXB 7599 E 10533/P 9059/odeon O-6522
7600
7601 E 10534/P 9060/odeon O-6523
7602
7603 E 10535/P 9061/odeon O-6524
7604
7605 E 10536/P 9062/odeon O-6525
7606

0249/16 and 18 february 1927/odeon sessions/**fritz zweig**
lotte lehmann, soprano
puccini turandot: del primo pianto
XXB 7610 O-9602/O-8720
cd issue: pearl GEMMCD 9409
puccini turandot: in questa reggia
XXB 7609 O-9602/O-8720
weber oberon: ozean du ungeheuer!
XXB 7611 O-8742
7612
giordano andrea chenier: la mamma morta
XXB 7613 parlophone R 20025
godard berceuse de jocelyn; jensen o lass dich halten!
XXB 7618 O-8709
7619
jensen mürmelndes lüftchen
XXB 7620 parlophone R 20025
mendelssohn auf flügeln des gesanges; brahms von ewiger liebe
XXB 7621 O-8713/O-8763
7622

0250/19 february 1927/parlophone session/**eduard mörike**
wagner lohengrin: orchestral fantasy
220141   E 10587/P 9087
220142

0251/21 february 1927/electrola session in the singakademie/**ernst viebig**
johann strauss eine nacht in venedig overture
BWR 800   hmv B 2547
    801

0252/23 february 1927/parlophone session/**frieder weissmann**
beethoven wellingtons sieg
220146   E 10555/P 9072
220147
220148   E 10556/P 9073
220149
kreutzer das nachtlager von grenada overture
220150   E 10622/odeon O-6545
220151

0253/24 february 1927/odeon session/**fritz zweig**
mafalda salvatini, soprano
catalani la wally: ebben ne andro lontana; bizet carmen: pres des remparts de seville
XXB 7623   unpublished recordings
    7624
puccini turandot: in questa reggia; del primo pianto
XXB 7625   unpublished recordings
    7626
halevy la juive: il va venir
XXB 7667   O-8712
the unpublished items were repeated on 1 april 1927 using same matrix numbers

0254/1 march 1927/electrola session in the singakademie/**ernst viebig**
suppe leichte kavallerie overture
CWR 823   EH 48
    824
suppe die schöne galathea overture
CWR 829   EH 53/hmv C 1527
    830

0255/18 march 1927/parlophone session/**frieder weissmann**
rossini l'italiana in algeri overture
220173   E 10891/P 8103
220174
attrib. beethoven jena symphony
220175   E 10610/P 9119
220176
220177   E 10611/P 9120
220178

0256/21 march 1927/parlophone session/**george szell**
cornelius der barbier von bagdad overture
XXB 7663   E 10613
    7664

0257/22 march 1927/parlophone session/**siegfried wagner**
wagner rienzi overture
220182   E 10576/P 9138
220183
220184   E 10577/P 9139
wagner götterdämmerung: siegfried's rhine journey
220185   E 10586/P 9117
220186

0258/28 march and 2 april 1927/grammophon sessions/**richard strauss**
mozart symphony no 40 in g minor k550
250bi   69864
251bi
252bi   69865
253bi
254bi   69866
255bi
cd issue: koch 3-7076-2
strauss intermezzo: interlude and waltz scene
261bi   69867
262bi
263bi   69868
264bi
cd issue: deutsche grammophon 429 9252
strauss der rosenkavalier: waltz sequence
265bi   69863
266bi
cd issue: deutsche grammophon 429 9252

0258a/april 1927/vox session/**erich kleiber**
wagner tannhäuser overture and venusberg music
1215AA   08434
1216AA
1217AA   08435
1218AA

0259/1 april 1927/*see 24 february 1927*

0260/6 april 1927/electrola session in the singakademie/**leo blech**
beethoven leonore no 3 overture
CWR 966   EJ 131
    967
    968   EJ 132
mozart der schauspieldirektor overture
CWR 965   EJ 132

0261/11 april 1927/odeon session/**fritz zweig**
thomas raymonda overture
XXB 7687   O-6530
    7688

0262/20 april 1927/electrola session in the singakademie/**ernst viebig**
max lorenz, tenor
wagner die meistersinger von nürnberg: morgenlich leuchtend
CWR 984   EH 300
cd issue: preiser 89232

0263/27 april 1927/parlophone session/**frieder weissmann**
jovita fuentes, soprano
puccini madama butterfly: un bel di; tu piccolo addio
220215   E 11047/P 9106
220216

0264/29 april 1927/odeon session/**fritz zweig**
suppe leichte kavallerie overture
XXB 7689   O-6536
    7690

0265/29 april 1927/odeon session/**eduard mörike**/staatsopernchor/
emmy bettendorf, soprano
mascagni cavalleria rusticana: regina coeli
XXB 7691   O-8711/O-7528
    7692
verdi aida: gloria all'egitto
XXB 7693   O-8710/O-6812
    7694

0266/4-5 may 1927/parlophone sessions/**frieder weissmann**
meta seinemeyer, soprano
mozart le nozze di figaro: porgi amor
220254   unpublished recording
mozart le nozze di figaro: dove sono
220255   E 11130/P 9832/P 9360/odeon O-7569
220256
verdi la forza del destino: son giunta!
220258   E 10605/P 9116/odeon O-7834
220259
verdi la forza del destino: pace pace mio dio!
220260   P 9865/P 9657/odeon O-7648
cd issue of the published arias: preiser 89402

0267/11 may 1927/electrola session in the singakademie/**leo blech**
jaro dworsky, tenor
mascagni cavalleria rusticana: prelude and siciliano
CDR 4578   EJ 135
puccini tosca: recondita armonia
BDR 4579   EW 36

0268/23 and 26 may 1927/electrola sessions in the singakademie/
leo blech/tino pattiera, tenor
leoncavallo i pagliacci: vesti la giubba; verdi il trovatore: di quella pira
BDR 4620 EW 21
    4621
puccini tosca: recondita armonia; e lucevan le stelle
BDR 4630 EW 23
    4631
verdi rigoletto: la donna e mobile; leoncavallo i pagliacci: un tal gioco
BDR 4622 EW 22
    4632

0269/8 june 1927/electrola session in the singakademie/**leo blech**
flotow martha overture
CWR 292 EH 92/hmv C 1502
CDR 4676
recording completed on 28 october 1927

0270/8-9 june 1927/electrola sessions in the singakademie/**leo blech**
fritz krauss, tenor
wagner lohengrin: mein lieber schwan; in fernem land
CDR 4673 EJ 140
    4674
flotow martha: ach so fromm; gounod faust: salut demeure
CDR 4675 EJ 141
    4679
wagner die walküre: winterstürme; siegmund bin ich!
CDR 4677 EJ 142
    4678

0271/10 june 1927/electrola session in the singakademie/**leo blech**
barbara kemp, soprano
strauss der rosenkavalier: da geht er hin
CDR 4682 EJ 146/hmv D 143
    4683
wagner tristan und isolde: mild und leise
CDR 4684 unpublished recording
    4685

0272/17 june 1927/electrola session in the singakademie/**leo blech**
friedrich schorr, bass-baritone
wagner die walküre: leb wohl du kühnes herrliches kind....to end of opera
CDR 4695 EJ 214/hmv D 1332
    4696
    4697 EJ 215/hmv D 1333
    4698
cd issue: pearl GEMMCDS 9137

0273/18 june 1927/electrola session in the singakademie/**leo blech**
staatsopernchor; friedrich schorr, bass-baritone
wagner das rheingold: abendlich strahlt der sonne auge
CDR 4700 EJ 157/hmv D 1319
    4701
cd issue: pearl GEMMCDS 9137
wagner die meistersinger von nürnberg: ehrt ihre deutschen meister; verachtet mir die meister nicht
BDR 4699 unpublished recordings
    4702

0274/20 june 1927/electrola session in the singakademie/**leo blech**
wagner lohengrin prelude
CDR 4703 EJ 147
    4704
wagner lohengrin act three prelude
CDR 4705 EJ 91
beethoven leonore no 3 overture, second part
CDR 4706 EJ 131
this presumably replaced CWR 967 (see 6 april 1927)
johann strauss perpetuum mobile
BDR 4707 unpublished recording

0275/21-22 june 1927/electrola sessions in the singakademie/**leo blech**
staatsopernchor/ivar andresen, bass
wagner götterdämmerung: ho ho ihr gibichsmannen!
CDR 4708 EJ 150/hmv D 1578
    4709
cd issue: pearl GEMMCDS 9137
wagner parsifal: das ist karfreitagszauber herr!
CDR 4710 EJ 151
    4711

0276/23 june 1927/electrola session in the singakademie/**otto klemperer**
brahms academic festival overture
CDR 4713 EJ 152/hmv D 1853
    4714
    4715 EJ 153/hmv D 1854
wagner tristan und isolde prelude
CDR 4716 EW 27/hmv E 476
    4717
    4718 EW 28/hmv E 477
    4719
cd issue of both items: archiphon ARC 121-125

0277/4 july 1927/electrola session in the singakademie/**leo blech**
friedrich schorr, bass-baritone
wagner die meistersinger von nürnberg: verachtet mir die meister nicht
CDR 4739   EJ 220/hmv D 1354
cd issue: pearl GEMMCDS 9137
wagner tannhäuser: o du mein holder abendstern
CDR 4740   unpublished recording
wagner der fliegende holländer: wie aus der ferne
CDR 4741   unpublished recording
wagner die meistersinger von nürnberg: was duftet doch der flieder
CDR 4742   victor 7425
cd issue of flieder-monolog: sanctus SCSH 006

0278/3 august 1927/parlophone session/**eduard mörike**
saint-saens danse macabre
XXB 7723   P 9111
    7724
    7725   P 9112

0279/25 and 27 august 1927/electrola sessions in the singakademie/**leo blech**
frida leider, soprano; rudolf laubenthal, tenor
wagner siegfried: nothung neidliches schwert; dass der mein vater nicht war
CWR 1057   EJ 340/hmv D 1530/victor M 53
    1058
    1059   EJ 371/hmv D 1532/victor M 53
wagner siegfried: heil dir sonne
CWR 1064   EJ 371/hmv D 1532/victor M 53
    1065   EJ 370/hmv D 1535/victor M 53
    1066
cd issue: pearl GEMMCDS 9137

0280/2 september 1927/parlophone session/**frieder weissmann**
gotthelf pistor, tenor
wagner parsifal: amfortas die wunde!; nur eine waffe taugt
220345   E 10771/P 9817
220346

0281/7 september 1927/electrola session in the singakademie/**leo blech**
friedrich schorr, bass-baritone
wagner tannhäuser: o du mein holder abendstern
CWR 1105   EJ 220/hmv D 1354
wagner der fliegende holländer: wie aus der ferne
CWR 1106   EJ 219/hmv D 1355
cd issue of holländer aria: nimbus NI 7848

0282/9-10 september 1927/parlophone sessions/**artur bodansky**
wagner die meistersinger von nürnberg overture
220325   E 10633/odeon O-6715/O-8320/am.decca 25555
220326
220327   E 10634/odeon O-6716/O-8321/am.decca 25556
wagner lohengrin act three prelude
220328   E 10634/odeon O-6716/O-8321/am.decca 25556
suppe die schöne galathea overture
220329   E 10943/P 9147
220330
johann strauss wein weib und gesang
220331   E 10651/odeon O-6719/O-8323
220332
wagner lohengrin prelude
220333   E 10635/P 9150
220334
cd issue of lohengrin prelude: pearl GEMS 0024

0283/12 september 1927/electrola session in the singakademie/**leo blech**
frida leider, soprano; friedrich schorr, bass-baritone
wagner die walküre: nun zäume dein ross
CWR 1116   EJ 205/hmv D 1323/victor M26-27
wagner die walküre: o heilige schmach!; so nimm meinen segen
CWR 1117   EJ 205/hmv D 1324/victor M26-27
     1118
cd issue: pearl GEMMCDS 9137

0284/14 september 1927/parlophone session/unnamed conductor
margret pfahl-wallenstein, soprano; gotthelf pistor, tenor
wagner siegfried: wie sah wohl mein vater aus?
220340   E 10658/P 9164
220341

0285/17 september 1927/electrola recording from a public performance in the krolloper/**leo blech**/violetta da strozzi, soprano; karin branzell, mezzo-soprano; robert hutt, tenor; michael bohnen, bass-baritone; emanuel list, bass
verdi aida: pur ti riveggio; l'abborita rivale!
CWR 1147   EJ 174
     1149
further unpublished sides CWR 1140, 1141, 1142, 1143, 1144, 1145, 1146, 1148 and 1150

0286/19 september 1927/electrola session in the singakademie/**leo blech**
gounod faust prelude and waltz
CWR 1155   EJ 180
     1156
lortzing zar und zimmermann overture
BWR 1157   EW 32/victor 4164
     1158

0287/20 september 1927/parlophone session/frieder weissmann
gotthelf pistor, tenor; ivar andresen, bass
suppe dichter und bauer overture
220344   E 10650/P 9213
220345
wagner parsifal: vom bade kehrt der könig heim; act one transformation
220347   E 10641/P 9155
220348
wagner tristan und isolde: tatest du es wirklich?
220349   E 10829
E 10641 issued on lp by discocorp but with incorrect attribution

0288/21 september 1927/electrola session in the singakademie/leo blech
frida leider, soprano; göta ljungberg, soprano; elfriede marherr-wagner, soprano; genia guszalewicz, mezzo-soprano; lydia kindermann, contralto; friedrich schorr, bass-baritone
wagner die walküre: wo ist brünnhild', wo die verbrecherin?; deinen leichten sinn
CWR 1161   EJ 212/hmv D 1330/victor M26-27
    1162
wagner die walküre: ride of the valkyries
CWR 1163   EJ 210/hmv D 1329/victor M26-27
    1164
wagner die walküre: rette mich kühne!
CWR 1188   EJ 211/hmv D 1327/victor M26-27
wagner die walküre: du zeugtest ein edles geschlecht
CWR 1189   EJ 213/hmv D 1331/victor M26-27
wagner die walküre: war es so schmählich?
CWR 1190   EJ 238/hmv D 1331/victor M26-27
CWR 1190 re-recorded on 1 november 1927
cd issue of all tracks: pearl GEMMCDS 9137

0289/30 september 1927/odeon session/frieder weissmann
hans reinmar, baritone
wagner tannhäuser: als du in kühnem sange; blick' ich umher in diesem edlen kreise
XXB 7777   O-6569
    7778
meyerbeer l'africaine: fille des rois
XXB 7779   O-6599/O-3682
offenbach les contes d'hoffmann: scintille diamant
XXB 7780   O-6600/O-3682
gounod faust: avant de quitter ces lieux
XXB 7781   O-6600/O-7783
verdi otello: credo in un dio
XXB 7782   O-6599/O-7783
cd issue of all arias: preiser 89112

0290/3 october 1927/electrola session in the singakademie/leo blech
verdi la forza del destino overture
CWR 1199   EJ 198/ES 364
    1200
meyerbeer le prophete: coronation march
CWR 1201   EJ 190/ES 340

0291/5 october 1927/parlophone session/**frieder weissmann**
mendelssohn a midsummer night's dream: wedding march and scherzo
220365   E 10649/P 9214
220366
weber preciosa overture
220367   E 10662/odeon O-6591
220368

0292/12 october 1927/parlophone session/**pietro mascagni**
rossini il barbiere di siviglia overture
220397   E 11148/odeon O-6807
220398

0293/12 october 1927/odeon session/**pietro mascagni**
rossini william tell overture
XXB 7897   O-8031/O-6810
    7898
    7899   O-8032/O-6811
    7900

0294/13 october 1927/parlophone session/**frieder weissmann**
eduard habich, baritone; ivar andresen, bass
wagner lohengrin: gott grüss' euch liebe männer von brabant; mein herr und gott!
220401   E 10670/P 9249
220402
wagner lohengrin: heil könig heinrich!; wo weilt nun der, den gott gesandt?
220403   E 10693
220404

0295/14 october 1927/electrola session in the singakademie/**leo blech**
bizet carmen entr'actes acts two and four
CWR 1241   EJ 188
      1242
verdi aida: triumphal march
CWR 1243   EJ 189
      1244

0296/18 october 1927/electrola session in the singakademie/**leo blech**
staatsopernchor
wagner lohengrin: bridal chorus
BWR 1249   EW 60
      1250
wagner lohengrin: procession to the minster
BWR 1251   EW 33
      1252
verdi aida prelude
BWR 1253   EJ 190

0297/26 october 1927/electrola session in the singakademie/**leo blech**
frida leider, soprano
wagner götterdämmerung: starke scheite schichtet mir dort
CLR 4666   EJ 420/hmv D 2025
       4667   EJ 421/hmv D 2026
       4668
cd issues: pearl GEMMCDS 9137 and preiser 89088

0298/26 and 30 october 1927/electrola sessions in the singakademie/**leo blech**
liszt hungarian rhapsody no 1
BLR 4718   EG 1341/hmv B 3135
BWR 1283
       1284   EG 1342/hmv B 3136
       1285
schubert rosamunde ballet music
BWR 1286   unpublished recording
       1287

0299/27 and 28 october 1927/electrola sessions in the singakademie/**leo blech**
maria olczewska, contralto
saint-saens samson et dalila: mon coeur s'ouvre a ta voix
CWR 1290   unpublished recording
saint-saens samson et dalila: printemps qui commence; bizet carmen: l'amour est
un oiseau rebelle
CWR 1291   EJ 238/hmv D 1386
       1295
bizet carmen: en vain pour eviter
CWR 1296   EJ 178/hmv D 1363
       1297

0300/28 october 1927/*see 8 june 1927*

0301/1 november 1927/*see 21 september 1927*

0302/1 november 1927/electrola session in the singakademie/**leo blech**
saint-saens samson et dalila: bacchanale
CWR 1309   EJ 191/hmv D 1444
       1310

0303/1-2 november 1927/parlophone sessions/**frieder weismann**/
staatsopernchor/meta seinemeyer, soprano; helene jung, contralto;
max hirzel, tenor; robert burg, baritone; willy bader, bass;
ivar andresen, bass
verdi aida: i sacri nomi
220417   E 10746/odeon O-8717/O-7522
220418
verdi aida: gloria all' egitto
220419   E 10747/odeon O-8718/O-7523
220420
puccini manon lescaut: in quelle trine morbide
220424   E 11153/P 9819/P 9621/odeon O-7568
rimsky-korsakov the tsar's bride: come into the garden
220425   P 9819/P 9621/odeon O-7832

1-2 november 1927/parlophone sessions/frieder weissmann/ concluded
verdi don carlo: tu che la vanita
220426   P 9873/P 9665/odeon O-7650
220427
cd issue of all items: preiser 89402

0304/4 november 1927/parlophone session/**franz schreker**
bizet l'arlesienne, incidental music
                                         P 9052/odeon O-6551
                                         P 9053/odeon O-6552
                                         P 9068/odeon O-6559
                                         P 9069/odeon O-6560
                                         P 9070/odeon O-6561
parts of the recording also published on E 10597-10598

0305/7 november 1927/electrola session in the singakademie/**leo blech**
mozart 7 deutsche tänze from k600, k602 and k605
CWR 1318   EJ 192/hmv D 1624
     1319
cd issue: archiphon ARC 135
gluck-mottl ballet suite
CWR 1320   ES 196/hmv D 1529
     1321

0306/7 november 1927/parlophone session/**frieder weissmann**
emmy bettendorf, soprano; karin branzell, contralto
rimsky-korsakov sadko: chanson indoue
220437   E 10836
offenbach les contes d'hoffmann: barcarolle
221102   E 10836

0307/9 november 1927/electrola session in the singakademie/**leo blech**
genia guszalewicz, mezzo-soprano; marcel noe, tenor;
eduard habich, baritone; ivar andresen, bass
wagner tristan und isolde: he kurwenal! ein zweites schiff!
CWR 1327   ES 265/hmv D 1416
wagner tristan und isolde: tot denn alles?
CWR 1328   hmv D 1417

0308/9 november 1927/electrola session in the singakademie/**fritz zweig**
elisabeth rethberg, soprano
wagner tannhäuser: dich teure halle; lohengrin: einsam in trüben tagen
CWR 1329   EJ 184/hmv D 1420/victor M633
     1330
cd issue: pearl GEMMCD 9199
verdi aida: o patria mia; ritorna vincitor
CWR 1332   EJ 185/hmv D 1451/victor 7106
     1331
cd issue: preiser 89971

0309/9 november 1927/parlophone session/**frieder weissmann**
rosa pauly, soprano
beethoven fidelio: abscheulicher wo eilst du hin?
220443-4   E 11036/P 9179

0310/11 november 1927/electrola session in the singakademie/**fritz zweig**
lotte schöne, soprano
puccini turandot: tu che di gel sei cinta
CWR 1343   EW 41/hmv E 503

0311/15 november 1927/parlophone session/**frieder weissmann**
margherita salvi, soprano
rossini il barbiere di siviglia: una voce poco fa
XXB 7841   E 10708/odeon O-6803/O-8328
    7842
orejon por un pajano; carnival of venice
XXB 7840   E 10828/odeon O-8339
    7845

0312/19 november 1927/odeon session/**manfred gurlitt**
mafalda salvatini, soprano; ludwig hofmann, bass-baritone
meyerbeer les huguenots: ach dies herz!
XXB 7849   unpublished recording
    7850
offenbach les contes d'hoffmann: barcarolle; cornelius verratene liebe
XXB 7851   O-8723/O-7529
    7852

0313/21 november 1927/odeon session/**frieder weissmann**
berta kiurina, soprano
puccini madama butterfly: un bel di; mozart le nozze di figaro: porgi amor
XXB 7853   O-6566
    7854

0314/21, 23 and 25 november 1927/electrola sessions in the singakademie/
leo blech/fritz kreisler, violin
brahms violin concerto in d op 77
CWR 1355   hmv DB 1120/victor 8098
    1356
    1357   hmv DB 1121/victor 8099
    1358
    1366   hmv DB 1122/victor 8100
    1367
    1368   hmv DB 1123/victor 8101
    1369
    1376   hmv DB 1124/victor 8102
cd issues: biddulph LAB 049-050, pearl GEMMCDS 9996 and music and arts CD 290

0315/28 november 1927/electrola session in the singakademie/**erich kleiber**
mozart symphony no 39 in e flat k543
CWR 1377   EJ 199/hmv D 1448
    1378
    1381   EJ 200/hmv D 1449
    1382
    1379   EJ 201/hmv D 1450
    1380

0316/29 november 1927/electrola session in the singakademie/**leo blech**
schubert marche militaire
CWR 1383   EJ 387/hmv D 1987/victor 11435

0317/30 november 1927/parlophone session/**max von schillings**
schubert symphony no 8 in b minor d759 "unfinished"
220486   E 10672/P 9800
220487
220488   E 10673/P 9801
220489
220490   E 10674/P 9802
220491

0318/december 1927/grammophon session/**oskar fried**
tchaikovsky casse noisette suite
326be   95030/90416/decca CA 8132
327be
329be   95031/90417/decca CA 8133
330be
331be   95032/90418/decca CA 8134
332be
cd issue: dante LYS 200; fried re-recorded the suite in 1929 in london with the orchestra of the royal philharmonic society

0319/2 december 1927/electrola session in the singakademie/**bruno seidler-winkler/**gita lau, soprano; cornelis bronsgeest, tenor
loewe archibald douglas
CWR 1398   EH 100/hmv C 2396
    1399
johann strauss g'schichten aus dem wienerwald; frühlingsstimmen
CWR 1400   EH 99/hmv C 1539
    1401

0320/7 december 1927/parlophone session/**frieder weissmann**
robert burg, bass-baritone
wagner die walküre: leb wohl du kühnes herrliches kind
220496   P 9216/odeon O-7575
220497
wagner tannhäuser: o du mein holder abendstern; als du in kühnem sange
220498   P 9200
220499

0321/8 and 11 december 1927/electrola sessions in the singakademie/
karl muck
wagner die meistersinger von nürnberg overture
CWR 1402   EJ 223/victor 6858
    1403
    1404   EJ 224/victor 6859
cd issues: preiser 90269 and centaur CRC 2142

8 and 11 december 1927/electrola sessions/karl muck/concluded
wagner götterdämmerung: siegfried's rhine journey
CWR 1418	EJ 224/victor 6859
cd issues: preiser 90269 and centaur CRC 2142
wagner siegfried's funeral march
CWR 1419	EJ 225/victor 6860
    1420
cd issues: preiser 90269 and centaur CRC 2142
wagner parsifal prelude
CWR 1421	EJ 226/victor 6861
    1422
    1423	EJ 227/victor 6862
    1424
cd issues: preiser 90269, centaur CRC 2142, pearl CDS 9843 and naxos 8.11049-50

0322/9 december 1927/electrola recording from a public performance in the krolloper/**leo blech**/maria müller and gitta alpar, sopranos; tino pattiera, tenor; eduard habich, baritone; otto helgers, bass-baritone; theodor scheidl, bass
puccini la boheme: che gelida manina; si mi chiamano mimi
CWR 1405	EJ 218
    1406
puccini la boheme: o soave fanciulla; sono andati?
CWR 1407	EJ 217
    1415
cd issue: preiser 89235
further unpublished sides CWR 1409-1414 and 1416-1417

0323/10 december 1927/parlophone session/**max von schillings**
wagner tristan und isolde: hörst du sie noch?....sink hernieder nacht der liebe, orchestral arrangement
220501	E 10661/P 9606
220502
220503	E 10685/P 9807
220548
recording completed on 29 december 1927

0324/10 and 13 december 1927/odeon sessions/**manfred gurlitt**
lotte lehmann, soprano; jan kiepura, tenor
puccini tosca: ah quegli occhi; o dolci mani
XXB 7881	O-9603/O-8743/parlophone R 20048
    7882
cd issue: pearl GEMMCD 9409
puccini turandot: nessun dorma; non piangere liu
XXB 7883	O-9604/O-9700/O-7536
    7884
beethoven fidelio: abscheulicher wo eilst du hin?
XXB 7885	O-8721/parlophone R 20053
    7886
strauss der rosenkavalier: die zeit sie ist ein sonderbar ding
XXB 7887	O-8726/parlophone R 20054
cd issue: pearl GEMMCD 9410
mozart le nozze di figaro: porgi amor
XXB 7888	O-8726/parlophone R 20054

0325/12 december 1927/odeon session/**frieder weissmann**
jan berlik, tenor; wilhelm zitek, bass
halevy die jüdin: wenn ewiger hass; verdi don carlo: ella giammai m'amo
XXB 7889 unpublished recordings
7890
puccini tosca: recondita armonia; e lucevan le stelle
XXB 7891 O-6590
7892

0326/13 december 1927/odeon session/**hermann weigert**
emmy land, soprano
wagner lohengrin: einsam in trüben tagen; euch lüften die mein klagen
XXB 7903 O-7508/parlophone E 10732
7904
mozart die zauberflöte: ach ich fühl's; mozart le nozze di figaro: venite inginocchiatevi
XXB 7905 O-7509
7906
verdi un ballo in maschera: morro ma prima in grazia; mascagni cavalleria rusticana: voi lo sapete
XXB 7907 O-7510
7908

0327/14 december 1927/odeon session/**manfred gurlitt**
ludwig hofmann, bass-baritone
krenek jonny spielt auf: hymn and blues song
XXB 7909 O-6565/parlophone E 10698
7910

0328/14 december 1927/electrola session in the singakademie/**leo blech**
staatsopernchor/genia guszalewicz, mezzo soprano; waldemar henke, tenor; eduard habich, baritone
auber fra diavolo: tanzet dem frühling fröhlich entgegen
CWR 1435 EJ 221
1436
verdi la forza del destino: rataplan!; popper tarantella
CWR 1437 EJ 222
1438

0329/27 december 1927/parlophone session/**frieder weissmann**
meta seinemeyer, soprano; ivar andresen, bass
verdi la forza del destino: la vergine degli angeli
220542 E 10709/P 9808/odeon O-7567
220545 E 11153
220547 P 9865/odeon O-7648
cd issue: preiser 89042; 220544 and 220546 remained unpublished

0330/29 december 1927/*see 10 december 1927*

0331/1928/grammophon sessions/**oskar fried**
mozart eine kleine nachtmusik
922be   66669/90144
923be
924be   66670/90145
925be
cd issue of 925be only: arbiter 153
thomas mignon overture
241be   19744
242be
weber euryanthe overture
205bs I   19988
206bs I
cd issue: music and arts CD 1198
wagner eine faust-ouvertüre
1390bm I   95318/90077
1391bm I
6811bi I   95319/90078
cd issue: music and arts CD 1167
donizetti don pasquale overture
1400bm I   27003
1401bm I

0332/1928/grammophon session/**julius prüwer**
rosette anday, contralto
wagner götterdämmerung: seit er von dir geschieden
1224bm   66778
1225bm
cd issue: preiser 89046

0333/1928/grammophon sessions/**richard strauss**
mozart symphony no 40 in g minor k550
296be   69869/95442/brunswick 90082
297be
298be   69870/95443/brunswick 90083
299be
300be   69871/95444/brunswick 90084
301be
302be   69872/95445/brunswick 90085
cd issues: deutsche grammophon 431 8742 and koch 3-7119-2
beethoven symphony no 5 in c minor op 67
1383bm I   66814/brunswick 90172
1384bm I
1385bm I   66815/brunswick 90173
1386bm I
1402bm I   66816/brunswick 90174
1403bm I
1404bm I   66817/brunswick 90175
1405bm I
cd issues: naxos 8.110926 and dutton CDBP 9813
mozart die zauberflöte overture
1406bm I   66826/brunswick 90255/decca CA 8106
1407bm I
cd issues: deutsche grammophon 431 8742, koch 3-7119-2 and dutton CDBP 9785; matrix numbers 1406bm and 1407bm were replaced in 1939 by 1239GS and 1240GS respectively

0334/1928/parlophone session/**frieder weissmann**
nanny larsen-todsen, soprano
wagner göttedämmerung: starke scheite schichtet mir dort
220694   E 10756/P 9827/american decca 25054
220695

0335/1928/parlophone session/**eduard mörike**
nanny larsen-todsen, soprano
wagner siegfried: ewig war ich
220771   P 9534/odeon O-7643

0336/1928/grammophon session/**manfred gurlitt**
willi domgraf-fassbaender, baritone
rossini il barbiere di siviglia: largo al factotum
596bi   95242
gluck iphigenie auf tauris: ihr die ihr mich verfolgt
1044bh   90053/24323
1045bh

0337/1928/grammophon session/**hans pfitzner**
schumann symphony no 2 in c, third movement
872bi   95414
1470bm   95415
1471bm
cd issue: zyx music PD 50222

0338/1928/grammophon session/**erich kleiber**
smetana the moldau/ma vlast
1563 bm I   66652
1564 ½ bm I
1015 ½ bm   66653
cd issue: naxos 8.110907

0339/1928/grammophon session/**joseph snaga**
staatsopernchor/franz völker, tenor
czernik es reiten die kosaken; ich bin ein freier mann und singe
                                                 27062
millöcker der bettelstudent: ich hab' sie ja nur!
                                                 27068
cd issue: preiser 89221
oscar strauss ein walzertraum: da draussen im duftenden garten
                                                 22254
zeller der vogelhändler: schenkt man sich rosen im tirol
                                             27068/15182/57414/57441
cd issue: preiser 89221
johann strauss der zigeunerbaron: werbelied und czardas
                                                 27072
cd issue: preiser 89221

0340/1928/grammophon session/**joseph snaga**/else kochhahn, soprano; irene eisinger, soprano; hertha klust, contralto; franz völker, tenor; gerhard witting, tenor; eduard kandl, baritone
johann strauss die fledermaus: im feuerstrom der reben; brüderlein und schwesterlein
22173/10017

cd issue: preiser 89221

0341/1928/electrola session/**leo blech**/lotte schöne, soprano
johann strauss die fledermaus: mein herr was dächten sie von mir?
EJ 429/hmv D 1733
lehar friederike: sah ein knab' ein röslein steh'n
EH 216/hmv C 1843

cd issue of both items: bbc records BBCCD 716

0342/12 january 1928/parlophone session/unnamed conductor
adele kern, soprano; alfred strauss, tenor
johann strauss wiener blut: grüss gott mein liebes kind!; offenbach les contes d'hoffmann: les oiseaux dans la chamille
220568   E 11091/P 9226
220564

0343/12 january 1928/odeon session/**franz schalk**
schubert symphony no 8 in b minor d759 "unfinished"
XXB 7918   O-8344/O-6813
    7919
    7920   O-8345/O-6814
    7921
    7922   O-8346/O-6815
    7923
re-recorded on 2 march 1928

0344/19 january 1928/parlophone session/**frieder weissmann**
meta seinemeyer, soprano
wagner tristan und isolde: mild und leise
220577   E 10829
re-recorded on 8 march 1928

0345/23 january 1928/odeon session/**frieder weissmann**
riele queling, violin
beethoven violin concerto in d op 61
XXB 7539   O-6951
    7540
    7541   O-6952
    7542
    7543   O-6953
    7544
    8093   O-6954
    8094
    8095   O-6955
recording completed on 15 may 1928

0346/25 january 1928/electrola session/**fritz zweig**/lotte schöne, soprano
puccini turandot: signore ascolta
BLR 3793　　　　　　　　　　　　EW 41/hmv E 503

0347/27 january 1928/parlophone session/**klaus nettstraeter**
wagner tannhäuser overture
220583　　　　　　　　　　　　E 10699/P 9189
220584
220585　　　　　　　　　　　　E 10700/P 9190
220586

0348/3 february 1928/parlophone sessions/**otto klemperer**
brahms symphony no 1 in c minor op 68
220511　　　　　　　　　　　　E 10807/P 9812/odeon O-6890/am.decca 25487
220512
220528　　　　　　　　　　　　E 10808/P 9813/odeon O-6891/am.decca 25488
220529
220530　　　　　　　　　　　　E 10809/P 9818/odeon O-6892/am.decca 25489
220531
220590　　　　　　　　　　　　E 10810/P 9838/odeon O-6893/am.decca 25490
220591
220858　　　　　　　　　　　　E 10811/P 9839/odeon O-6894/am.decca 25491
220859
220860　　　　　　　　　　　　E 10812/P 9840/odeon O-6895/am.decca 25492
220861
cd issue: archiphon ARC 121-125

0349/7 february 1928/parlophone session/**frieder weissmann**
helge rosvaenge, tenor
mozart cosi fan tutte: un aura amorosa
220595　　　　　　　　　　　　P 9227/odeon O-6923
mozart don giovanni: dalla sua pace
220596　　　　　　　　　　　　P 9227/odeon O-6588
adam der postillon von lonjumeau: freunde vernehmet die geschichte
220597　　　　　　　　　　　　P 9210
boieldieu la dame blanche: viens gentille dame
220598　　　　　　　　　　　　P 9210/odeon O-6923
cd issues of all arias: preiser 89201 and pearl GEMMCD 9394

0350/7 february 1928/odeon session/**frieder weissmann**
helge rosvaenge, tenor
mozart don giovanni: il mio tesoro
XXB 7963　　　　　　　　　　　O-6588/O-7981
cd issues: preiser 89201 and pearl GEMMCD 9394

0351/8 february 1928/parlophone session/**frieder weissmann**
mascagni cavalleria rusticana intermezzo; handel largo
220599　　　　　　　　　　　　E 10701/P 9206
220600

0352/8 february 1928/electrola session/**fritz zweig**/helge rosvaenge, tenor
verdi la traviata: de miei bollenti spiriti
BLR 3851   EG 814
bizet carmen: la fleur que tu m'avais jetee
CLR 3852   EH 126
cd issue of both arias: preiser 89201

0353/9 february 1928/odeon session/**frieder weissmann**
johann strauss an der schönen blauen donau
XXB 7965   O-6581
    7966
johann strauss g'schichten aus dem wienerwald
XXB 7967   O-6605
    7968

0354/13 february 1928/odeon session/**manfred gurlitt**
lotte lehmann, soprano
korngold das wunder der heliane: ich ging zu ihm
XXB 7997   O-8722/american decca 25805
    7998

0355/15-16 february 1928/electrola sessions/**hans knappertsbusch**
johann strauss freut euch des lebens
CLR 3874   EH 119/victor 5009
    3878
johann strauss acclerationen waltz
CLR 3879   EH 123/victor 56025
    3880
johann strauss g'schichten aus dem wienerwald
CLR 3881   EH 120/hmv C 1828
    3882
cd issues of all items: preiser 90236, archiphon ARC 110-111 and tahra TAH 358-361

0356/17 february 1928/electrola session/**fritz zweig**/ivar andresen, bass
wagner tannhäuser: gar viel und schön; lohengrin: gott grüss' euch liebe
männer von brabant!
CLR 3884   EH 122/hmv C 1853
    3885

0357/28 february 1928/odeon session/**manfred gurlitt**
iso golland, baritone
verdi un ballo in maschera: eri tu; rossini il barbiere di siviglia: largo al factotum
XXB 7983   O-6594
    7985
verdi rigoletto: cortigiani!; pari siamo
XXB 7984   O-6595
    7986

0358/29 february 1928/parlophone session/**frieder weissmann**
liszt hungarian rhapsody no 2
220650   E 10724/P 9230
220651
offenbach les contes d'hoffmann, orchestral selection
220652   E 20725/P 9231
220653

0359/2 march 1928/*see 12 january 1928*

0360/8 march 1928/parlophone session/**frieder weissmann**
meta seinemeyer, soprano; john glaser, baritone
verdi il trovatore: mira d'acerbe lagrime
220576   P 9815/P 9637/odeon O-7799
strauss traum durch die dämmerung
220578   P 9870/P 9662
see also 19 january 1928; cd issue of all items: preiser 89402

0361/12 march 1928/parlophone session/**frieder weissmann**
elisabeth gero, soprano
leoncavallo i pagliacci: stridono lassu
XXB 8051   E 11111

0362/12-13 march 1928/electrola sessions/**ernst viebig**/max lorenz, tenor
wagner die walküre: ein schwert verhiess mir der vater
BLR 3945   EG 860
      3946
wagner die walküre: winterstürme wichen dem wonnemond
BLR 3947   EG 861
wagner tannhäuser: inbrunst im herzen
CLR 3948   EH 136
      3949
cd issue of all items: preiser 89232

0363/14 march 1928/odeon session/**frieder weissmann**
margherita salvi, soprano
delibes lakme: ou va la jeune indoue?; meyerbeer dinorah: ombre legere
XXB 7999   O-8340/O-6897/parlophone E 10770
      8000

0364/14-15 march 1928/electrola sessions/**leo blech**
auber la muette de portici overture
CLR 3951   EJ 304
      3952
dvorak slavonic dance op 46 no 3
CLR 3953   EJ 290
      3954
beethoven coriolan overture
CLR 3959   EJ 303
      3960

0365/15 march 1928/electrola session/**fritz zweig**
maria olczewska, contralto
saint-saens samson et dalila: mon coeur s'ouvre a ta voix; handel rinaldo:
lascia ch'io pianga
CLR 3961 EJ 273/hmv D 1465
    3962

0365a/15 march 1928/electrola session/**erich kleiber**
schubert rosamunde: overture and ballet music in b minor
CLR 3963 EJ 369
    3964
    3965 EJ 370
    3966

0366/16 march 1928/parlophone session/**frieder weissmann**
wagner tannhäuser act three prelude
220666 E 10711/P 9252
220667

0367/19 march 1928/parlophone session/**eduard mörike**
wagner der fliegende holländer overture and act three introduction
220668 E 10761/P 9250
220669
220670 E 10762/P 9251
220671

0368/19 march 1928/parlophone session/**frieder weissmann**
margherita salvi, soprano
auber fra diavolo: cavatine de zerlina
220672 E 10817
220673

0369/19 and 21 march 1928/electrola sessions/**leo blech**
nanny larsen-todsen, soprano; erik enderlein, tenor; herbert
janssen, baritone; ivar andresen, bass
wagner götterdämmrung: zu neuen taten; helle wehr heilige waffe!
CLR 3967 unpublished recording
    3968
    3969 unpublished recording
    3975
    3976 unpublished recording
    3977

0370/22 march 1928/odeon session/**manfred gurlitt**
boieldieu le caliphe de bagdad overture
XXB 8020 O-6601/parlophone E 10797
    8021
rossini la gazza ladra overture
XXB 8022 O-6602/parlophone E 10788
    8023

0371/23 march 1928/parlophone session/**frieder weissmann**
elisabeth gero, soprano
verdi un ballo in maschera: saper vorreste
XXB 8052   E 11111/odeon O-6627

0372/23 march 1928/electrola session/**leo blech**
tchaikovsky capriccio italien
CLR 3991   EJ 294/hmv D 1593
    3992
verdi la traviata prelude; un ballo in maschera prelude
CLR 3993   EJ 292
    3994

0373/26 march 1928/parlophone session/**artur bodanzky**
meyerbeer le prophete: coronation march
220685   E 10841

0374/26 march 1928/parlophone session/**frieder weissmann**
grieg peer gynt: solveig's song, orchestral arrangement
220947   E 11042/P 9528
reissiger die felsenmühle overture
220683   E 11055/P 9232
220684
weber jubel overture
220686   E 10749/P 9233
220687

0375/27 march 1928/odeon session/**frieder weissmann**
tchaikovsky 1812 overture
XXB 8029   O-6803/parlophone E 10712
    8030
    8031   O-6804/parlophone E 10713
    8032

0376/27 march 1928/parlophone session/**max von schillings**
wagner götterdämmerung: starke scheite schichtet mir dort, orchestral
arrangement
220680   E 10773/P 9834
220681
wagner götterdämmerung: siegfried's funeral march
220690   E 10736/P 9827
220691

0377/27 march 1928/electrola session/**leo blech**
johann strauss kaiserwalzer
CLR 4000   EJ 328/hmv D 1991
    4001
liszt hungarian rhapsody no 2
CLR 4002   EJ 293/hmv D 1625
    4003

0378/3 april 1928/odeon session/**frieder weissmann**
weber der freischütz overture
XXB 8039   O-6633/parlophone E 10737
    8040
chopin polonaise militaire; brahms hungarian dances nos 5 and 6
XXB 8041   O-6634/parlophone E 10763
    8042
der freischütz overture was re-recorded on 7 june 1928

0379/11 and 14 april 1928/electrola sessions/**leo blech**/staatsopernchor
wagner parsifal: zum letzten liebesmahle
CLR 4021   unpublished recording
    4022
verdi aida: act two finale
CLR 4027   unpublished recording
    4028

0380/17 and 19 april 1928/electrola sessions/**leo blech**/staatsopernchor
lauritz melchior, tenor: herbert janssen, baritone
wagner lohengrin: höchstes vertrauen
CLR 4031   EJ 302/hmv D 1505
    4032
verdi otello: si per ciel
CLR 4033   unpublished recording
gounod faust: valentin's prayer and death
CLR 4044   EH 219/hmv C 1852
    4043

0381/19 april 1928/parlophone session/**frieder weissmann**
meta seinemeyer, soprano
schubert du bist die ruh
220716   unpublished recordng
schubert gretchen am spinnrade
220717   P 9817/P 9663/odeon O-7652/american decca 25832
cd issue: preiser 89402

0382/24 april 1928/parlophone session/**frieder weissmann**/staatsopernchor
meta seinemeyer, soprano; sigismund von pilinsky, tenor
schubert so lasst mich scheinen
220725   P 9871/P 9662/odeon O-7652
schubert die junge nonne
220726   P 9870/P 9662/american decca 25832
wagner die meistersinger von nürnberg: morgenlich leuchtend.....keiner wie du
220733   E 10947/P 9633
220734
cd issue of all items: preiser 89402

0383/25 april 1928/odeon session/**frieder weissmann**
sigismund von pilinsky, tenor
meyerbeer le prophete: roi du ciel et des anges
XXB 8063 O-6809/O-8354/parlophone E 11037

0384/26 april 1928/electrola session/**leo blech**
weber der freischütz overture
CLR 4064 unpublished recording
    4065
thomas mignon overture
CLR 4066 unpublished recording

0385/27 april 1928/parlophone session/**frieder weissmann**/staatsopernchor
joseph lindler, bass-baritone
wagner die meistersinger von nürnberg: verachtet mir die meister nicht
220747 E 10792/P 9271

0386/29 april 1928/electrola recording from a stage performance in the staatsoper unter den linden/**leo blech**/staatsopernchor
elfriede marherr-wagner, soprano; lydia kindermann, contralto; fritz wolff, tenor; karl jöken, tenor; friedrich schorr, bass-baritone; eduard kandl, baritone; emanuel list, bass
wagner die meistersinger von nürnberg: johannistag!
CLR 4072 EJ 279
cd issues: pearl GEMMCD 9340 and pristine PACO 065
wagner die meistersinger von nürnberg: jerum! jerum!; sieh evchen!
CLR 4073 unpublished recordings
    4075
cd issue: pristine PACO 065
further unpublished sides CLR 4070, 4071, 4074, 4076, 4077, 4078, 4079, 4080, 4081, 4082 and 4083
see also 22 may 1928

0387/30 april and 2 may 1928/parlophone sessions/**artur bodanzky**
mozart die zauberflöte overture
220758 E 10750/P 9829
220759
johann strauss die fledermaus overture
220760 E 10775/P 9449
220761
weber oberon overture
220762 E 10840
220763

0388/30 april 1928/parlophone session in the potsdamerstrasse studio/ **michael taube**/emanuel feuermann, cello
dvorak cello concerto in b minor
220748	E 10856/P 9667/odeon O-7537
220749	
220750	E 10857/P 9668/odeon O-7538
220751	
220752	E 10858/P 9669/odeon O-7539
220753	
221582	E 11071/P 9670/odeon O-7540
221583	
221584	E 11072/P 9671/odeon O-7541

recording completed on 27 september 1929
cd issues: pearl GEMMCD 9077 and naxos 8.110901

0389/1 may 1928/odeon session/**artur bodanzky**
wagner tannhäuser overture
XXB 8073	O-8348/O-6717
8074	
8075	O-8349/O-6718
8076	

0390/2 may 1928/parlophone session in the potsdamerstrasse studio/ **frieder weissmann**
bizet carmen preludes to acts one and three
220769	E 11015/P 9306
220768	

0391/11 may 1928/parlophone session in the potsdamerstrasse studio/ **frieder weissmann**/meta seinemeyer, soprano; tino pattiera, tenor
verdi otello: gia nella notte
220774	E 10816/P 9835/odeon O-7570
220775	

verdi aida: pur ti riveggo
220776	E 10905/odeon O-7798/american decca 25298
220777	

cd issue of both items: preiser 89402

0392/11 and 14 may 1928/parlophone sessions in the potsdamerstrasse studio/**frieder weissmann**/nino ederle, tenor
rossini il barbiere di siviglia: ecco ridente; donizetti la favorita: spirto gentil
284033	E 11276
284038	

0393/15 may 1928/*see 23 january 1928*

0394/15 may 1928/odeon session/**frieder weissmann**
flotow alessandro stradella overture
CLR XXB 8090   O-6704
       8091
bizet carmen preludes act one and four
XXB 8092   O-6653
       8096

0395/15 may 1928/electrola session in the singakademie/**karl muck**
wagner tristan und isolde prelude
CLR 4129   EJ 367/hmv D 2028
       4130   EJ 366/hmv D 2029
       4131
cd issues: preiser 90269 and centaur CRC 2142
wagner der fliegende holländer overture
CLR 4132   EJ 368/hmv D 2027
       4133
       4134   EJ 367/hmv D 2028
cd issues: preiser 90269 and centaur CRC 2142
wagner tannhäuser overture
CLR 4135   EJ 335
       4136
       4137   EJ 336
       4138
cd issue: preiser 90269

0396/22 may 1928/electrola recording from a stage performance in the staatsoper unter den linden/**leo blech**/staatsopernchor
elfriede marherr-wagner, soprano; lydia kindermann, contralto; robert hutt, tenor; karl jöken, tenor; friedrich schorr, bass-baritone; leo schützendorf, baritone; emanuel list, bass
wagner die meistersinger von nürnberg: will ich denn schuster sein?
CLR 4165   EJ 277
       4166
wagner die meistersinger von nürnberg: das schöne fest johannistag
CLR 4168   EJ 278
       4169
wagner die meistersinger von nürnberg: johannistag!
CLR 4171   EJ 279
wagner die meistersinger von nürnberg: jerum! jerum!
CLR 4174   EJ 280
       4175
       4176   EJ 281
       4177
       4178   EJ 282
wagner die meistersinger von nürnberg: gleich meister hier!
CLR 4181   EJ 282
       4182   EJ 283

22 may 1928 / electrola recording from staatsoper / leo blech / concluded
wagner die meistersinger von nürnberg: grüss gott mein evchen...o sachs mein freund!
CLR 4185 EJ 283
    4186 EJ 284
    4187
wagner die meistersinger von nürnberg: sankt krispin!...silentium!...wach auf!
CLR 4189 EJ 285
    4190
wagner die meistersinger von nürnberg: verachtet mir die meister nicht!...ehrt ihre deutschen meister!
CLR 4194 EJ 286
    4195

cd issues: pearl GEMMCD 9340 and pristine PACO 065
cd issue of 4165, 4166, 4168, 4169, 4189 and 4190 only: gebhardt JGCD 00352
further unpublished sides CLR 4167, 4170, 4172, 4173, 4179, 4180, 4183,
4184, 4188, 4191, 4192 and 4193
see also 29 april 1928

0397 / 24 may 1928 / odeon session / **hermann weigert** / hans reinmar, baritone
meyerbeer l'africaine: l'avoir tant adoree; bizet carmen: votre toast
XXB 8106 unpublished recordings
    8107
verdi rigoletto: pari siamo; la traviata: di provenza il mar
XXB 8108 unpublished recordings
    8109

0398 / 24 and 26 may 1928 / odeon sessions / **ernst hauke** / richard tauber, tenor
d'albert tiefland: wie ich nun gestern abend in der hütte liege
XXB 8100 O-8365
cd issue: emi 698 5422
d'albert tiefland: schau her das ist ein taler!
XXB 8103 O-8354
lehar friederike: sah ein knab' ein röslein steh'n; o mädchen mein mädchen
XXB 8110 unpublished recordings
    8111

0399 / 25 may 1928 / electrola session in the philharmonie / **otto klemperer**
strauss salome: dance of the 7 veils
CLR 4212 EJ 276 / hmv D 1633
    4213
cd issue: archiphon ARC 121-125

0400 / 4 june 1928 / odeon session / **frieder weissmann**
john o'sullivan, tenor
bizet carmen: la fleur que tu m'avais jetee
XXB 8112 unpublished recording

0401/6 june 1928/parlophone session in the potsdamerstrasse studio/
frieder weissmann
grieg peer gynt suite no 1
220797 E 11027
220799
220798 E 11028
220796

0402/7 june 1928/*see 3 april 1928*

0403/8 june 1928/electrola session/**leo blech**
mascagni cavalleria rusticana intermezzo
BLR 4246 EW 57
johann strauss an der schönen blauen donau
BLR 4247 unpublished recording
    4248

0404/8 june 1928/odeon session/**frieder weissmann**/
helene wildbrunn, soprano
wagner lohengrin: entweihte götter!
XXB 8115 unpublished recording

0405/10 june 1928/odeon session/**ernst hauke**/richard tauber, tenor
offenbach les contes d'hoffmann: o dieux de quelle ivresse; il etait une fois
XXB 8129 O-8356
    8130
cd issue: emi 698 5422

0406/11 june 1928/parlophone session in the potsdamerstrasse studio/
frieder weissmann/costa milona, tenor
massenet werther: pourquoi me reveiller?; verdi un ballo in maschera:
di tu se fedele
220803 E 10802/P 9316
220812
meyerbeer l'africaine: o paradis!; tosti ideale
220814 E 10888
220819

0407/12 june 1928/odeon session/**hermann weigert**/emmy land, soprano
offenbach les contes d'hoffmann: elle a fui la tourturelle; halevy la juive: il va venir
XXB 8119 unpublished recordings
    8120

0408/13 june 1928/parlophone session/**frieder weissmann**/costa milona, tenor
bizet les pecheurs de perles: romance de nadir
220817 E 10853

0409/13 june 1928/electrola session/**clemens schmalstich**/max lorenz, tenor
bizet carmen: la fleur que tu m'avais jetee; verdi aida: celeste aida
CLR 4257 EH 181
    4258
halevy la juive: quand du seigneur; kienzl der evangelimann: selig sind die verfolgung
CLR 4259 EH 182
    4260
cd issue of all arias: preiser 89232

0410/15-16 june 1928/odeon sessions/**eugen szenkar**
beethoven symphony no 5 in c minor op 67
XXB 8121 O-6688
     8122
     8123 O-6689
     8124
     8125 O-6690
     8126
     8127 O-6691
     8128

0411/18 june 1928/electrola session in the singakademie/**leo blech**
boieldieu la dame blanche overture
CLR 4270 EJ 306
    4271
adam si j'etais roi overture
CLR 4272 EJ 307
    4273
leoncavallo i pagliacci intermezzo
BLR 4274 EW 57

0412/19 june 1928/odeon session/**ernst hauke**
carlotta vanconti, soprano; richard tauber, tenor
lehar die rose von stambul: ein walzer muss es sein; berte das dreimädlerhaus:
was macht glücklich
XXB 8131 O-8380
     8132
lehar der rastelbinder: wenn zwei sich lieben; johann strauss der zigeunerbaron:
wer uns getraut
XXB 8133 O-8355/O-9174
     8134

0413/19-20 june 1928/electrola sessions in the singakademie/**leo blech**
genia guszalewicz, soprano; lauritz melchior, tenor
wagner die walküre: ein schwert verhiess mir der vater....siegumd heiss' ich!
CLR 4275 EJ 300
   4276
wagner tannhäuser: inbrunst im herzen
CLR 4277 ES 454/hmv D 1635
   4284

0414/21 june 1928/odeon session/**hermann weigert**/ludwig hofmann, bass
lortzing undine: lied an die flasche; zar und zimmermann: sonst spielt' ich
XXB 8143 O-6669
   8144
fischer in tiefem keller; nicolai die lustigen weiber: als büblein klein
XXB 8145 O-6661
   8146

0415/22 june 1928/parlophone session/**frieder weissmann**/staatsopernchor
meta seinemeyer, soprano
puccini madama butterfly: ancora un passo
220848 E 10805/P 9876/odeon O-7572
puccini tosca: a te quest' inno; vissi d'arte
220849 E 10851/P 9844/odeon O-7571
220850
puccini madama butterfly: un bel di
220851 E 10805/P 9841/odeon O-7572
giordano andrea chenier: la mamma morta
220852 P 9843/P 9640/odeon O-7569
cd issue of all items: preiser 89402

0416/25 june 1928/parlophone session/**frieder weissmann**/staatsopernchor
meta seinemeyer, soprano; helene jung, contralto; sigismund von
pilinsky, tenor; fritz düttbernd, baritone; robert burg, bass-baritone
wagner lohengrin: procession to the minster
220855 E 10933/P 9837/odeon O-7563/am.decca 25056
220856
wagner lohengrin: durch gottes sieg ist jetzt dein leben mein!
220857 E 10782/P 9842/odeon O-7654/am.decca 25065

0417/25 june 1928/odeon session/**frieder weissmann**
sigismund von pilinsky, tenor
wagner rienzi: erstehe hohe roma neu!
XXB 8147 O-8354/O-6809/parlophone E 11037

0418/26 june 1928/electrola session in the singakademie/**georg schumann**
berliner singakademie
brahms selig sind die da leid tragen/ein deutsches requiem
CLR 4309 EH 257/hmv C 2383
   4310
   4311 EH 258/hmv C 2384

0419/26-27 june 1928/electrola sessions in the singakademie/**leo blech**
rudolf laubenthal, tenor
wagner das rheingold: entry of the gods into valhalla
CLR 4303 EJ 298
    4304
wagner siegfried: dass der mein vater nicht ist
CLR 4305 EJ 299/hmv D 1531
    4306
cd issue: pearl GEMMCD 9137
liszt les preludes
CLR 4312 EJ 296
    4313
    4314 EJ 297
    4315

0420/29-30 august 1928/electrola sessions/**leo blech**
johann strauss tritsch-tratsch polka; ritter pasman polka
BLR 4457 EG 013
    4458
johann strauss ritter pasman czardas; josef strauss frauenherz polka
CLR 4456 EH 208
    4459
mozart eine kleine nachtmusik
CLR 4460 EJ 326/hmv D 2038
    4461
    4462 EJ 327/hmv D 2039
    4463

0421/3-4 september 1928/odeon sessions/**hermann weigert**
lotte lehmann, soprano
lehar eva: wär' es auch nichts als ein augenblick; meyer-helund zauberlied
XXB 8150 O-9730
    8151
strauss ariadne auf naxos: in den schönen feierkleidern...es gibt ein reich
XXB 8168 O-8731/parlophone R 20147/american decca 25816
    8169
cd issue: pearl GEMMCD 9410

0422/4-5 september 1928/odeon sessions/**hans knappertsbusch**
haydn symphony no 94 in g "surprise"

XXB 8152	O-6695/parlophone E 10844
8153	
8154	O-6696/parlophone E 10845
8155	
8156	O-6697/parlophone E 10846
8157	

strauss intermezzo: waltz scene

XXB 8158	O-6744/parlophone E 10860
8159	

cd issues: preiser 90260 and wing WCD 10
strauss salome: dance of the 7 veils

XXB 8160	O-6788/parlophone E 10894
8161	

cd issue: preiser 90260
strauss till eulenspiegels lustige streiche

XXB 8162	O-6772
8163	
8164	O-6773
8165	

cd issue: preiser 90260
johann strauss die fledermaus overture

XXB 8166	O-6663/O-10043
8167	

cd issues: preiser 90236, archiphon ARC 110-111 and wing WCD 10

0423/6 september 1928/odeon session/**artur bodanzky**
mendelssohn hebrides overture and a midsummer night's dream scherzo

XXB 8170	O-6722/O-25791
8171	
8172	O-6723/O-25792
8173	

johann strauss sphärenklänge

XXB 8174	O-8367/O-25767
8175	

0424/7 september 1928/parlophone session/**eduard mörike**
smetana the moldau/ma vlast

220897	E 10794/P 9366
220898	
220899	E 10795/P 9367
220900	

0425/7 and 10 september 1928/electrola sessions/**leo blech**/staatsopernchor
tilly de garmo, soprano; elfriede marherr-wagner, soprano;
lydia kindermann, contralto; rudolf laubenthal, tenor;
desider zador, baritone; emanuel list, bass
wagner götterdämmerung: mime hiess ein mürrischer zwerg
CLR 4483 EJ 418/hmv D 1583/D 7817
    4484 EJ 419/hmv D 1584/D 7816
wagner götterdämmerung: brünnhilde heilige braut!
CLR 4482 EJ 419/hmv D 1584/D 7816
wagner götterdämmerung: frau sonne sendet lichte strahlen
CLR 4488 EJ 416/hmv D 1581/D 7821
    4489 EJ 417/hmv D 1582/D 7820
    4490 EJ 417/hmv D 1582/D 7819
    4491 EJ 418/hmv D 1583/D 7818
cd issue of all items: pearl GEMMCDS 9137

0426/12 september 1928/parlophone session/**artur bodanzky**
berlioz la damnation de faust: hungarian march
220917 E 10993/american decca 25356

0427/15 and 19 september 1928/parlophone sessions/**frieder weissmann**
joseph wolfsthal, violin
mozart violin concerto no 5 in a k219
220911 E 10921/odeon O-7635/american decca 25102
220916
220918 E 10922/odeon O-7635/american decca 25103
220919
220927 E 10923/odeon O-7636/american decca 25104
220928
220929 E 10924/odeon O-7637/american decca 25105
220930
cd issue: pearl GEMMCD 9387

0428/18 september 1928/parlophone session/**frieder weissmann**
augusto garavello, bass
rossini il barbiere di siviglia: la calunnia!; boito mefistofele: son lo spirito
220909 E 10830
220910

0429/20 and 27 september 1928/odeon sessions/**erich kleiber**
stravinsky firebird suite
XXB 8179 O-6816/parlophone E 10964/american decca 25441
     8180
     8181 O-6762/parlophone E 11017/american decca 25442
     8182
     8183 O-6763/parlophone E 11018/american decca 25443
cd issue: preiser 90311

0430/21 september 1928/parlophone session/**frieder weissmann**
meta seinemeyer, soprano; grete merrem-nikisch, elisa stunzner, contralto; emanuel list, bass
strauss der rosenkavalier: nicht dort ist das vorzimmer!
220941   E 10864/P 9868/american decca 25237
cd issue: preiser 89402
strauss der rosenkavalier: bin von so viel finesse
220942   E 10864/P 9868/american decca 25237
strauss der rosenkavalier: es war nicht mehr wie eine farce
220943   E 10865/P 9869/american decca 25238
strauss der rosenkavalier: hab mir's gelobt
220944   E 10865/P 9869/american decca 25238
cd issue: preiser 89402

0431/25 september 1928/electrola session/**leo blech**/lotte schöne, soprano
johann strauss g'schichten aus dem wienerwald
CLR 4546   EJ 429/hmv D 1733
puccini madama butterfly: un bel di
CLR 4547   EJ 422/hmv D 1653

0432/26 september 1928/parlophone session/**frieder weissmann**
grieg peer gynt: ingrid's lament, orchestral arrangement
220946   E 11042/P 9528

0433/1 october 1928/parlophone session/**frieder weissmann**
fritzi jokl, soprano
donizetti don pasquale: so anch'io la virtu magica; flotow alessandro stradella: seid meiner wonne stille zeugen
220963   E 10884
220964
puccini la boheme: si mi chiamano mimi   unpublished recording

0434/2 october 1928/odeon session/**fritz busch**/rose pauly, soprano
strauss die ägyptische helena: helena's awakening
XXB 8185   O-6792/parlophone E 10787/american decca 25031
strauss die ägyptische helena: bei jener nacht
XXB 8186   O-6670/parlophone E 11356/american decca 25850
strauss die ägyptische helena: da-ud's funeral march
XXB 8187   O-6792/parlophone E 10787/american decca 25031
strauss die ägyptische helena: zweite brautnacht!
XXB 8188   O-6670/parlophone E 11356/american decca 25850
cd issue of all items: profil medien PH 07032

0435/2 october 1928/odeon session/**ernst hauke**/richard tauber, tenor
lehar friederike: sah ein knab' ein röslein steh'n
XXB 8110   O-8352
lehar friederike: o mädchen mein mädchen!
XXB 8111   O-8352/O-8815
cd issue of 8111 only: emi 698 5422

0436/3 october 1928/parlophone sesion/**frieder weissmann**
delibes coppelia, orchestral selection
220965   E 10813/P 9334/odeon O-6871
220966
mozart die entführung aus dem serail overture
220967   E 10847/P 9333/odeon O-7546
220968

0437/8 october 1928/parlophone session/**max von schillings**
weber euryanthe overture
220991   E 10872/odeon O-6916/american decca 25098
220992
220993   E 10873/odeon O-6917/american decca 25099

0438/8-9 october 1928/electrola sessions/**clemens schmalstich**
marcel wittrisch, tenor
lehar friederike: sah ein knab' ein röslein steh'n; o mädchen mein mädchen!
CLR 4593   EH 216/hmv C 1843
    4597

0439/10 october 1928/parlophone sesson/**frieder weissmann**
nino piccaluga, tenor
verdi otello: niun mi tema
220961   E 10946/P 9642/odeon O-7667

0440/10, 11, 13 and 14 october 1928/electrola sessions in the singakademie/
karl muck/staatsopernchor/gotthelf pistor, tenor;
cornelis bronsgeest, baritone; ludwig hofmann, bass
wagner parsifal, act three prelude and heil dir dass ich dich wieder finde…to end of act
CLR 4609   EJ 373/hmv D 1537/victor 7160
    4610
    4598   EJ 374/hmv D 1538/victor 7161
    4599
    4600   EJ 375/hmv D 1539/victor 7162
    4601
    4602   EJ 376/hmv D 1540/victor 7163
    4603
    4604   EJ 377/hmv D 1541/victor 7164
    4611
    4612   EJ 378/hmv D 1542/victor 7165
    4613
    4614   EJ 379/hmv D 1543/victor 7166
    4615
    4616   EJ 380/hmv D 1544/victor 7167
    4617

hmv set also available in automatic coupling with catalogue numbers D 7491-7498
cd issues: pearl opal CDS 9843 and naxos 8.110049-110050

0441/15 october 1928/electrola session in the singakademie/**leo blech**
strauss tod und verklärung
CLR 4618   EJ 476
    4619
    4620   EJ 477
    4621
    4622   EJ 478
    4623
recording completed on 7 november 1928

0442/18 october 1928/odeon session/**frieder weissmann**
liszt hungarian rhapsody no 2
XXB 8197   O-6675/parlophone E 10823
    8198

0443/19 october 1928/parlophone session/**frieder weissmann**
meta seinemeyer, soprano; robert burg, bass
puccini manon lescaut: buon giorno sorellina; in quelle trine morbide
221001   P 9866/odeon O-7794
221002
verdi aida: ciel mio padre!....su dunque sorgete egizie coorti!
221003   P 9876
221004
cd issue: preiser 89402

0444/20 october 1928/odeon session/**frieder weissmann**
mafalda salvatini, soprano
puccini madama butterfly: un bel di; tosca: vissi d'arte
XXB 8199   unpublished recordings
    8200
bizet carmen: l'amour est un oiseau rebelle
XXB 8201   unpublished recording
verdi aida: ritorna vincitor; o patria mia
XXB 8202   O-8732
    8203

0445/22 october 1928/electrola session/**leo blech**/lotte schöne, soprano
johann strauss die fledermaus: mein herr was dächten sie von mir?
CLR 4644   EJ 429//hmv D 1733
puccini madama butterfly: che tua madre
CLR 4645   EJ 422/hmv D 1653
mozart die zauberflöte: ach ich fühl's
CLR 4646   unpublished recording

0446/22 october 1928/parlophone session/unnamed conductor
gerhard hüsch, baritone
verdi la traviata: di provenza al mar; lortzing zar und zimmermann:
sonst spielt' ich
221015   E 11091
221017
cd issue of lortzing item: bbc records CD 716

0447/24 october 1928/parlophone session/**frieder weissmann**
nino piccaluga, tenor
verdi il trovatore: ah si ben mio
221014   E 10946/P 9642/odeon O-7667

0448/28 october 1928/electrola session in the singakademie/**leo blech**
frida leider, soprano
wagner götterdämmerung: starke scheite schichtet mir dort
CLR 4666   EJ 420/hmv D 2025
     4667   EJ 421/hmv D 2025
     4668
cd issue: pearl GEMMCDS 9137

0449/29 october 1928/odeon session/**frieder weismann**
vera schwarz, soprano; richard tauber, tenor
johann strauss die fledermaus: dieser anstand so manierlich; kalman
zigeunerliebe: es liegt im blauen fernen
XXB 8205   O-8815
     8206
puccini madama butterfly: viene la sera
XXB 8207   unpublished recording
     8208

0450/1 november 1928/odeon session/**frieder weissmann**
strauss der rosenkavalier: waltz sequence
XXB 8209   O-6681/parlophone E 10832
     8210
dvorak slavonic dances nos 6 and 8
XXB 8211   O-6782
     8212

0451/2 november 1928/parlophone session/**frieder weissmann**
leopold mozart toy symphony
221047   E 10821/P 9424
221050

0452/5 november 1928/parlophone session/**eduard mörike**/staatsopernchor
else knepel, soprano; hans clemens, tenor; emanuel list, bass
wagner tannhäuser: frau holda kam aus dem berg hervor; pilgrims' chorus
221052   E 10890/P 9346
221053
wagner götterdämmerung: ho ho ihr mannen!
221054   E 10904
221055
wagner götterdämmerung: hier sitz' ich zur wacht
221056   E 11359/P 9384
221057

0453/6 november 1928/odeon session/**frieder weissmann**/björn talen, tenor
wagner die walküre: winterstürme wichen dem wonnemond
XXB 8216   E 11177/american decca 25030

0454/7 november 1928/parlophone session/**frieder weissmann**
verdi la traviata prelude
221059   E 10876/P 9347
rossini semiramide overture
221060   E 10911/P 8517/odeon O-6794
221061
ponchielli la gioconda: dance of the hours
221062   E 10859/odeon O-6980
221063

0455/7 november 1928/electrola session in the philharmonie/**leo blech**
liszt hungarian rhapsody no 1
BLR 4718   EG 1341/hmv B 3135/victor 4187
    4719
BWR 1283   EG 1342/hmv B 3136/victor 4188
    1285
cd issue: koch 3-7072-2
see also 15 october 1928

0456/7 november 1928/parlophone session/**frieder weissmann**
costa milona, tenor
mascagni cavalleria rusticana: siciliana
221069   E 10853

0457/8 november 1928/electrola session in the philharmonie/**leo blech**
frida leider, soprano; elfriede marherr-wagner, soprano
wagner tristan und isolde: doch nun von tristan....er schwur mit tausend eiden
CLR 4722   EJ 301/hmv D 1667/victor 7603
    4723
cd issues: nimbus NI 7848, preiser 89984, pearl GEMMCD 9331 and emi 764 0082
wagner götterdämmerung: schweigt eures jammers jauchzenden schwall
CLR 4724   EJ 420/hmv D 2025
cd issuse: pearl GEMMCDS 9137, GEMMCD 9331 and preiser 89098

0458/19 november 1928/electrola session/**leo blech**
mozart die zauberflöte overture
BLR 4758   EW 58
    4759
bizet carmen prelude
BLR 4760   EW 59
    4761

0459/20 november 1928/parlophone session/**frieder weissmann**
rossini il barbiere di siviglia overture
221086   E 10928
221087
bellini norma overture
221088   E 10876/P 9347
221089

0460/20 november 1928/odeon session/**frieder weissmann**
siede chinese street serenade; zimmer japanese lantern dance
XXB 8230   O-6676
    8231

0461/20 november 1928/odeon session/**hugo rüdel**
berliner lehrergesangverein
johann strauss rosen aus dem süden
XXB 8232 O-6677
　　 8233
johann strauss an der schönen blauen donau
XXB 8234 O-6678
　　 8235

0462/26 november 1928/electrola session in the philharmonie/**leo blech**
wagner tannhäuser overture and venusberg music
CLR 4785 EH 346/hmv C 2181
　　 4786
　　 4787 EH 347/hmv C 2182
　　 4788

0463/28 november 1928/parlophone session/**frieder weissmann**
emmy bettendorf, soprano; karin branzell, contralto
wagner lohengrin: ortrud bist du's?
221103 E 10852/P 9497
221104
verdi aida: fu la sorte dell' armi
221105 E 10916/odeon O-6801
221106

0464/29 november 1928/parlophone session/**frieder weissmann**
corelli concerto in g minor "christmas concerto"
221107 E 11064/P 9422
221108
221109 E 11065/P 9423
221110

0465/december 1928/electrola session/**georg schumann**/berliner singakademie
brahms denn alles fleisch/ein deutsches requiem
CLR 4860 EH 265/hmv C 2377
　　 4861
brahms wie lieblich sind deine wohnungen/ein deutsches requiem
CLR 4862 EH 266/hmv C 2381
　　 4863

0466/1 december 1928/odeon session/**frieder weissmann**/björn talen, tenor
verdi aida: celeste aida
XXB 8256 unpublished recording
wagner die meistersinger von nürnberg: morgenlich leuchtend
XXB 8257 E 11177
verdi un ballo in maschera: di tu se fedele
XXB 8258 unpublished recording

0467/6 december 1928/electrola session in the philharmonie/**leo blech**
staatsopernchor/genia guszalewicz, mezzo-soprano
weber der freischütz bridesmaids'chorus; wagner der fliegende holländer:
spinning chorus
CLR 4831 EJ 427
4832
wagner lohengrin: bridal chorus
BLR 4833 EW 60
wagner der fliegende holländer: sailors' chorus
BLR 4834 EW 70/hmv E 557

0468/10 and 12 december 1928/electrola sessions in the philharmonie/**leo blech**
smetana the moldau/ma vlast
CLR 4840 EJ 386/hmv D 1986/victor 11434
4841
4842 EJ 387/hmv D 1987/victor 11435
cd issue: koch 3-7072-2
chabrier espana
CLR 4849 EJ 385
4850
strauss der rosenkavalier: waltz sequence
CLR 4851 EH 350/hmv C 1819
4852

0469/14 december 1928/parlophone session/**max von schillings**
beethoven egmont overture
221126 E 10953/P 9456/odeon O-6899
221127
weber abu hassan overture
E 10873/P 9849/odeon O-6917/am.decca 25099

0470/17 december 1928/parlophone session/**frieder weissmann**
gerhard hüsch, baritone
wagner tannhäuser: wohl wusst' ich hier; o du mein holder abendstern
221018 E 10839
221025
wagner tannhäuser: blick' ich umher in diesem edlen kreise
221130 E 11046

0471/17 december 1928/odeon session/**frieder weissmann**/staatsopernchor
lotte lehmann, soprano; grete merrem-nikisch, soprano; karin
branzell, contralto; richard tauber, tenor; walter stägemann,
baritone; karl lange, bass
johann strauss die fledermaus, act two finale
XXB 8266 O-8734/parlophone R 20085/am.decca 29015
8267
johann strauss der zigeunerbaron, acts one and two finales
XXB 8268 O-8735/parlophone R 20104/am.decca 29013
8269
cd issue: bbc CD 716

0472/19 december 1928/electrola session in the philharmonie/**leo blech**
puccini madama butterfly intermezzo; manon lescaut intermezzo
CLR 4875 EH 349
    4876
meyerbeer torch dance
CLR 4877 EH 348
    4878

0473/21 december 1928/parlophone session/**fritz stiedry**
mozart serenade no 10 k361, abridged version
221150 E 11197/P 9538
221151
221182 E 11198/P 9539
221181
recording completed on 18 january 1929

0474/28 and 30 december 1928/columbia sessions/**william steinberg**
bronislav huberman, violin
tchaikovsky violin concerto in d op 35
WAX 4509 L 2335/odeon O-8737/american decca 25470
    4510
    4511 L 2336/odeon O-8738/american decca 25471
    4512
    4513 L 2337/odeon O-8739/american decca 25472
    4514
    4515 L 2338/odeon O-8740/american decca 25473
cd issue: classical collector EPM 150 032

0475/1929/grammophon sessions/**oskar fried**/bruno kittel chor/lotte leonard, soprano; jenny sonnenberg, contralto; eugene transky, tenor; wilhelm guttmann, bass
beethoven symphony no 9 in d minor op 125 "choral"
633bm 66657/brunswick 90179
634bm
635bm 66658/brunswick 90180
585 ¾ bm
636bm 66659/brunswick 90181
637bm
638bm 66660/brunswick 90182
639 ½ bm
586 ½ bm 66661/brunswick 90183
587bm
566 ½ bm 66662/brunswick 90184
564 ½ bm
565 ½ bm 66663/brunswick 90185
567 ½ bm
cd issues: pearl GEMMCD 9372 and naxos 8.110929

0476/1929/grammophon sessions/**hans pfitzner**
mozart le nozze di figaro overture; cosi fan tutte overture
255bs II   27066
256bs II
lortzing zar und zimmermann overture
1627bm I   27069
1628bm I
cd issue of all items: pristine PASC 305

0477/1929/grammophon sessions/**erich kleiber**
beethoven symphony no 2 in d op 36
755bi I   66905/brunswick 90140
756bi I
757bi I   66906/brunswick 90141
758bi I
759bi I   66907/brunswick 90142
252bv I
761bi I   66908/brunswick 90143
762bi I
cd issues: naxos 8.110919 and dutton CDBP 9716
dvorak symphony no 9 in e minor "from the new world"
773bi   66909/brunswick 90150
774bi
824bi   66910/brunswick 90151
825bi
826bi   66911/brunswick 90152
775bi
615bi   66912/brunswick 90153
827bi
828bi   66913/brunswick 90154
829bi
cd issue: naxos 8.110901

0478/1929/grammophon sessions/**manfred gurlitt**/julius patzak, tenor
massenet manon: oh fuyez douce image!
708bi   95267
verdi la traviata: de miei bollenti spiriti; smetana the bartered bride: es muss gelingen
709 ½ bi   95268
710bi
cd issue of all items: preiser 89075

0479/1929/grammophon session/**manfred gurlitt**/elisabeth ohms, soprano
beethoven fidelio: abscheulicher wo eilst du hin?
803b   66904
804b
strauss der rosenkavalier: kann mich auch an ein mädel erinnern
805bi   95385
cd issue of both items: preiser 89987

0480/1929/grammophon session/**julius prüwer**
elisabeth ohms, soprano; theodor scheidl, bass-baritone
wagner der fliegende holländer: versank ich jetzt in wunderbaren träumen
878b   95407
879b
cd issue: preiser 89987

0481/1929/grammophon sessions/**hermann weigert**/staatsopernchor
hella toros, soprano; hertha klust, soprano; lotte dörwald, contralto; franz völker, tenor; armin weltner, baritone
verdi il trovatore, kurzoper (abridged version on 4 discs)
691bi I   95260/59084/15277
692bi I
693bi I   95261/59085/15278
694 ½ bi
695 ½ bi   95262/59086/15279
696 ½ bi
697bi I   95263/59087/15280
698 ½ bi

0482/1929/grammophon sessions/**hermann weigert**/sabine meyen, soprano; julius patzak, tenor; armin weltner, bass-baritone; eduard kandl, bass
rossini il barbiere di siviglia, kurzoper (abridged version on 4 discs)
832 ½ bi   95282/27352/15250
833 ½ bi
834 ½ bi   95283/27353/15251
839 ½ bi
835 ½ bi   95284/27354/15252
836bi
837 ½ bi   95285/27355/15253
838bi

0483/1929/grammophon sessions/**hermann weigert**/staatsopernchor
margret pfahl, soprano; hertha klust, soprano; else ruzicka,
contralto; franz völker, tenor; willi domgraf-fassbaender, baritone
johann strauss die fledermaus, kurzoperette (abridged version on 5 discs)

905bi	95313/15289/27415/decca CA 8118
906bi	
907bi	95314/15290/27416/decca CA 8119
908bi	
909bi	95315/15291/27417/decca CA 8120
910bi	
911 ½ bi	95316/15292/27418/decca CA 8121
912bi	
914bi I	95317/15293/27419/decca CA 8122
915bi I	

cd issue: pearl GEMM 0087

0484/1929/grammophon sessions/**hermann weigert**/staatsopernchor
elfriede marherr-wagner, soprano; tilly de garmo, soprano;
fritz soot, tenor; eduard kandl, baritone; armin weltner,
baritone; deszö ernster, bass; waldemar henke, speaker
weber der freischütz, kurzoper (abridged version on 4 discs)

1523bm I	95234/27387/decca CA 8132
1524bm I	
1525bm I	95235/27388/decca CA 8133
1526bm I	
1527bm I	95236/27389/decca CA 8134
1528 ½ bm I	
1529bm	95237/27390/decca CA 8135
1530bm	

cd issue: sanctus SCSH 006

0485/1929/grammophon sessions/**hermann weigert**/staatsopernchor
tilly de garmo, soprano; willy frey, tenor; eduard kandl, baritone;
willi domgraf-fassbaender, baritone; waldemar henke, bass
lortzing zar und zimmermann, kurzoper (abridged version on 4 discs)

742 ½ bi	95291/15281/27407
743 ½ bi	
744 ½ bi	95292/15282/27408
745 ½ bi	
746 ½ bi	95293/15283/27409
747 ½ bi	
748 ½ bi	95294/15284/27410
749 ½ bi	

0486/1929/grammophon sessions/**hermann weigert**/staatsopernchor
elfriede marherr-wagner, soprano; margret pfahl, soprano
else ruzicka, contralto; willy frey, tenor; eduard kandl, baritone;
armin weltner, baritone; hermann kant, bass
nicolai die lustigen weiber von windsor, kurzoper (abridged version on 4 discs)
810bi   95273/15268/27399
811bi
812bi   95274/15269/27400
813bi
814bi   95275/15270/27401
815bi
816bi   95276/15271/27402
834bi

0487/1929/grammophon session/**manfred gurlitt**/julius patzak, tenor
massenet manon: en fermant les yeux
1528bh   90062
tchakovsky evgeny onegin: faint echo of my youth
1531bh   90060
1532bh
cd issue of both items: preiser 89075

0488/1929/grammophon sessions/**manfred gurlitt**/joseph wolfsthal, violin
beethoven violin concerto in d op 61
1534 ½ bm   95243
1535 ½ bm
1536bm   95244
1537bm
1538bm   95245
1547 ½ bm
1548 ½ bm   95246
1549bm
1550bm   95247
1551bm
cd issue: deutsche grammophon 453 8042

0489/1929/grammophon session/**alexander kitschin**
xenia belmas, soprano; willi domgraf-fassbaender, baritone
leoncavallo i pagliacci: nedda! silvio!....no piu non m'ami
1590bm   66847
1591bm
mascagni cavalleria rusticana: oh il signore vi manda…comare santa
1592bm   66848
1593bm
verdi aida: ciel mio padre!....su dunque sorgete
1594bm   66849
1595bm

0490/1929/grammophon sessiom/**julius prüwer**
hedwig von debicka, soprano; willi domgraf fassbaender, baritone
verdi rigoletto: tutte le feste; ah solo per me l'infamia
751 ½ bi 66878
752 ½ bi
verdi rigoletto: o figlia! mio padre!; v'ho ingannato…colpevoli fui!
750bi 66879
753 ½ bi

0491/1929/odeon session/**frieder weissmann**/staatsopernchor
nanny larsen-todsen, soprano
wagner der fliegende holländer: traft ihr das schiff?
XXB 8786 O-2979/parlophone R 1079
   8787
cd issue: preiser 89984

0492/1929/odeon session/**ernst römer**/staatsopernchor
vera schwarz, soprano; else knepel, contralto; richard tauber, tenor; leo schützendorf, tenor; max kuttner, baritone
millöcker der bettelstudent, kurzoper (abridged version on 4 discs)
BE 8913 O-4862
   8914
   8915 O-4863
   8916
   8917 O-4864
   8918
   8919 O-4865
   8920

0493/1929/telefunken session/**carl schuricht**
grieg peer gynt suite no 1
 A 161/clangor M 1557/D 69

 A 162/clangor M 1569/D 70

johann strauss die fledermaus overture
30159
30160 E 145/clangor MD 535/decca K 638
weber der freischütz overture E 265/clangor D 70/decca K 460

0494/1929/parlophone session/**frieder weissmann**
sibelius finlandia
 E 11170/american decca 25418

0495/january 1929/columbia sessons/**bruno walter**
mozart symphony no 40 in g minor k550
WAX 4570 DX 31/DOX 25/american columbia 68109
     4571
     4572 DX 32/DOX 26/american columbia 68110
     4573
     4574 DX 33/DOX 27/american columbia 68111
     4575
cd issue: wing WCD 26
johann strauss die fledermaus overture
WAX 4576 L 2311/american columbia 9080
     4577
johann strauss wiener blut waltz
WAX 4578 L 2270
     4579
cd issue of both johann strauss items: dante LYS 358

0496/january 1929/electrola session/**leo blech**
mendelssohn a midsummer night's dream overture and wedding march
CLR 4895 EH 330/hmv C 1883
     4896
     4897 EH 331/hmv C 1884
     4898

0497/3 january 1929/odeon session/**frieder weissmann**/vera schwarz, soprano
puccini tosca: vissi d'arte; madama butterfly: un bel di
XXB 8270 unpublished recordings
     8271

0498/4 january 1929/parlophone session/**frieder weissmann**
popy suite orientale
221166 E 10896/P 9368
221167
221168 E 10897/P 9369
221169
weber-berlioz aufforderung zum tanz
221170 E 10927/P 9399
221171

0499/12 january 1929/odeon session/**frieder weissmann**/heinrich knote, tenor
wagner die meistersinger von nürnberg: am stillen herd; morgenlich leuchtend
XXB 8273 O-6992
     8276
wagner lohengrin: mein lieber schwan; in fernem land
XXB 8274 O-6708
     8275

0500/14 january 1929/parlophone session/**frieder weissmann**/staatsopernchor
meta seinemeyer, soprano; jaro dworsky, tenor; emanuel list, bass
gounod faust: prison scene
221175   E 10834/P 9852/odeon O-7644
221176
gounod faust: church scene
221177   E 10835/P 9850/odeon O-7573
221178
verdi un ballo in maschera: ecco l'orrido campo!
221179   E 11300/P 9867/odeon O-7649
221180
cd issue of all items: preiser 89402

0501/17 january 1929/odeon session/**frieder weissmann**
elisabeth feuge, soprano
wagner tannhäuser: dich teure halle!; allmächtige jungfrau
XXB 8287   E 10877
      8288
weber der freischütz: leise leise
XXB 8285   unpublished recording
      8286

0502/17 january 1929/odeon session/**erich kleiber**
dvorak slavonic dance op 46 no 8
XXB 8282   O-6763/parlophone E 11018
cd issue: preiser 90207
schubert symphony no 3, second and third movements
XXB 8283   O-6820/parlophone E 11248
      8284

0503/18 january 1929/*see 21 december 1928*

0504/february 1929/electrola session/**clemens schmalstich**
rudolf bockelmann, bass-baritone
bizet carmen: votre toast; offenbach les contes d'hoffmann: scintille diamant!
CLR 5045   EH 278/hmv C 1680
      5046

0505/february 1929/electrola session/**clemens schmalstich**
max lorenz, tenor
wagner tannhäuser overture; albumblatt arranged for violin and orchestra
CLR 5057   EH 430/hmv C 2184
    5058
    5059   EH 431/hmv C 2185
    5814
wagner die meistersinger von nürnberg: am stillen herd
CLR 5078   EH 300/hmv C 2153
meyerbeer l'africaine: o paradis!; verdi la forza del destino: tu che in seno
CLR 5079   EH 287
    5080
leoncavallo i pagliacci: un tal gioco
CLR 5081   EH 294
wagner lohengrin: atmest du nicht mit mr die süssen düfte; mein lieber schwan
CLR 5082   EH 288
    5084
cd issue of all items: preiser 89232

0506/4 february 1929/parlophone session/**frieder weissmann**
verdi un ballo in maschera prelude
221201   E 11040

0507/5 february 1929/odeon session/**frieder weissmann**
verdi il trovatore, orchestral selection
XXB 8295   O-6693/parlophone E 10895
    8296
puccini la boheme, orchestral selection
XXB 8297   O-6700
    8298
waldteufel estudianita waltz; espana waltz
XXB 8299   O-6698
    8300
zimmer grosse marsch-revue
XXB 8301   O-6701
    8302

0508/15 february 1929/parlophone session/**frieder weissmann**
meta seinemeyer, soprano; helene jung, contralto
puccini madama butterfly: scuoti quella fronda
221222   E 10883/P 9864/odeon O-7647/am.decca 25193
221223
humperdinck hänsel und gretel: abends will ich schlafen geh'n; juchhei nun ist die hexe tot!
221224   E 10870/P 9415/odeon O-7796/am.decca 25431
221225
cd issue of all items: preiser 89402

0509/21 february 1929/odeon session/**frieder weissmann**
marta schellenberg, soprano
mozart don giovanni: vedrai carino; le nozze di figaro: porgi amor
XXB 8303   unpublished recordings
    8304

0510/26 february 1929/odeon session/**frieder weissmann**
lotte lehmann, soprano
weber der freischütz: leise leise
XXB 8305   O-8741/parlophone R 20087/am.decca 29007
     8306

0511/7 march 1929/electrola session/**leo blech**
tchaikovsky serenade for strings, waltz and finale
CLR 5132   EH 351/hmv C 2257
     5133
unknown title
CLR 5134   unpublished recording
     5135
wagner tannhäuser overture, part three
CLR 5136   EJ 522

0512/8 march 1929/parlophone session/**frieder weissmann**
luise helletsgruber, soprano
puccini la boheme: si mi chiamano mimi
221261   E 10945/P 9382
gounod faust: il etait un roi de thule; ah je ris!
221262   E 10932
221263
bizet carmen: je dis que rien ne m'epouvante
221264   E 11358/P 9382
puccini turandot: signore ascolta
221265   E 11358

0513/8 march 1929/electrola session/**erich kleiber**
heuberger der opernball overture
CLR 5145   EH 352/hmv C 1799
     5146

0514/8 march 1929/electrola session/**leo blech**
mendelssohn a midsummer night's dream, scherzo and intermezzo
CLR 5147   EH 332
     5148

0515/12 march 1929/odeon session/**frieder weissmann**
d'albert tiefland, orchestral fantasy
XXB 8311   O-6714
     8312

0516/14-20 march 1929/parlophone sessions/**issay dobrowen**
borodin prince igor: polovtsian dances
221276   E 10979/P 9411
221290
dvorak slavonic dances op 46 nos 1 and 2
221282   E 10936/P 9390
221283
dvorak slavonic dances op 46 no 8 and op 72 no 8
221289
221291

0517/15 march 1929/electrola session/**leo blech**
wagner huldigungsmarsch
CLR 5184   EH 353/hmv C 2190
    5185
meyerbeer les huguenots: prelude and ballet music
CLR 5186   EH 340
    5187

0518/18 march 1929/parlophone session/**frieder weissmann**
meta seinemeyer, soprano
liszt liebestraum
221278   E 10901/P 9861/odeon O-7645
weingartner liebesfeier
221279   P 9872/odeon O-7651
rubinstein es blinkt der tau
221280   P 9872/odeon O-7651/am.decca 25751
rubinstein die nacht
221281   E 10901/P 9861/odeon O-7645/am.decca 25751
cd issue of all items: preiser 89402

0519/19 march 1929/odeon session/**frieder weissmann**/fritz krauss, tenor
weber der freischütz: nein länger trag' ich nicht die qualen!
XXB 8313   O-6703
    8314
wagner der fliegende holländer: mit gewitter und sturm; meyerbeer huguenotten: ihr wangenpaar
BE 8097   O-11058
    8098

0520/22 march 1929/electrola session/**leo blech**
goldmark die königin von saba: processional march
CLR 5226   EH 354
    5227

0521/23 march 1929/odeon session/**manfred gurlitt**/robert hager, baritone
wagner tannhäuser: blick' ich umher in diesem edlen kreise; wie todesahnung
XXB 8315
    8316

0522/25 march 1929/parlophone session/**max von schillings**
wagner tannhäuser venusberg music
221303   E 10886/P 9853
221304
wagner tannhäuser act three prelude
221305   E 10887/P 9854
221407
act three prelude completed on 10 may 1929

0523/28 march 1929/electrola session/**leo blech**
mendelsohn a midsummer night's dream: nocturne
CLR 5258   EH 333
    5259
johann strauss der zigeunerbaron: schatzwalzer
CLR 5260   EH 335/hmv C 1942/victor 9991
    5261
weber preciosa overture
CLR 5262   EH 336
    5263

0524/april 1929/electrola session/**clemens schmalstich**/max lorenz, tenor
weingartner liebesfeier; schmalstich trinkspruch
BLR 5324   EG 1356
    5325
hildach der lenz ist da!
BLR 5326   unpublished recording
cd issue of all three items: preiser 89232

0525/2 april 1929/odeon session/**frieder weissmann**/karol szreter, piano
saint-saens danse macabre, arrangement for piano and orchestra
XXB 8317   O-6729/parlophone E 10903/am.decca 25323
    8318

0526/9 april 1929/odeon session/**frieder weissmann**/beate malkin, soprano
verdi la forza del destino: pace pace; madre pietosa vergine
XXB 8319   unpublished recordings
    8320

0527/10 and 12 april 1929/parlophone sessions/**frieder weissmann**
emil prill, flute
ciardi russian carnival for flute and orchestra
221351   E 10948
221352
respighi fontane di roma
221358   E 10941/P 8523/am.decca 25375
221359
221360   E 10942/P 8524/am.decca 25376
221361

0528/16 april 1929/odeon session/**frieder weissmann**/lotte lehmann, soprano
puccini tosca: vissi d'arte; la boheme: si mi chiamano mimi
XXB 8321   unpublished recordings
    8322
recordings repeated on 13 june 1929 using same matrix numbers

0529/17 april 1929/parlophone session/**joseph rosenstock**
beethoven symphony no 5 in c minor op 67
221365   E 10906/P 9407
221366
221367   E 10907/P 9408
221368
221369   E 10908/P 9409
221466
221467   E 10909/P 9410
221468
recording completed on 3 june 1929

0530/24 april 1929/parlophone session/**frieder weissmann**
meta seinemeyer, soprano; curt taucher, tenor
wagner die walküre: der männer sippe sass hier im saal
221378   P 9874/odeon O-7565
221379
221380   P 9875/odeon O-7566
221381
cd issue: preiser 89402
wagner die walküre: war wälse dein vater?
221382   unpublished recording

0531/29 april 1929/parlophone session/**artur bodanzky**
suppe ein morgen ein mittag ein abend in wien
221387   E 10882/P 9403
221388

0532/1 may 1929/odeon session/**artur bodanzky**
thomas mignon overture
XXB 8323   O-6739
    8324

0533/2 may 1929/odeon session/**frieder weissmann**
verdi aida, orchestral selection
XXB 8325   O-6705/parlophone E 10937
    8326

0534/3 may 1929/parlophone session/**max von schillings**
schillings mona lisa prelude and arrigo's serenade
221383   P 9462
221384
cd issue: preiser 90294
schumann manfred overture
221393   E 11131/P 9484/odeon O-6913/am.decca 25474
221394
221395   E 11132/P 9485/odeon O-6914/am.decca 25475

0535/3 may 1929/parlophone session/**frieder weissmann**
meta seinemeyer, soprano; robert burg, bass-baritone
wagner der fliegende holländer: wie aus der ferne längst vergang'ner zeiten
221396 unpublished recording
221397
221398 unpublished recording
221399

0536/4 may 1929/odeon session/**frieder weissmann**/cida lau, soprano
mozart die entführung aus dem serail: martern aller arten; johann strauss
g'schichten aus dem wienerwald
XXB 8327 unpublished recordings
    8328
johann strauss dorfschwalben aus österreich; mozart le nozze di figaro: deh vieni non tardar
XXB 8329 unpublished recordings
    8330
8327, 8328 and 8329 repeated on 31 october 1929 but remained unpublished

0537/4 and 6 may 1929/electrola sessions/**leo blech**/lotte schöne, soprano
schubert der hirt auf dem felsen
CLR 5345 EJ 558/hmv D 2004
    5346
verdi un ballo in maschera: saper vorreste
BLR 5347 EW 70
massenet manon: adieu notre petite table; profitons bien de la jeunesse!
CLR 5348 EJ 669
    5349
puccini la boheme: quando m'en vo
CLR 5350 EW 70

0538/6 may 1929/odeon session/**artur bodanzky**
adam si j'etais roi overture
XXB 8331 O-6721/parlophone E 11008
    8332

0539/8 may 1929/parlophone session/**otto dobrindt**/emanuel list, bass
kremser andreas hofer; lortzing zar und zimmermann: auch ich war ein jüngling
221402 E 11250/P 9418
221403

0540/10 may 1929/*see 25 march 1929*

0541/14 may 1929/odeon session/**frieder weissmann**/max hirzel, tenor
mozart don giovanni: il mio tesoro; dalla sua pace
XXB 8335 O-7805
    8336

0542/16 may 1929/parlophone session/**frieder weissmann**
dvorak rusalka, orchestral selection
221420 E 11216/P 9572
221421
221422 E 11217/P 9573
221423

0543/17 may 1929/odeon session/**frieder weissmann**
potpourri of themes from the operettas of franz lehar
XXB 8337   O-6707/parlophone E 10960
      8338

0544/21-22 may 1929/electrola sessions in the philharmonie/**leo blech**
göta ljungberg, soprano; friedrich schorr, bass-baritone
strauss salome: du wolltest mich nicht dich küssen lassen
CLR 5395   EJ 481/hmv D 1699
      5396
cd issue: pearl GEMMCD 9257
wagner die meistersinger von nürnberg: wahn wahn überall wahn!
CLR 5397   EJ 472/hmv D 1734/DB 10129
      5398
puccini madama butterfly: un bel di
CLR 5399   EJ 571/hmv D 2036
mascagni cavalleria rusticana: voi lo sapete
CLR 5400   EJ 571/hmv D 2036
cd issue: pearl GEMMCD 9257
wagner der fliegende holländer: die frist ist um
CLR 5401   EJ 473/hmv D 1813
      5402

0545/22 may 1929/parlophone session/**otto klemperer**
auber fra diavolo overture
220862   E 11201/P 9406/american columbia 50250
221431
offenbach la belle helene overture
221432   E 10935/P 9469/odeon O-6889/am.decca 25145
221433
cd issue of both items: archiphon ARC 121-125

0546/24 may 1929/parlophone session/**max von schillings**
beethoven symphony no 3 in e flat op 55 "eroica"
221435   E 10965/P 9434/american columbia 67763
221436
221437   E 10966/P 9435/american columbia 67764
221438
221492   E 10967/P 9436/american columbia 67765
221493
221494   E 10968/P 9437/american columbia 67766
221495
221519   E 10969/P 9438/american columbia 67767
221520
221521   E 10970/P 9439/american columbia 67768
221522
recording completed on 13 and 27 june 1929

0547/24-27 may 1929/electrola sessions in the philharmonie/**leo blech**
staatsopernchor/anton baumann, tenor
meyerbeer l'africaine prelude; le prophete: quadrille skating scene
CLR 5411   EH 305
    5412
meyerbeer l'africaine: marche indienne
CLR 5413   EH 306
    5414
meyerbeer robert le diable: march and ballet music
CLR 5415   EH 307
    5416
meyerbeer les huguenots: gloire au grand dieu vengeur
CLR 5417   EH 365/hmv C 1861
    5418
les huguenots item has sometimes been attributed to conductor hans knappertsbusch

0548/28 may 1929/electrola session in the philharmonie/**leo blech**
göta ljungberg, soprano; joseph schmidt, tenor
puccini tosca: vissi d'arte; amaro sol per te
CLR 5421   EJ 468/hmv D 2019
    5422

0549/28 may 1929/odeon session/**frieder weissmann**
fucik marinella overture
XXB 8342   O-6712/parlophone E 10980
     8343

0550/3 june 1929/*see 17 april 1929*

0551/3 june 1929/parlophone session/**otto klemperer**
strauss till eulenspiegels lustige streiche
221452   E 10925/P 9859/odeon O-7628/am.decca 25421
221453
221513   E 10926/P 9860/odeon O-7629/am.decca 25422
221514
recording completed on 24 june 1929; cd issue: archiphon ARC 121-125

0552/3-4 june 1929/parlophone sessions/**joseph rosenstock**
berlioz le carnaval romain overture
221454   E 10971/P 9561/american decca 25256
221455
berlioz benvenuto cellini overture
221456   E 10992/american decca 25355
221459
221464   E 10993/american decca 25356
mendelssohn hebrides overture
221469   E 11053
221470
221471   E 11054

0553/5 june 1929/grammophon session in the hochschule/**richard strauss**
strauss till eulenspiegels lustige streiche
779 ½ bi I   66887/brunswick 90044
780 ½ bi I
781 ½ bi I   66888/brunswick 90045
782 ½ bi I
matrix numbers 779-782 were replaced in 1939 by 1244gs-1247gs respectively
strauss don juan
791b   66902/brunswick 90046/decca CA 8126
792b
793n   66903/brunswick 90047/decca CA 8127
794b
matrix numbers 791-794 were replaced in 1939 by 1248gs-1251gs respectively
cd issue of both works: deutsche grammophon 429 9252

0554/6 june 1929/odeon session/**frieder weissmann**/violetta de strozzi, soprano
verdi un ballo in maschera: ecco l'orrido campo
XXB 8351   unpublished recording
verdi la forza del destino: pace pace!
XXB 8352   unpublished recording
bizet carmen: en vain pour eviter
XXB 8353   unpublished recording

0555/7 june 1929/parlophone session/**armas järnefelt**
sibelius finlandia, abridged version; valse triste
XXSTO 3050   E 10774/odeon O-7090
      3052
moszowski from foreign parts, suite
XXSTO 3329   E 11084/odeon O-7686/am.decca 25818
      3330
      3331   R 841/odeon O-25765/am.decca 202238
      3332
glazunov the seasons, abridged version
XXSTO 3478   E 11219/odeon O-6056/am.decca 25423
      3479
      3480   E 11220/odeon O-6059/am.decca 25424
      3481
      3482   E 11221/odeon O-6060/am.decca 25425
      3483
handel largo; järnefelt prelude funebre
XXSTO 3484   E 11147
      3485

0556/10 june 1929/parlophone session/**frieder weissmann**
gounod faust ballet music; delibes naila: flower waltz
221485   E 11006
221486
221487   E 11007
221488

0557/11-12 june 1929/electrola sessions in the philharmonie/**leo blech**
halevy la juive prelude
CLR 5449   EH 371
verdi aida: ballet music
CLR 5450   EH 372
    5451
meyerbeer robert le diable overture
CLR 5452   EH 371
unidentified title
CLR 5457   unpublished recordng

0558/13 june 1929/*see 24 may 1929*

0559/13 june 1929/odeon session/**frieder weissmann**/lotte lehmann, soprano
puccini tosca: vissi d'arte; la boheme: si mi chiamano mimi
XXB 8321   O-8746
    8322
cd issue of both arias: pearl GEMMCD 9409

0560/15 june 1929/electrola session in the philharmonie/**leo blech**
liselotte krumrey-topas, soprano; lauritz melchior, tenor;
friedrich schorr, bass-baritone; rudolf watzke, bass
wagner götterdämmerung: hast du gunther ein weib?....was nahmst du am eide nicht teil?
CLR 5458   EJ 471/hmv D 1700
    5459
wagner die walküre: ein schwert verhiess mir der vater...siegmund heiss' ich!
CLR 5460   EJ 475/hmv D 2022
    5461
cd issue: pearl GEMMCDS 9137

0561/19 june 1929/electrola session in the philharmonie/**leo blech**
friedrich schorr, bass-baritone
schumann die beiden grenadiere
CLR 5496   EJ 573/hmv D 2112
unidentified titles
CLR 5497   unpublished recordings
    5498

0562/19 june 1929/parlophone session/**fritz stiedry**
brahms academic festival overture
221498   E 10943/P 9569/american decca 25146
221499

0563/20 june 1929/parlophone session/**issay dobrowen**
sinding rustle of spring
221506   E 11054

0564/21 june 1929/parlophone session/**frieder weissmann**/mikhail szekely, bass
mozart die zauberflöte: in diesen heiligen hallen; wagner tannhäuser:
gar viel und schön
221508   E 10939
221509

0565/23 june 1929/parlophone session/**frieder weissmann**/georg baklanoff, bass
borodin prince igor: no rest no peace
221512   E 11014
221513

0566/24 june 1929/*see 3 june 1929*

0567/26 june 1929/parlophone session/**issay dobrowen**
grieg symphonic dances
221515   E 11171/P 9487/odeon O-6873/am.dccca 25241
221516
221517   E 11172/P 9488/odeon O-6874/am.decca 25242
221518

0568/27 june 1929/*see 24 may 1929*

0569/27-28 june 1929/odeon session/**ernst hauke**/richard tauber, tenor
loewe die uhr; tom der reimer
XXB 8366   O-8375
    8367
schumann die beiden grenadiere
XXB 8368   O-8377

0570/28 june 1929/parlophone session/**otto klemperer**
strauss don juan
221523   E 11051/P 9495/american decca 25444
221524
221615   E 11052/P 9496/american decca 25445
221616
recording completed on 25 october 1929; cd issue: archiphon ARC 121-125

0571/september 1929/electrola session/**clemens schmalstich**/joseph schmidt, tenor
flotow martha: ach so fromm
BLR 5591   EG 1698/hmv B 8036/odeon O-4718
boieldieu le caliphe de bagdad overture
BLR 5593   EG 1536/hmv B 3482
    5594

0572/9 september 1929/parlophone session/**frieder weissmann**
lacorne la feria, spanish suite
221555   E 11029
221556

0573/10 september 1929/odeon session/**frieder weissmann**
männecke potpourri on graf zeppelins weltreise
XXB 8393   O-6727
    8394

0574/13 september 1929/electrola session in the philharmonie/**albert coates**
frida leider, soprano; lauritz melchior, tenor
wagner tristan und isolde: isolde! geliebte! ....doch es rächte sich
CLR 5612 EJ 482/hmv D 1723/victor 7273
    5613
this complemented second part of the duet "sink hernieder nacht der liebe" recorded earlier by these artists in london
cd issues: preiser 89004 and danacord DACOD 315-316

0575/16, 21 and 30 september 1929/parlophone sessions/**max von schillings**
beethoven symphony no 6 in f op 68 "pastoral"
221560   E 11222/P 9463/odeon O-6907
221561
221562   E 11223/P 9464/odeon O-6908
221563
221564   E 11224/P 9465/odeon O-6909
221565
221566   E 11225/P 9466/odeon O-6910
221572
221573   E 11226/P 9467/odeon O-6911
221586
221587   E 11227/P 9468/odeon O-6912
221588

0576/19 september 1929/electrola session in the philharmonie/**leo blech**
jensen hochzeitsmusik
CLR 5628   EH 398
    5629
unidentified title
CLR 5630   unpublished recording
strauss der bürger als edelmann: intermezzo
CLR 5631   EJ 478

0577/20 september 1929/parlophone session/**frieder weissmann**
margarete bäumer, soprano
wagner tannhäuser: dich teure halle!; zurück von ihm!
221568   E 11035/P 9471/american decca 25120
221569
wagner tristan und isolde: isolde's narration and curse
221570   E 10996/odeon O-7801/am.decca 25338
221571

0578/26 september 1929/odeon session/**frieder weissmann**
georg baklanoff, bass
mussorgsky khovantschina: alles schläft im lager; rubinstein der dämon:
ich bin's den du so oft vernahmst
XXB 8395   unpublished recordings
    8396
rubinstein der dämon: kind weine nicht!; was ist ihr leben?
XXB 8397   unpublished recordings
    8398
mussorgsky boris godunov: i have attained the highest power; death of boris
XXB 8399   O-7726
    8400
8398 was repeated on 4 november 1929 but remained unpublished

0579/27 september 1929/*see 30 april 1928*

0580/28 september 1929/parlophone session/**frieder weissmann**
keler-bela ungarische lustspielouvertüre
221580 E 11302
221581

0581/october 1929/electrola sessions/**clemens schmalstich**
käte heidersbach, soprano; max lorenz, tenor
wagner tannhäuser: o fürstin!
CLR 5696 EH 414/hmv C 1897
    5697
wagner lohengrin: das süsse lied verhallt
CLR 5698 EH 406/hmv C 1899
    5699
cd issue of both items: preiser 89232

0582/october 1929/electrola sessions/**clemens schmalstich**
joseph schmidt, tenor; laszio szentgyörgi, violin
meyerbeer l'africaine: o paradis!
BNR 829 EG 1698
paganini violin concerto no 1, abridged version
CWR 794 EH 418/hmv C 2457
    795
    796 EH 419/hmv C 2458
    797
potpourri on themes from composers from gluck to wagner
2D 378 EH 688/hmv C 2467
   383

0583/1 october 1929/parlophone session/**hans knappertsbusch**
mozart symphony no 39 in e flat k543
XXB 8401 E 11003/odeon O-6735
     8402
     8403 E 11004/odeon O-6736
     8404
     8405 E 11005/odeon O-6737
     8406
also issued by parlophone in automatic coupling as E 15202-15204
cd issues: toshiba SGR 3001-3003, music and arts CD 4897 and archipel ARPCD 0078

0584/3-4 october 1929/odeon sessions/**franz lehar**
vera schwarz, soprano; richard tauber, tenor
lehar das land des lächelns, querchnitt

XXB 8409	O-8376/parlophone RO 20112
8410	O-8376/parlophone RO 20112/american decca 25779
8596	O-4951/parlophone RO 20136/american decca 20391
8597	O-4949/electrola EG 1583/american decca 23036
8598	O-4949/parlophone RO 20107/american decca 23036
8599	parlophone RO 20136
8633	O-11105/american decca 20392

XXB 8633 recorded on 22 october 1929
cd issues: emi 754 8382 (except XXB 8633) and pearl GEMMCD 9310

0585/7 october 1929/parlophone session/**max von schillings**/elisabeth kuhnlein, soprano; alfhild petzet, soprano; paula lindberg. mezzo-soprano
wagner götterdämmerung: frau sonne sendet lichte strahlen

221598	E 10987/odeon O-7827/american decca 25216
221599	
221600	E 10988/odeon O-7828/american decca 25217
221601	

0586/9 october 1929/parlophone session/**frieder weissmann**
mozart eine kleine nachtmusik

221557	E 11241/P 9478/odeon O-6790
221602	
221603	E 11242/P 9479/odeon O-6791
221604	

0587/18 and 22 october 1929/electrola sessions in the philharmonie/**leo blech**
haydn symphony no 94 in g "surprise"

CLR 5705	EJ 493/hmv D 2040
5706	
5707	EJ 494/hmv D 2041
5708	
5713	EJ 495/hmv D 2042
5714	

mozart die entführung aus dem serail overture; maurerische trauermusik

CLR 5715	EJ 496/hmv D 2050
5718	

cd issue of mozart items: archiphon ARC 135

0588/22 october 1929/*see 3-4 october 1929*

0589/22-24 october 1929/telefunken sessions/**selmar meyrowitz**
irene eisinger, soprano; joseph schmidt, tenor
lehar das land des lächelns: wer hat die liebe uns ins herz gesenkt?;
von apfelblüten einen kranz

030353	E 247
030354	E 242

cd issue of both items: teldec 3984 284062

0590/25 october 1929/*see 28 june 1929*

0591/31 october 1929/odeon session/**frieder weissmann**/cida lau, soprano
mozart die gärtnerin aus liebe: fern von ihrem neste
XXB 8416 unpublished recording
see also 4 may 1929

0592/november 1929/electrola sessions/**clemens schmalstich**/richard crooks, tenor
mascagni cavalleria rusticana: o lola ch'hai di latti cammisa; puccini tosca: recondita armonia
BLR 5752 EW 75/hmv E 601
    5753
humperdinck hänsel und gretel: gingerbread waltz and witches' ride
BLR 5755 EG 1612/hmv B 3654/victor 25169
    5760
moszkovski from foreign lands, suite
BLR 5777 EG 1687/hmv B 3624
    5778
    5779 EG 1688/hmv B 3625
    5780
smetana the bartered bride overture
BLR 5802 EG 1691/hmv B 3501/victor 80701
    5803

0593/1 and 6 november 1929/parlophone sessions/**frieder weissmann**
strauss tod und verklärung
221619 E 11243/P 9525/american decca 25350
221620
221621 E 11244/P 9526/american decca 25351
221622
221623 E 11245/P 9527/american decca 25352
221624

0594/3 november 1929/parlophone session/**fritz stiedry**
wolf italian serenade
221625 E 11173/P 9486/odeon O-7554/am.decca 25259
221626

0595/4 november 1929/*see 26 september 1969*

0596/7, 12 and 19 november 1929/electrola sessions in philharmonie/**leo blech** staatsopernchor/sigrid onegin, contralto
weber der freischütz: huntsmens' chorus
BLR 5769 EW 77/hmv E 557
gluck iphigenie in aulis overture and musette from ballet suite arr. mottl
BLR 5772 EG 1671/hmv B 4113
    5773
    5774 EG 1672/hmv B 4114
    5775
weber jubel overture
CLR 5776 EH 428/hmv C 2041
    5801
saint-saens samson et dalila: printemps qui commence; mon coeur s'ouvre a ta voix
CLR 5799 hmv DB 1420/victor 7305/7320
    5800

0597/19 november 1929/odeon session/**hans knappertsbusch**
beethoven symphony no 7 in a op 92
XXB 8417 O-6775/parlophone E 11103
    8418
    8419 O-6776/parlophone E 11104
    8420
    8421 O-6777/parlophone E 11105
    8422
    8423 O-6778/parlophone E 11106
    8424
    8425 O-6779/parlophone E 11107
    8426
also issued by parlophone in automatic coupling as E 15211-15215
cd issues: tahra TAH 309, documents 205229 and urania URN 22217

0598/13 december 1929/reichsrundfunk recording from a performance in the staatsoper unter den linden/**leo blech**/carl martin oehmann, tenor; heinrich schlusnus, baritone
leoncavallo i pagliacci, act one finale
RRG 106 unpublished recording

0599/1930/grammophon sessions/**hermann weigert**/franz völker, tenor
wagner rienzi: allmächtiger vater!
940bi I 95377/95491/67100/brunswick 90380
cd issues: nimbus NI 7848, preiser 89005 and deutsche grammophon 459 0062
verdi otello: niun mi tema
942bi 95494/67159/67992/27325
cd issue: preiser 89005
czernik liebesbrief an grammophon; erwin schenk mir doch nie eine frau
943bi I 27206
944bi I
cd issue of erwin item only: franz-völker-kreis RR 501
verdi aida: celeste aida
945bi 95377/67159/67205
cd issue: preiser 89005
leoncavallo i pagliacci: un tal gioco; vesti la giubba
2301bh I 90166
2302 ½ bh
cd issue of vesti la giubba: preiser 89005

0600/1930/grammophon session/**hermann weigert**/julius patzak, tenor
mozart die zauberflöte: dies bildnis ist bezaubernd schön
958bi   95437
cd issue: preiser 89075
offenbach les contes d'hoffmann: o dieu! quelle ivresse!; air de kleinzack
960bi   66985
961bi
cd issues: preiser 89075 and pearl GEMMCD 9383

0601/1930/grammophon session/**hans pfitzner**
beethoven symphony no 6 in f op 68 "pastoral"
977bi   66467
978bi
979bi   66468
980bi
981bi   66469
982bi
983bi   66470
985bi
986bi   66471
987bi
988bi   66472
cd issue: naxos 8.110927

0602/1930/grammophon session/**max fiedler**
brahms symphony no 4 in e minor op 98
993bi   95356
994bi
995bi   95357
997bi
998bi   95358
999bi
1000bi   95359
1001bi
1002bi   95360
1003bi
1004bi   95361
cd issues: biddulph WHL 003-004 and pristine PASC 363

0603/1930/grammophon session/**hermann weigert**/else ruziczka, mezzo-soprano; elfriede marherr-wagner, soprano; helge rosvaenge, tenor; karl armster, baritone; willi domgraf-fassbaender, baritone
bizet carmen, kurzoper (abridged version on 5 discs)
1847 ½ bm   95337/27367/15259
1848bm
1849bm   95338/27368/15260
1850bm
1851bm   95339/27369/15261
1852bm
1853bm   95340/27370/15262
1854bm
1855bm   95341/27371/15263
1856bm

0604/1930/grammophon session/**hermann weigert**/margret pfahl, soprano; irene eisinger, soprano; julius patzak, tenor; eduard kandl, baritone; waldemar henke, bass
millöcker der bettelstudent, kurzoperette (abridged version on 4 discs)
1881bm   95342/27411/15285
1882bm
1883 ½ bm   95343/27412/15286
1884bm
1885 ½ bm   95344/27413/15287
1886 ½ bm
1887 ½ bm   95345/27414/15288
1888 ½ bm

0605/1930/grammophon session/**hermann weigert**/felicie hüni-mihacsek, soprano; hedwig jungkurth, soprano; helge rosvaenge, tenor; armin weltner, baritone
puccini la boheme, kurzoper (abridged version on 5 discs)
1013bi   95362/27357/15254
1014bi
1015bi   95363/27358/15255
1016bi
1017bi   95364/27359/15256
1023bi
1024bi   95365/27360/15257
1025bi
1026bi   95366/27361/15258
1027bi

0606/1930/grammophon session/**hermann weigert**/felicie hüni-mihacsek, soprano; adele kern, soprano; helge rosvaenge, tenor; waldemar henke, bass
kalman die czardasfürstin, kurzoperette (abridged version on 4 discs)
1053bi I   95397
1054bi I
1055bi I   95398
1056bi I
1057bi I   95399
1058bi I
1059bi I   95400
1060bi I

0607/1930/grammophon session/**hermann weigert**/hedwig von debicka, soprano; hedwig jungkurth, soprano; helge rosvaenge, tenor; heinrich schlusnus, bass-baritone; eduard kandl, bass
gounod faust, kurzoper (abridged version on 4 discs)
1173 ½ bi I   95447/27378/15273
1174 bi I
1175 ½ bi I   95448/27379/15274
1176 bi I
1177 bi I   95449/27380/15275
1178 ½ bi I
1179 ½ bi I   95450/27381/15276

0608/1930/grammophon session/**hermann weigert**/staatsopernchor beate malkin, soprano; henriette gottlieb, soprano; fritz wolff, tenor; otto helgers, bass
wagner lohengrin, kurzoper (abridged version on 4 discs)
1599 bm I   95238/27395
1600 bm I
1601 bm I   95239/27396
1602 bm I
1603 bm I   95240/27397
1604 bm I
1605 bm I   95241/27398
1606 bm I

0609/1930/grammophon session/**hermann weigert**/staatsopernchor tilly de garmo, soprano; else ruziczka, contralto; eduard kandl, bass
humperdinck hänsel und gretel, kurzoper (abridged version on 4 discs)
890bi I   95297/27391/15264/decca CA 8000
891bi I
892bi I   95298/27392/15265/decca CA 8001
893bi I
894bi I   95299/27393/15266/decca CA 8002
895bi I
896bi I   95300/27394/15267/decca CA 8003
897bi I

0610/1930/ultraphon session/**selmar meyrowitz**/mme. charles cahier, contralto
mahler urlicht; ich bin der welt abhanden gekommen
          E 228

cd issue: pearl GEMMCDS 9929

0611/1930/parlophone session/**frieder weissmann**/margarita carosio, soprano
thomas mignon: je suis titania; verdi il trovatore: spargi d'amaro pianto
228048   E 11024
228047

0612/16 and 21 january 1930/odeon sessions/**frieder weissmann**
heinrich knote, tenor
weinberger schwanda der dudelsackpfeifer, orchestral fantasy
XXB 8444   O-6745/parlophone E 11000
  8445
wagner götterdämmerung: brünnhilde heilige braut!; parsifal: nur eine waffe taugt
XXB 8450   O-6822/parlophone E 11162
  8451
wagner tannhäuser: inbrunst im herzen
XXB 8452   O-6766
  8453

0613/february 1930/electrola session/**clemens schmalstich**/joseph schmidt, tenor
verdi il trovatore: di quella pira
BLR 6083   EG 1698/hmv B 8036/odeon O-4718

0614/3 february 1930/odeon session/**frieder weissmann**
potpourri on themes from kalman operettas
XXB 8456   O-6749/parlophone E 11016
  8457

0615/24 and 27 february 1930/electrola sessions/**leo blech**
chopin funeral march, arranged for orchestra by gustav schmidt
BLR 6099   EG 1838
  6100
weber der freischütz overture, first part
CLR 6101   EJ 520
brahms hungarian dances nos 5 and 6
BLR 6102   EW 79
  6103
dvorak slavonic dances nos 1 and 2
CLR 6116   EJ 534
  6117
weinberger schwanda der dudelsackpfeifer: polka and furiant
BLR 6118   EG 1851/hmv B 8173
  6119

0616/28 february 1930/parlophone sesson/**frieder weissmann**
barbara kemp, mezzo-soprano; tino pattiera, tenor
bizet carmen: c'est toi! c'est moi!
221661   E 11013/P 9506
221662
cd issue: preiser 89222

0617/march 1930/electrola session/**leo blech**/lotte schöne, soprano
nicolai die lustigen weiber von windsor: nun eilt herbei!
CLR 6358   EJ 528/hmv D 2021/DB 1562
    6359

0618/march 1930/electrola session/**clemens schmalstich**/max lorenz, tenor
wagner die meistersinger von nürnberg: morgenlich leuchtend
CLR 6158   EH 504
wagner der fliegende holländer: willst jenes tages du dich nicht mehr entsinnen?
BLR 6159   unpublished recording
wagner rienzi: allmächtiger vater!
CLR 6160   EH 504
cd issue of all items: preiser 89232

0619/11 march 1930/electrola session/**leo blech**
unidentified title
CLR 6153   unpublished recording
    6154
schubert symphony no 8 in b minor d759 "unfinished"
CLR 6155   EJ 604
    6156
    6157   EJ 605
    6350
    6351   EJ 606
    6352
recording completed on 15 june 1930

0620/13 and 18 march 1930/odeon sessions/**frieder weissmann**/salvatini, soprano
schestak fantasy on operatic themes
XXB 8472   O-6753/parlophone E 11066
    8473
verdi ernani: ernani involami!; thomas mignon: kennst du das land?
XXB 8475   unpublished recordings
    8476

0621/21 march 1930/parlophone session/**frieder weissmann**/staatsopernchor
tino pattiera, tenor; paul schöffler, bass-baritone
verdi il trovatore, scenes
221675   E 11048/P 9516
221676
221677   E 11049/P 9517
221678
221679   E 11050/P 9518
221680

0622/31 march 1930/odeon session/**frieder weissmann**
verdi aida: triumphal march
XXB 8479   O-6746/parlophone E 11041
     8480
wagner die walküre: ride of the valkyries; berlioz marche hongroise
XXB 8481   O-6740/parlophone E 11077
     8482

0623/april 1930/electrola session/**clemens schmalstich**/alexander kipnis, bass
mozart don giovanni: madamina!
BLR 6263   EW 89/hmv E 599
     6264
verdi don carlo: ella giammai m'amo
BLR 6297   EW 88/hmv E 610
     6298
flotow martha: lasst mich euch fragen; weber der freischütz: hier im irdischen jammertal
BLR 6301   EW 91/hmv E 591
     6302
gounod faust: vous qui faites l'endormie; le veau d'or
BLR 6303   EW 90/hmv E 592
     6304

0624/1 april 1930/parlophone session/**frieder weissmann**
gerhard hüsch, baritone
mozart die zauberflöte: ein mädchen oder weibchen
221683   E 11046
verdi rigoletto: pari siamo; cortigiani!
221684   E 11034/P 9550
221685

0625/9 april 1930/ultraphon session in studio wilhelmsaue/**erich kleiber**
joseph wolfsthal, violin
saint-saens danse macabre
30450   E 461
30451
cd issue: teldec 0927 426642

0626/may 1930/electrola session/**clemens schmalstich**
else gentner-fischer, soprano; max lorenz, tenor
verdi aida: o terra addio!
CLR 6401   EH 593
     6402
this version of the duet is listed in neither world's encyclopedia of recorded music nor in the gramophone shop encyclopedia
wagner tannhäuser: dir töne lob!
BLR 6403   unpublished recording
cd issue of both items: preiser 89232

0627/ 1 may 1930/parlophone session/**frieder weissmann**/moriz rosenthal, piano
chopin piano concerto no 1 in e minor

                                                E 11113/P 9558

                                                E 11114/P 9559

                                                R 902/B 12451

                                                R 903/B 12452

                                                R 904/B 12453

recording completed on 28 november 1930 and also published by odeon as O-25231-25233
cd issue: pearl GEMMCD 9339

0628/ 21 may 1930/odeon session/**frieder weissmann**/elisabeth rethberg, soprano
bizet carmen: je dis que rien ne m'epouvante; puccini madama butterfly: un bel di
XXB 8486   O-8372/parlophone R 20123/american decca 25285
    8487

0629/ 27-30 may 1930/parlophone sessions/**frieder weissmann**
emmy bettendorf, soprano; john glaser, tenor
wagner der fliegende holländer: mit gewitter und sturm; lohengrin: in fernem land
221717   E 11272
221718
gounod faust: il se fait tard
221719   E 11092/P 9549
221720

0630/ 7 june 1930/parlophone session/**frieder weissmann**/valeria barsowa, soprano
thomas mignon: je suis titania; gounod romeo et juliette: je veux vivre dans cette reve
XXRO 616   E 11186
    617
david charmant oiseau; masse along my pathway
XXRO 618   E 11176
    619

0631/ 15 june 1930/*see 11 march 1930*

0632/ 16 june 1930/parlophone session/**frieder weissmann**
margarete bäumer, soprano; gotthelf pistor, tenor
wagner die walküre: siegmund sieh auf mich!
221728   E 11257/P 9555
221729
221730   E 11258/P 9556
221731

0633/17 june 1930/odeon session/**frieder weissmann**
vera schwarz, soprano; max hirzel, tenor; arturo rubini, baritone
bizet carmen: votre toast; verdi la traviata: di provenza al mar
XXB 8450   parlophone E 11061
    8451
verdi il trovatore: miserere
XXB 8488   O-6841/parlophone E 11137
    8489
puccini madama butterfly: vieni la sera
XXB 8490   O-6780/parlophone E 11101
    8491
puccini tosca: mario! mario!
XXB 8492   O-6767
    8493

0634/20, 25 and 28 june 1930/grammophon sessions/**richard strauss**
strauss der bürger als edelmann, suite
408bs II   95392/brunswick 90130
409 ½ bs II
410bs II   95393/brunswick 90131
414bs II
415bs II   95394/brunswick 90132
416bs II
417bs II   95395/brunswick 90133
418bs II
419bs II   95396/brunswick 90134
cd issues: deutsche grammophon 429 9252 and dutton CDBP 9746

0635/21 june 1930/odeon session/**frieder weissmann**
lehar das land des lächelns, orchestral potpourri
XXB 8500   O-6768
    8501
recording completed on 4 september 1930

0636/august 1930/electrola session/**clemens schmalstich**
rudolf bockelmann, bass
wagner die walküre: leb wohl du kühnes herrliches kind!
CLR 8960   EH 607/hmv C 2179
    8961
wagner die meistersinger von nürnberg: jerum jerum!; verachtet mir die meister nicht
CLR 8963   EH 608/hmv C 2255
    8964

0637/4 september 1930/*see 21 june 1930*

0638/23 september 1930/electrola session/**leo blech**
mozart symphony no 34 in c k338
CD 9063   EJ 607/ES 753
   9064
   9065   EJ 608/ES 754
   9066
cd issue: archiphon ARC 135

0639/october 1930/electrola session/**clemens schmalstich**/ewald böhmer, baritone
mozart die zauberflöte: der vogelfänger bin ich ja!; ein mädchen oder weibchen
BD 9218   EG 2138/hmv B 3781
    9219

0640/2 october 1930/electrola session/**leo blech**
schubert symphony no 5 in b flat d485
CD 9099   EJ 664/hmv D 2070/victor 11476
    9100
    9101   EJ 665/hmv D 2071/victor 11477
    9102
    9103   EJ 666/hmv D 2072/victor 11478
    9104
also published by hmv in automatic coupling with numbers D 7464-7466

0641/7 october 1930/electrola session/**leo blech**
borodin prince igor: polovtsian dances and march
CD 9120   EJ 609
    9123
    9121   EJ 610
    9122

0642/13 and 17 october 1930/electrola sessions/**leo blech**
tchaikovsky symphony no 5 in e minor op 64
CD 9138   EJ 659/EH 718/hmv C 2276
    9139
    9140   EJ 660/EH 719/hmv C 2277
    9141
    9142   EJ 661/EH 720/hmv C 2278
    9167
    9168   EJ 662/EH 721/hmv C 2279
    9169
    9170   EJ 663/EH 722/hmv C 2280
    9171

0643/29 october 1930/electrola session/**leo blech**/staatsopernchor
beethoven fidelio: prisoners' chorus
BD 9203   EW 95
    9204
bizet carmen: choeurs des cigarieres and ballet music
BD 9205   EJ 654
    9206
unidentified title
BD 9207   unpublished recording

0644/28 november 1930/*see 1 may 1930*

139

0645/12 december 1930/parlophone session/**frieder weissmann**
gitta alpar, soprano
delibes lakme: dove l'indiana bruna?
221769   E 11214/P 9553/odeon O-6999
221770

0646/1931/columbia session/**erich orthmann**
charles kullmann, tenor; walter grossmann, bass
verdi la forza del destino: solenne in quest' ora; aida: celeste aida
WRX 16   DX 822/DWX 5038
    17
cd issue of both items: preiser 89057

0647/1931/columbia session/**otto dobrindt**/charles kullmann, tenor
offenbach les contes d'hoffmann: o dieu de quelle ivresse!
WR 223   DW 3011
    224
cd issue: preiser 89057

0648/1931/electrola session/**clemens schmalstich**/staatsopernchor
käthe heidersbach, soprano; willi domgraf-fassbaender, baritone
wagner lohengrin: sei gegrüsst du gottgesandter held!
2D 514   DB 4400
    515
cd issue: preiser 89989

0649/1931/grammophon session/**fritz zweig**/franz völker, tenor
millöcker der feldprediger: traumwalzer; lehar der rastelbinder: wenn zwei sich lieben
2622bh   24177
2624bh
cd issue: preiser 89221
lortzing undine: vater mutter!; zar und zimmermann: lebwohl du flandrisch mädchen
                             24193/26509
gounod chanson de printemps; sullivan let me dream again
                             24200
verdi il trovatore: di quella pira
                             24240/62776
komm mit mir ins reich der träume
                             23917

0650/1931/grammophon session/**otto klemperer**
weill kleine dreigroschenmusik
2743 ½ bh II   24172
2744bh II
2746bh II   24173
2745bh II
cd issue: archiphon ARC 121-125

0651/1931/grammophon session/**alois melichar**
hedwig von debicka, soprano; helge rosvaenge, tenor
ries wo du hingehst; böhm still wie die nacht
3013bh   24615
3014bh

0652/1931/grammophon session/**alois melichar**/staatsopernchor/hedwig von debicka, soprano; else ruczicka, contralto; helge rosvaenge, tenor
offenbach les contes d'hoffmann, scenes
3328 ½ bh II   24969
3329 ½ bh II
3330 ½ bh II   24970
3331 ½ bh II
3332 ½ bh II   24971
3338 ½ bh II

0653/1931/grammophon sessions/**julius prüwer**/staatsopernchor/julius patzak, tenor
offenbach der goldschmied von toledo: lieblichste aller frauen
2643 ½ bh I   23921/decca PO 5021
cd issues: preiser 89174 and pearl GEMMCD 9383
zeller der obersteiger: sei nicht bös; wie mein ahn'l zwanzig jahr'
2644bh I   23922
2647bh I
cd issue of both items: preiser 89174
strauss cäcilie; ständchen
2645bh I   23923
2646 ½ bh I
cd issues of both items: preiser 89075 and pearl GEMM 0156
mozart cosi fan tutte: un aura amorosa
1118bh I   95437/decca CA 8196
cd issues: preiser 89075 and 89233 and pearl GEMM 0156
wagner die meistersinger von nürnberg: am stillen herd; morgenlich leuchtend
2976bh I   90181
2977bh I
cd issue: preiser 89233
puccini la boheme: che gelida manina; la fanciulla del west: ch'ella mi creda
2978bh I   90182
2981bh I
cd issues: preiser 89233 and pearl GEMMCD 9383
verdi aida: celeste aida; bizet carmen: la fleur que tu m'avais jetee
2979bh I   90183
2980bh I
cd issue: preiser 89233
flotow martha: mag der himmel euch vergeben
4323bd I   90180
cd issue: preiser 89233
puccini madama butterfly: addio fiorito asil; mascagni cavalleria rusticana: siciliana
4325bd I   24327
4328bd I
puccini item also published by decca on PO 5007
cd issue of both items: preiser 89233
zeller der landstreicher: sei gepriesen du lauschige nacht; dellinger don cesar: komm herab o madonna theresa!
4326bd I   24326
4327bd I
cd issue of both items: preiser 89174

0654/1931/grammophon session/**hermann weigert**
hedwig von debicka, soprano; helge rosvaenge, tenor
bizet carmen: ma mere je la vois
1187 ½ bi   95451
offenbach les contes d'hoffmann: c'est une chanson d'amour
1186bi   95464/decca CA 8057
cd issue of both items: preiser 89209

0655/1931/grammophon session/**alois melichar**/staatsopernchor
hedwig von debicka, soprano; julius patzak, tenor
verdi la traviata: libiamo!
4324 ½ bd   90180
cd issues: preiser 89075 and 89233

0656/1931/electrola session/**clemens schmalstich**
willi domgraf-fassbaender, baritone
mozart le nozze di figaro: non piu andrai; aprite un po
OD 206   EG 2323
    207

0657/1931/odeon session/**frieder weissmann**/joseph schmidt, tenor
johann strauss der zigeunerbaron: als flotter geist
133349   O-25982/parlophone R 1332
cd issue: bbc records CD 716

0658/1931/odeon session/**frieder weissmann**/richard tauber, tenor
kalman gräfin maritza: komm zigany!
                                        O-4502/parlophone RO 20183
cd issue: bbc records CD 716

0659/1931/parlophone session/**frieder weissmann**/fritz krauss, tenor
verdi la traviata: libiamo!
37250   B 12145
flotow martha: ach so fromm
37251   B 12145

0660/21 january 1931/parlophone session/**frieder weissmann**
friedmann slavonic rhapsody
221779   E 11094/P 9557
221780

0661/march 1931/electrola session/**erich orthmann**/lotte schöne, soprano;
willi domgraf-fassbaender, baritone
donizetti don pasquale: pronto io…vado corro
2D 270   DB 1546 (version in italian)
   271
   272   DB 1563 (version in german)
   273

0662/10, 13 and 17 april 1931/electrola sessions/**leo blech**/alexander kipnis, bass
rossini il barbiere di siviglia: la calumnia!
2D 298   EJ 689/hmv D 2088
verdi simon boccanegra: il lacerato spirito
2D 309   EJ 689/hmv D 2088/victor 15820
nicolai die lustigen weiber von windsor: als büblein klein
2D 311   EJ 686/hmv D 2018
lortzing der wildschütz: fünftausend taler!
2D 330   EJ 686/hmv D 2018

0663/june-july 1931/electrola sessions/**clemens schmalstich**/staatsopernchor willi domgraf-fassbaender, baritone
johann strauss der zigeunerbaron: werbelied; kreutzer der verchwender: da streiten sich die leut' herum
OD 450   EG 2336
   451
verdi un ballo in maschera: eri tu; la traviata: di provenza al mar
OD 452   EG 2341
   453
wagner tannhäuser: wie todesahnung
2D 517   EH 724

0664/august 1931/electrola session/**erich orthmann**/else ruzicka, contralto; alexander kipnis, bass
strauss der rosenkavalier: herr kavalier!
2D 213   DB 1543/victor 7894
cd issue: nimbus NI 7848

0665/october 1931/electrola session/**leo blech**/maria ivogün, soprano
strauss ariadne auf naxos: grossmächtige prinzessin!
2D 391   DB 4405
   392
cd issue: nimbus NI 7812

0666/october 1931/electrola sessions/**leo blech**
mozart serenade no 10 for wind k361, abridged version
2D 424   EJ 697/hmv DB 4401
   425
   426   EJ 698/hmv DB 4402
   427
cd issue: archiphon ARC 135
mozart idomeneo: chaconne and gavotte; andante for flute k315
2D 432   EJ 691/hmv D 2065
   433
cd issue: archiphon ARC 135

october 1931/ electrola sessions/ leo blech/ concluded
mozart divertimento no 6 k188
2D 434   DA 4400
  435
mozart divertimento no 9 k240
2D 436   EJ 692/hmv D 2069
  437
cd issue of both items: archiphon ARC 135

0667/november 1931/electrola session/**erich orthmann**/staatsopernchor willi domgraf-fassbaender, baritone
lortzing undine: nun ist's vollbrachr; kreutzer das nachtlager von granada: ein schütz bin ich
OD 674   EG 2510
   675

0668/22 november 1931/electrola session/**fritz zweig/**chor der städtischen oper/margarete teschemacher, soprano; marcel wittrisch, tenor
puccini madama butterfly: ancora un paso; tosca: vissi d'arte
OD 1294   EG 2726
   1295
cd issue of both items: preiser 89971
grieg peer gynt: solveigs lied; schlaf du teuerster knabe mein
2D 1296   EH 814/hmv DB 5598
   1297
verdi la traviata: libiamo!
2D 1298   DB 4416
cd issue: pearl GEMMCD 9256
verdi il trovatore: miserere
2D 1299   DB 4416
cd issue: hamburger archiv für gesangskunst HAG 1034

0669/1932/grammophon sessions/**alois melichar**/franz völker, tenor
wagner die walküre: ein schwert verhiess mir der vater; siegmund heiss' ich!
1238bi I   27291/brunswick 90312
1239bi I
schubert-berte das dreimädlerhaus potpourri
3185 ½ bh VIII   24807
3186bh VIII
von wien durch die welt, operetta potpourri
3183 ½ bn VIII   24939
3184 ½ bh VIII
spoliansky heut' nacht oder nie
3189 ½ bh I   24790
cd issue: franz-völker-kreis RR 501
höser deutschland du darfst nicht untergeh'n; meyer-helmund deutschland blühe neu auf!
3190bh   24806
3192 ½ bh
knauer übers meer möcht' ich flieh'n
3191bh   25200/10603

0670/1932/grammophon session/**alois melichar**/heinrich schlusnus, baritone
tchaikovsky pique dame: i love you dear!
1257bi   35003/67050
cd issues: preiser 89006 and 89212

0671/1932/electrola session/**fritz zweig**/erna berger, soprano; henriette gottlieb, soprano;
marcel wittrisch, tenor; willi domgraf-fassbaender, baritone
beethoven fidelio: mir ist so wunderbar; er sterbe doch er soll erst wissen!
2D 1336   DB 4417
   1337
cd issue: preiser 89989
rossini il barbiere di siviglia: una voce poco fa
2D 1338   EH 819
   1339
cd issues: preiser 89035 and emi 763 7592

0672/1932/electrola session/**fritz zweig**/staatsopernchor/margarete klose, contralto; therese gerson, soprano; susanne fischer, mezzo-soprano; marcel wittrisch, tenor; walter grossmann, bass-baritone
bizet carmen: si tu m'aimes
2D 1359   DB 4418
   1360
verdi il trovatore: ai nostri monti
OD 1361   DA 4407
cd issue of both items: preiser 89082

0673/1932/electrola session/**fritz zaun**/elsa oehme-foerster, soprano; erna berger, soprano; elisabeth friedrich, soprano; margarete klose, contralto; walter ludwig, tenor; willi domgraf-fassbaender, baritone
puccini la boheme: addio dolce svegliare
2D 1470   EH 813
   1471
lortzing der wildschütz: kann es im erdenleben
2D 1865   EH 850

0674/1932/electrola session/**willem van hoogstraten**/elly ney, piano
strauss burleske for piano and orchestra
2D 2109   DB 4424
   2110
   2111   DB 4425
   2112
cd: biddulph BID 82045

0675/1932/columbia session/**clemens schmalstich**/erna berger, soprano; charles kullmann, tenor
puccini turandot: non piangere liu; nessun dorma
WR 479   DW 3068
  480
verdi rigoletto: caro nome
WR 485   DW 3071
  486
johann strauss der zigeunerbaron: wer uns getraut; als flotter geist
WR 487
  488
cd issue of all items: preiser 89035; rigoletto also on emi 763 7592

0676/1932/clangor session/**franz alfred schmidt**/ludwig hofmann, bass-baritone
wagner die meistersinger von nürnberg: was duftet doch der flieder
9643   MD 9643
9644
cd issues: preiser 89102 and 90232 and hamburger archiv für gesangskunst HAGHOF 1
wagner die meistersinger von nürnberg: verachtet mir die meister nicht
9645   MD 9645
cd issue: preiser 89102
wagner die meistersinger von nürnberg, act three prelude
9646   MD 9646
gounod faust: le veau d'or; vous qui faites l'endormie
9647   MD 9647
9648

0677/1932/parlophone session/**otto dobrindt**/gitta alpar, soprano; herbert ernst groh, tenor
kalman die bajadere: ob sie wohl kommt?
133554   RO 20210/odeon O-11672
cd issue: bbc records CD 716

0678/12 january 1932/electrola session/**erich orthmann**
margarete teschemacher, soprano; marcel wittrisch, tenor
bizet carmen: ma mere je la vois
2D 7451   EH 732
   7452
cd issue: pearl GEMMCD 9256

0679/23 april 1932/odeon session/**manfred gurlitt**/staatsopernchor/ lotte lehmann, soprano
puccini madama butterfly: ancora un passo
BE 9908   O-4832/O-4839/parlophone PO 157/RO 20104
cd issue: pearl GEMMCD 9409

0680/may 1932/electrola session/**leo blech**/maria ivogün, soprano
johann strauss an der schönen blauen donau; die fledermaus: klänge der heimat
2D 1198   DB 4412
   1205
cd issues: nimbus NI 7832 and bbc records CD 716

0681/12 may 1932/electrola session/**erich orthmann**/margarete teschemacher, soprano; margarete klose, contralto; marcel wittrisch, tenor; willi domgraf-fassbaender, baritone
verdi aida: o terra addio!
2D 919   DB 4409
   920
offenbach les contes d'hoffmann: barcarolle; ecoute antonia!
2D 921   DB 4410
   922
cd issues of ecoute antonia!: preiser 89228 and 89989
verdi il trovatore: mira d'acerbe lagrime
OD 936   DA 4403
   937
cd issue: preiser 89980

0682/june 1932/telefunken session/**selmar meyrowitz**/pearl yoder, soprano; lydia kindermann, contralto; helge rosvaenge, tenor; hans reinmar, baritone
verdi rigoletto: bella figlia dell' amore
018469   SK 1162
cd issue: preiser 89209

0683/8 october 1932/grammophon session/**alois melichar**/julius patzak, tenor
donizetti l'elisir d'amore: una furtiva lagrima
3382bh VIII   25011/decca PO 5067
cd issues: preiser 89233 and pearl GEMMCD 9383
flotow martha: ach so fromm
3383 ½ bh VIII   25012
cd issues: preiser 89075 and 89233 and pearl GEMMCD 9383
rossini la danza
3384 ½ bh VIII   25011
cd issue: pearl GEMM 0156
kienzl der evangelimann: selig sind die verfolgung leiden
3385bh VIII   25012
cd issues: preiser 89075 and 89233

0684/28 october 1932/grammophon session/**alois melichar**/franz völker, tenor
millöcker der bettelstudent: ich knüpfe manche zarte band'; weber der freischütz: hat denn der himmel mich verlassen?
238db   unpublished recordings
239db

0685/12 november 1932/telefunken session/**franz alfred schmidt**/helge rosvaenge, tenor
meyerbeer les huguenots: plus blanche que la blanche hermine
018776   SK 1272
cd issues: preiser 89209 and teldec 3984 284102
verdi i vespril siciliani: giorno di pianto
018777   SK 1272
cd issues: teldec 3984 284102
wagner die meistersinger von nürnberg: am stillen herd; morgenlich leuchtend
018796   SK 1297
018797
cd issue of both items: preiser 89209 and teldec 3984 269192

0686/1933/grammophon session/**alois melichar**/franz völker, tenor
wagner rienzi: erstehe hohe roma neu
667 ½ be VIII   27325/95491/67100/67208
cd issue: preiser 89005
halevy la juive: quand du seigneur; o dieu de nos peres!
668be VIII   27328
669be VIII
cd issue of both arias: preiser 89401
wagner tannhäuser: inbrunst im herzen
670be VIII   27306/95483/67141
671be VIII
cd issue: preiser 89070
beethoven fidelio: gott welch dunkel hier?
672 ½ be   27311/95984/15452
673be VIII
cd issues: preiser 89070 and 89401

0687/1933/grammophon session/**hans pfitzner**
lanner pesther-walzer
5294 ½ bd   10133
5295 ½ bd
cd issue: pristine PASC 305

0688/1933/grammophon session/**hermann weigert**/julius patzak, tenor
johann strauss eine nacht in venedig: komm in die gondel
2341bh   23921
cd issues: bbc records CD 716 and preiser 89174

0689/1933/grammophon session/**alois melichar**/heinrich schlusnus, baritone
verdi simon boccanegra: plebe! patrizi!
695be   67150
verdi i vespri siciliani: in braccio alle dovizie
696be   67050/68119
bizet carmen: votre toast
697be   73086
borodin prince igor: no sleep no rest
698be   69057/decca CA 8185
cd issues of all items: preiser 89006 and 89212

0690/1933/grammophon session/**johannes schüler**/helge rosvaenge, tenor; heinrich schlusnus, baritone
verdi i vespri siciliani: quando al mio sen
5460 ½ bd VIII   90204
5461 ½ bd VIII
cd issues: preiser 89209 and symposium 1280

0691/1933/grammophon session/**clemens krauss**/viorica ursuleac, soprano; margit bokor, soprano; alfred jerger, baritone
strauss arabella: das war sehr gut mandryka
5577 ½ bd VIII   62711/american decca DE 7025/brunswick 85025
5578bd VIII
strauss arabella: so wie sie sind; aber der richtige
5579bd VIII   62712/american decca DE 7024/brunswick 85026
5580 ½ bd VIII

0692/1933/grammophon sessions/**richard strauss**/enrico mainardi, cello
strauss don quixote
724be I   27320/95485/35007/brunswick 90319/decca LY 6087
725be I
726be I   27321/95486/35008/brunswick 90320/decca LY 6088
727 ½ be I
728be I   27322/95487/35009/brunswick 90321/decca LY 6089
729 ½ be I
730be I   27323/95488/35010/brunswick 90322/decca LY 6090
731be I
732 ½ be I   27324/95489/35011/brunswick 90323/decca LY 6091
cd issues: deutsche grammophon 429 9252 and dutton CDBP 9746

0693/1933/columbia session/**clemens schmalstich**/erna berger, soprano; else ruzicz contralto; emma zador, contralto; charles kullmann, tenor; walther beck, tenor; walter grossmann, bass-baritone; eugen fuchs, bass
smetana the bartered bride: think it over marie!; everyone praises his own girl
WRX 18   DWX 5037/LX 316/american columbia 9096M
    19

0694/1933/electrola session/**fritz zaun**/elisabeth friedrich, soprano; margarete klose, contralto; walther ludwig, tenor; willi domgraf-fassbaender, baritone; eugen fuchs, ba
lortzing der wildschütz: kann es im erdenleben; mozart don giovanni: taci ingiusto core
2D 1783   EH 850
   1784
mozart don giovanni: deh vieni alla finestra; le nozze d figaro: si vuol ballare
2D 1785   EG 2906
   1786

0695/1933/electrola session/**fritz zaun**/elisabeth friedrich, soprano; walther ludwig, tenor; gerhard hüsch, baritone; wilhelm strienz, bass
kreutzer das nachtlager von granada: schon die abendglocken klangen; trenne nicht das band der liebe
2D 1959   EH 864
   1958
cd issue of both items: preiser 89989

0696/6 january 1933/odeon session/**frieder weissmann**/joseph schmidt, tenor
puccini la fanciulla del west: or son sei mesi; ch'ella mi creda libero
133723 O-25987/parlophone R 2292
133745
recordings completed on 17 february 1933

0697/3 february 1933/telefunken session/**franz alfred schmidt**
rudolf bockelmann, bass-baritone
wagner das rheingold: abendlich strahlt der sonne auge
018938 SK 1342/ultraphon G 22603
cd issue: teldec 8573 830222

0698/april 1933/odeon session/**max von schillings**
schillings der pfeifertag, act three prelude
XXB 8552 O-6830/parlophone P 67502
    8553
schillings moloch: das erntefest
BE 10292 O-25010/parlophone B 49793
    10293
cd issue of both items: preiser 90294

0699/april 1933/odeon session/**hans knappertsbusch**
deutsche tänze k509; deutsche tänze k600
BE 10306 O-11862/parlophone R 1561/american decca 20057
    10307
    10328 O-11863/parlophone R 1562/american decca 20058
    10329
cd issues of both items: preiser 90183, archiphon ARC 110-111 and wing WCD 10
liszt mazeppa
BE 10322 O-11897/parlophone R 1579/american decca 20082
    10323
    10324 O-11898/parlophone R 1580/american decca 20083
    10325
    10326 O-11899/parlophone R 1581/american decca 20084
    10327
cd issues: preiser 90183, archiphon ARC 110-111 and documents 205 229

0700/september 1933/grammophon session/**leo blech**/adele kern, soprano
rossini il barbiere di siviglia: uns voce poco fa
5449 ½ bd VIII 10303/decca PO 5119
5450 ½ bd VIII

0701/22 september 1933/electrola session/**fritz zaun**
margarethe teschemacher, soprano; marcel wittrisch, tenor
wagner lohengrin: das süsse lied verhallt
2D 1729 EH 842
cd issues: preiser 89049 and hamburger archiv für gesangskunst HAG 1033
wagner lohengrin: einsam in trüben tagen
2D 1731 EH 840
cd issue: hamburger archiv für gesangskust HAG 1033

0702/october 1933/electrola session/**fritz zaun**
bruckner symphony no "0" in d minor, scherzo and trio
2D 1787 EH 844/hmv C 2659/victor 11726
cd issue: emi 566 2062

0703/october-december 1933/grammophon sessions/**leo blech**/staatsopernchor erna berger, soprano; else ruziczak, mezzo-soprano; max hirzel, tenor; carl jöken, tenor; artur cavara, tenor; karl august neumann, bass-baritone; hans batteux, baritone; felix fleischer-janczak, bass; eduard kandl, bass
verdi rigoletto: non v'e piu alcuno che qui rispondami; un ballo in maschera: e scherzo ed e follia!
686 ½ be VIII 35004/decca CA 8168
687 ½ be VIII
wagner die meistersinger von nürnberg: selig wie die sonne
688 ½ be VIII 35006/brunswick 90273
cd issue of all items: preiser 89989

0704/1933-1934/grammophon sessions/**leo blech**/august seider, tenor
flotow martha: horch die lerche singt im hain; adam der postillon von lonjumeau: freunde vernehmet die geschichte!
5720bd VIII 10197
5724bd VIII
mascagni cavalleria rusticana: mamma quel vino!; thomas mignon: lebwohl mignon!
5721bd VIII 10254
5723bd VIII
verdi rigoletto: la donna e mobile; il trovatore: di quella pira
5722bd VIII 10215/decca PO 5095
5725bd VIII

0705/1934/grammophon session/**leo blech**/börner, soprano
puccini la boheme: si mi chiamano mimi; tosca: vissi d'arte
468 ½ gs VIII 15078
469 ½ gs VIII
gounod faust: ah je ris!; bizet carmen: je dis que rien ne m'epouvante
5729 ½ gr VIII 10295
5730 ½ gr VIII

0706/1934/grammophon session/**leo blech**/heinrich schlusnus, baritone
gumbert an des rheines grünen ufern
470 ½ gs VIII 35016
tchaikovsky evgeny onegin: written words
471gs VIII 35016/67107
cd issues: preiser 89006 and 89121

0707/1934/grammophon session/**leo blech**/tiana lemnitz, soprano
wagner tannhäuser: dich teure halle; allmächtige jungfrau
472gs VIII					15079/67058/decca CA 8243
473gs VIII
weber der freischütz: leise leise; und ob die wolke
476gs VIII					15081/decca CA 8233/LY 6108
477 ½ gs VIII
cd issue of all items: preiser 89025

0708/1934/grammophon sessions/**leo blech**/julius patzak, tenor
mozart don giovanni: dalla sua pace; die entführung aus dem serail: konstanze dich wiederzuseh'n!
474gs VIII					15080
475 ½ gs VIII
cd issue of both items: preiser 89233
millöcker der betteltudent: ich knüpfe manche zarte band; suppe boccaccio: hab' ich nur deine liebe
5675 ½ gr					10284
6144 ½ gd
cd issue of both items: pearl GEMMCD 9383
millöcker gasparone: o dass ich doch der räuber wär'; johann strauss waldmeister: die ganze nacht durchschwärmt
5814 ½ gr					10324
5815 ½ gr VIII
cd issue of both items: preiser 89174

0709/1934/grammophon sessions/**leo blech**/erna berger, soprano
auber fra diavolo: welches glück ich atme freier; bizet les pecheurs de perles: me voila seule!
5693 ½ gr VIII				10285/26500
5694gr VIII
grieg peer gynt: solveig's song
5696gr VIII					10429/11518/26502/62387
puccini madama butterfly: un bel di
5697gr VIII					10267/11518
flotow martha: letzte rose; donizetti la fille du regiment: tirolienne
5856gr						10329/26501/62386
5857gr VIII

0710/1934/grammophon session/**alois melichar**/erna berger, soprano
puccini la boheme: quando m'en vo
6137 ½ gd VIII				10267
cd issue: preiser 89035

0711/ 1934/grammophon session/**walter schütze**
adele kern, soprano; franz völker, tenor
lehar giuditta: schaut der mond abends spät; schön wie die blaue sommernacht
5505 ½ br   25369/90207
5506br
lehar guditta: du bist meine sonne; freunde das leben ist lebenswert!
5507br VIII   25368
5508br VIII
cd issue of all items: preiser 89221

0712/ 1934/grammophon session/**walter schütze**/erna berger, soprano; elly völkel, soprano; hilde scheppan, soprano; günther treptow, tenor; fritz wolf, baritone
johann strauss die fledermaus: mein herr marquis; spiel' ich die unschuld vom lande
5883bd   10169
5884bd
cd issue of both items: preiser 89035
weber der freischütz, potpourri
                                       decca LY 6126

0713/ 1934/electrola session/**fritz zaun**
walther ludwig, tenor; gerhard hüsch, baritone
puccini madama butterfly: amore o grillo; addio fiorito asil
OD 1961   EG 3035
   1960
cd issue of both items: preiser 89088

0714/ january 1934/grammophon session/**leo blech**/erna berger, soprano; adele kern, soprano; else ruziczka, mezzo-soprano; max hirzel, tenor; carl jöken, tenor; karl august neumann, baritone; eduard kandl, bass
mozart die zauberflöte: hm! hm! hm!
689 ½ be VIII   35003/brunswick 90273/decca CA 8169
mozart die entführung aus dem serail: nie werd' ich deine huld verkennen
690 ½ be VIII   35003/decca CA 8169
cd issue of both items: preiser 89989

0715/ january 1934/electrola session/**ludwig roth**/miliza korjus, soprano
johann strauss fruhlingsstimmen
2D 1910   EH 860/hmv C 2664/C 3122/victor 12829

0716/ february 1934/electrola session/**fritz zaun**
strauss arabella, orchestral selection
OD 1952   B 8175
   1953
bruckner symphony no 1: scherzo and trio; symphony no 2: scherzo and trio
2D 1954   EH 865/hmv C 2685
   1955
cd issue of bruckner items: emi 566 2062

0717/ june 1934/electrola session/**edmund nick**/miliza korjus, soprano
rossini il barbiere di siviglia: una voce poco fa
2D 2113   EH 867/hmv C 2688

0718/26 june 1934/grammophon session/**alois melichar**
erna berger, soprano; julius patzak, tenor
zeller der vogelhändler, potpourri
6139 ¾ gd VIII   10248
6140 ½ gd VIII
cd issue: preiser 89174
lieder der liebe, potpourri
6141 ½ gd VIII   10250
6142 ½ gd VIII

0719/september 1934/electrola session/**fritz schönbaumsfeld**/staatsopernchor
hedwig jungkurth, soprano; walther ludwig, tenor
zeller der vogelhändler: schenkt man sich rosen im tirol; millöcker
der bettelstudent: ich setz' den fall
2RA 64   EH 893
    65

0720/20 october 1934/grammophon session/**alois melichar**/franz völker, tenor
millöcker der bettelstudent: ich knüpfe manche zarte band; ich hab kein geld
5674 ½ gr VIII   10269
5675 ½ gr VIII
cd issue of both items: preiser 89221
friml rose marie: über die prärie; rimsky-korsakov sadko: hindulied
5676 ½ gr VIII   10270
5677 ½ ge VIII

0721/november 1934/electrola session/**fritz schönbaumsfeld**/staatsopernchor/
5 parodisters/anni frind, soprano; walther ludwig, tenor
kalman die czardasfürstin, selection
2RA 159   EH 902
    160

0722/26 november 1934/electrola session/**leo blech**/margarethe teschemacher, soprano; marcel wittrisch, tenor; gerhard hüsch, baritone
verdi aida: ah no fuggiamo!....ma dimmi!
2RA 231   DB 4431
    232

0723/december 1934/electrola session/**fritz schönbaumsfeld**
miliza korjus, soprano
weber aufforderung zum tanz, vocal version; chopin maiden's wish
2RA 63   EH 889/hmv C 2721
    115
meyerbeer dinorah: ombre leggiera; offenbach les contes d'hoffmann:
les oiseaux dans la charmlle
2RA 263   EH 905/hmv C 2770
    264

0724 / 20 and 22 december 1934/odeon sessions/**robert heger**
tchaikovsky casse noisette suite
XXB 8566 O-6961/parlophone E 11269/am.decca 25182
    8567
    8568 O-6962/parlophone E 11270/am.decca 25183
    8569
    8570 O-6963/parlophone E 11271/am.decca 25184
    8571
lortzing zar und zimmermann: holzschuhtanz; schubert marche militaire
XXB 8572 O-6967/parlophone E 11283
    8573
johann strauss kaiserwalzer
XXB 8574 O-6965/parlophone E 11278/am.decca 25764
    8575

0725 / 1934-1935/telefunken session/**hans schmidt-isserstedt**
erna sack, soprano
weber der freischütz: einst träumte meiner seligen base
20464 A 1771/capitol 77-80035
20465

0726 / 1935/grammophon session/**leo blech**/heinrich schlusnus, baritone
leoncavallo i pagliacci: si puo signore!; verdi un ballo in maschera: eri tu
514 ½ gs 35022
517gs
wagner tannhäuser: blick' ich umher; wie todesahnung
515gs 35023
516 ½ gs
marschner hans heiling: an jenem tag
521gs 35027
cd issue of all arias: preiser 89006 and 89212

0727 / 1935/grammophon session/**alois melichar**/helge rosvaenge, tenor
puccini turandot: non piangere liu; nessun dorma
2827 ½ gn 10447
2828gn
cd issue of both arias: preiser 89209

0728/1935/grammophon session/**leo blech**/erna berger, soprano
verdi la traviata: addio del passato
2779gn 10444
cd issue: preiser 89035
verdi rigoletto: caro nome
5854 ½ gr 10444
cd issue: preiser 89092

0729/1935/grammophon session/**eduard künneke**/tiana lemnitz, soprano; helge rosvaenge, tenor
künneke die grosse sünderin: immerzu singt dein herz meinem herzen zu; das lied vom leben des schrenk
490 ½ gs 15099
491 ¾ gs
cd issue of both items: preiser 89209

0730/january 1935/electrola session/**fritz schönbaumsfeld**/miliza korjus, soprano
arditi parla-walzer
2RA 338 EH 908/hmv C 2789
arditi bacio-walzer
2RA 339 EH 908/hmv C 2789/C 3152

0731/11 january 1935/electrola session/**hans udo müller**/margarethe teschemacher, soprano; walther ludwig, tenor
verdi la forza del destino: ah per sempre; un ballo in maschera: non sai che se l'anima mia
2RA 304 EH 909
    305
cd issue of ballo duet: hamburger archiv für gesangskunst HAG 4054

0732/4 march 1935/grammophon session/**alois melichar**/franz völker, tenor
de curtis vergissmeinnicht
6136 ½ gr 10411/decca F 5930
cd issue: franz-völker-kreis RR 501

0733/april 1935/electrola session/**bruno seidler-winkler**
favres solistenvereinigung
margherita perras, soprano
verdi 4 pezzi: ave maria; messa da requiem: requiem aeternam
2RA 544 EH 915/hmv C 2794
    545

0734/9 april 1935/odeon session/**robert heger**/maria cebotari, soprano
verdi rigoletto: tutte le feste; caro nome
BE 10958 O-25427
    10959
mozart die entführung aus dem serail: martern aller arten
BE 10960 O-25399/parlophone RO 20285
    10961
cd issue of all items: preiser 89161

0735/10 april 1935/reichsrundfunk recording made at the wedding ceremony of hermann goering and emmy sondermann/**paul graener**/viorica ursuleac, soprano; franz völker, tenor
graener hochzeitsspruch for soprano, tenor and orchestra
                         unpublshed radio broadcast

0736/may 1935/electrola sessions/**bruno seidler-winkler**/miliza korjus, soprano
dell' aqua vilanelle; johann strauss 1001 nacht, waltz in vocal arrangement
2RA 615   EH 922/hmv C 2784
      616
denzi funiculi funicula; rossini la danza
2RA 756   EH 937/hmv C 2813
      757
chopin two nocturnes in vocal arrangement
2RA 932   EH 948/hmv C 2832
      933

0737/may 1935/electrola session/**leo blech**/marcel wittrisch, tenor; wilhelm strienz, bass
mascagni cavalleria rusticana: brindisi; verdi ernani: a te scegli…seguimi!
2RA 639   DB 4434
      640

0738/may 1935/electrola session/**bruno seidler-winkler**/helge rosvaenge, tenor
künneke die grosse sünderin: das lied vom indischen märchen
2RA 927   EH 947
künneke die grosse sünderin: historchen! geschichten!
2RA 929   EG 3519
cd issue of both items: preiser 89209

0739/may 1935/grammophon session/**eduard künneke**/tiana lemnitz, soprano; helge rosvaenge, tenor
künneke die grosse sünderin: immerzu singt dein herz meinem herzen zu; das lied vom leben des schrenk
490 ½ gs   15099
491 ½ gs
cd issue of both items: preiser 89209

0740/26-27 august 1935/grammophon sessions/**wolfgang martin** julius patzak, tenor
verdi rigoletto: parmi veder; la donna e mobile
6096 ½ gr   30008
6097gr
thomas mignon: lebwohl mignon!
6098 ½ gr   30014
massenet werther: un autre est son epoux
6094gs VIII   35083
cd issue of all arias: preiser 89233
lehar eva: wär' es nichts als ein traum vom glück; der graf von luxemburg: bist du's lachendes glück?
6101gr   10385
6102 ½ gr
cd issue of both arias: preiser 89174

0741/28 august 1935/grammophon session/**alois melichar**/julius patzak, tenor
di capua: o meine sonne; maria maria
6103 ½ gr 10423
6104 ½ gr
cd issue of maria maria: deutsche grammophon 459 0072

0742/4 september 1935/grammophon session/**alois melichar**/franz völker, tenor
de curtis serenata veneziana
6137 ½ gr 10411/decca F 5930
stolz ob blond oder braun; schenk mir dein herz heut' nacht
6138 ½ gr VIII 10412/decca F 5931
6139gr

0743/25 october 1935/grammophon session/**wolfgang martin**
helge rosvaenge, tenor
flotow martha: ach so fromm; letzte rose
6267 ¾ gr 10434/decca DE 7051
6270 ½ gr
thomas mignon: froh und frei will ich eilen
6268 ½ gr 10422
cd issue of all items: preiser 89209

0744/6 november 1935/electrola session/**bruno seidler-winkler**/staatsopernchor
margherita perras, soprano; walther ludwig, tenor; gerhard hüsch, baritone
verdi la traviata, selection
2RA 870 EH 930
    871

0745/11 november 1935/grammophon session/**franz alfred schmidt**
helge rosvaenge, tenor
verdi la forza del destino: tu che in seno agli angeli; un ballo in maschera:
ma se m'e forza perdeti
324 ½ go 67211
325 ½ go
cd issue of both arias: preiser 89209

0746/12 december 1935/odeon session/**robert heger**/maria cebotari, soprano;
herbert ernst groh, tenor
puccini madama butterfly: bimba degli occhi
BE 11193 O-25627
    11194
johann strauss frühlingsstimmen, vocal version
BE 11195 O-25647
    11196

0747/1936/grammophon session/**clemens krauss**/viorica ursuleac, soprano
puccini tosca: vissi d'arte; turandot: in questa reggia
592gs 35033/decca CA 8227
593 ½ gs
strauss cäcilie; frühlingsfeier
2924 ½ gn VIII 30017/decca DE 7063
2925 ½ gn VIII
cd issue of all items: preiser 89953

0748/1936/grammophon session/**clemens krauss**/viorica ursuleac, soprano; erna berger, soprano; tiana lemnitz, soprano
strauss der rosenkavalier: hab mir's gelobt; ist ein traum kann nicht wirklich sein
594 ½ gs VIII   67075/decca CA 8238
606 ½ gs
cd issues: preiser 89035 and 89953

0749/1936/grammophon session/**clemens krauss**/viorica ursuleac, soprano; erna berger, soprano; heinrich schlusnus, baritone; alexander sved, bass-baritone
verdi il trovatore: mira d'acerbe lagrime
600 ½ gs VIII   67173
cd issue: preiser 89953
mozart don giovanni: la ci darem la mano
2933gn   62755
mozart le nozze di figaro: che soave zeffiretti
6400gr   62755
cd issue of mozart items: preiser 89035

0750/1936/grammophon session/**wolfgang martin**/erna berger, soprano; gertrud rünger, contralto; julius patzak, tenor
verdi il trovatore: mal reggendo
404go VIII   67106/decca CA 8264
cd issue: pearl GEMMCD 9383
verdi rigoletto: quest o quella; la traviata: parigi o cara
406go   67535
407go
cd issue of both arias: 89092
nicolai die lustigen weiber von windsor: horch die lerche singt im hain
2969gn   30014
cd issue: preiser 89075

0751/1936/electrola session/**bruno seidler-winkler**/miliza korjus, soprano
delibes lakme: ou va la jeune hindoue?; blanche dourga
2RA 1012   EH 961/hmv C 2839/victor 12136
    1011

0752/1936/electrola session/**bruno seidler-wikler**/walther ludwig, tenor
mozart die entführung aus dem serail: o wie ängstlich!; cosi fan tutte:
un aura amorosa
2RA 1013   EH 957
    1014
cd issue of cosi aria only: preiser 89088

0753/march 1936/electrola session/**bruno seidler-winkler**/miliza korjus, soprano; margherita perras, soprano; helge rosvaenge, tenor
verdi rigoletto: e il sol dell' anima; un ballo in maschera: di tu se fedele
2RA 1104   DB 4445/victor 17560
    1105
verdi la traviata: un di felice
2RA 1220   DB 4458
cd issue of all items: preiser 89209

0754/march 1936/electrola session/**bruno seidler-winkler**/adelheid armhold, soprano; anni frind, soprano; walther ludwig, tenor; wilhelm strienz, bass
weber der freischütz, selection
2RA 1115   EH 963
    1116

0755/march 1936/electrola session/**bruno seidler-winkler**/hedwig jungkurth, soprano; walther ludwig, tenor
lehar der rastelbinder: wenn zwei sich lieben; millöcker gasparone: dunkelrote rosen
ORA 1152   EG 3633
    1153
lehar paganini: niemand liebt dich so wie ich; der zarewitsch: hab' nur dich allein
ORA 1154   EG 3641
    1155

0756/28 april 1936/electrola session/**bruno seidler-winkler**/margarethe teschemacher, soprano; marcel wittrisch, tenor
gounod faust: il se fait tard; mascagni cavalleria rusticana: tu qui santuzza?
2RA 1251   DB 4459
    1252
cd issue of gounod item: hamburger archiv für gesangskunst

0757/20 may 1936/electrola session/**bruno seidler-winkler**/ilonka rosvaenge, soprano; helge rosvaenge, tenor
auber fra diavolo: pour toujours disait-elle; adam der postillon von lonjumeau: freunde vernehmet die geschichte!
ORA 1297   DA 4414
    1298
cd issue of both items: preiser 89209
emborg agnes mein reizender schmetterling; vollmond am see
ORA 1314   DA 4415
    1315
friis mein herz hat dich so viel zu fragen; aus meiner jugend
ORA 1316   EG 3693
    1317
cd issue of emborg and friis items: preiser 89225

0758/22 may 1936/odeon session/**robert heger**
wolf-ferrari il segreto di susanna overture; reznicek donna diana overture
XXB 8590   O-7692/parlophone E 11305/am.decca 25772
    8591

0759/june 1936/electrola session/**bruno seidler-winkler**/helge rosvaenge, tenor
weber oberon: vater hör mein flehen!
ORA 1458   DA 4417
weber oberon: von jugend auf im kampfgefilde
ORA 1459   DA 4416
    1460
weber der freischütz: länger trag' ich nicht die qualen
ORA 1562   DA 4418
    1563
cd issue of all arias: preiser 89209

0760/4 june 1936/odeon session/**robert heger**/maria cebotari, soprano
verdi la traviata: e strano!.....sempre libera!
BE 11376   O-25834/parlophone RO 20328
    11377
cd issue: preiser 89161

0760a/11 june 1936/grammophon session/**clemens krauss**
heinrich schlusnus, baritone
wagner tannhäuser: als du in kühnem sange
2394gn   30015
2385gn
cd issue: preiser 89212

0761/23-24 june 1936/grammophon sessions/**wolfgang martin**/erna berger, soprano
gertrud rünger, contralto; julius patzak, tenor
verdi il trovatore: mal reggendo; ai nostri monti
404go VIII   67106/decca CA 8264
405go VIII
cd issues of both duets: preiser 89233 and pearl GEMM 0156
verdi rigoletto: e il sol dell' anima; la traviata: parigi o cara
406go VIII   67535
407go VIII
cd issues of both duets: preiser 89233 and decca 467 9172

0762/24 june 1936/grammophon session/**alois melichar**/julius patzak, tenor
melichar wann kommt die stunde; de curtis nur du maria
2967gn VIII   30013
2968gn VIII
nicolai die lustigen weiber von windsor: horch die lerche singt im hain
2969gn VIII   30014
cd issues of nicolai item: preiser 89233 and pearl GEMM 0156 and GEMMCD 9383

0763/september 1936/electrola sessions/**bruno seidler-winkler**/anni frind, soprano;
margarete klose, contralto; marcel wittrisch, tenor; wilhelm strienz, bass
millöcker der bettelstudent, potpourri
2RA 1644   EH 1006
    1645
cd issue: bbc records CD 716
verdi don carlo: o don fatale; un ballo in maschera: re dell' abisso
2RA 1661   DB 4461
    1662
cd issue of both arias: preiser 89082

0764/september 1936/electrola session/**bruno seidler-winkler** /walther ludwig, tenor
mozart die zauberflöte: wie stark ist nicht dein zauberton; nicolai die
lustigen weiber von windsor: horch die lerche singt im hain
2RA 1700   EH 1020
    1702
cd issue of both arias: preiser 89088

0765/29 september 1936/columbia session/**hans rosbaud**/walter gieseking, piano
mozart piano concerto no 9 in e flat k271
CBX 30	LX 559/american columbia 68895
31	
32	LX 560/american columbia 68896
33	
34	LX 561/american columbia 68897
35	
36	LX 562/american columbia 68898
37	

also issued by columbia on automatic coupling as LX 8291-8294

0766/2 october 1936/odeon session/**hermann abendroth**
sibelius finlandia
XXNSK 14   O-7896/parlophone E 11418
       15
cd issue: pristine PASC 258

0767/1937/telefunken session/**hansgeorg otto**
johann strauss der zigeunerbaron: einzugsmarsch
021957   A 2193
cd issue: teldec 3984 284112

0768/1937/telefunken session/**hans schmidt-isserstedt**/hilde konetzni, soprano; marie-luise schilp, contralto
puccini madama butterfly: scuoti quella fronda
022034   E 2320
022035
puccini madama butterfly: ancora un passo; tosca: vissi d'arte
022036   E 2246
022039
beethoven fidelio: abscheulicher wo eilst du hin?
022037   E 2290
022038
cd issue of all items: preiser 90078

0769/1937/telefunken session/**hans schindler**/staatsopernchor
karl schmitt-walter, baritone; willy stech, piano
unter italienischer sonne, potpourri
022460   E 2343
022461
der heimat schönste lieder, potpourri
022462   E 2344
022463

0770/1937/grammophon session/**johannes schüler**/erna berger, soprano
weber non paventar mia vita, concert aria
647gs   57083/decca LY 6181
648 ½ gs
cd issues: preiser 89035 and sanctus SCSH 006

0771/1937/grammophon session/**johannes schüler**/tiana lemnitz, soprano
wagner lohengrin: einsam in trüben tagen; euch lüften die mein klagen
696gs VIII   35081/decca LY 6144
697 ½ gs VIII
cd issue of both items: preiser 89025

0772/1937/grammophon session/**johannes schüler**/heinrich schlusnus, baritone
lortzing zar und zimmermann: sonst spielt' ich
699 ½ gs   67151
verdi il trovatore: il balen del suo sorriso; la traviata: di provenza al mar
700 ½ gs   67362
701gs
cd issues of all items: preiser 89006 and 89212

0773/1937/reichsrundfunk recording/**artur rother**/margarete klose, contralto
saint-saens samson et dalila: mon coeur s'ouvre a ta voix
issued only on acanta lp 22.21484

0774/5 january 1937/electrola session/**hans udo müller**/gerhard hüsch, baritone
besenbinderlied
2RA 1704   EH 1024
cd issue: preiser 89071

0775/12 january 1937/electrola session/**erich orthmann**/margarethe teschemacher, soprano; marcel wittrisch, tenor
meyerbeer les huguenots: oh ciel ou courez-vous?
2D 746   EH 734/hmv DB 21511
   747
cd issues: preiser 89024 and pearl GEMMCD 9256

0776/25 january 1937/grammophon session/**franz alfred schmidt**
tiana lemnitz, soprano
verdi aida: ritorna vincitor
6946 ½ gd I   30018
6947gd I
cd issue: preiser 89025

0777/28 january 1937/electrola session/**bruno seidler-winkler**
margarete teschemacher, soprano
smetana the bartered bride: the dream of love; mascagni cavalleria rusticana: voi lo sapete
2RA 1782   EH 1032
   1783
cd issue of smetana item: hamburger archiv für gesangskunst HAG 1033
weber oberon: ozean du ungeheuer
2RA 1784   DB 5568
   1785
cd issue: preiser 89971

0778/8 february 1937/electrola session/**bruno seidler-winkler**
helge rosvaenge, tenor
cornelius der barbier von bagdad: o holdes bild in engelsschöne; verdi la traviata:
de miei bollenti spriti
2RA 1812 DB 4495
1814
cd issues: preiser 89209 and nimbus NI 7848
nimbus issue incorrectly dated 1935
mozart die enrführung aus dem serail: hier soll ich dich denn sehen?
2RA 1813 DB 4417
cd issues: preiser 89209 and pearl GEMMCD 9129

0779/march 1937/electrola session/**bruno seidler-winkler**/max lorenz, tenor
wagner siegfried: nothung neidliches schwert!; schmiede mein hammer!
2RA 1860 DB 4470
1861
cd issues: preiser 89232 and 90213

0780/march 1937/electrola sessions/**bruno seidler-winkler**/margherita perras, soprano; walther ludwig, tenor; wilhelm strienz, bass
smetana the bartered bride: each man praises his own
2RA 1952 EH 1036
1953
cd issue: preiser 89089
puccini tosca: ah quegli occhi!
2RA 1976 DB 4475
cd issue: preiser 89209
bizet carmen: parle-moi de ma mere
2RA 1991 DB 4498
1992
cd issue: preiser 89088

0781/8-9 april 1937/telefunken sessions/**artur rother**/karl schmitt-walter, baritone
verdi la traviata: di provenza al mar; rigoletto: cortigiani!
021973 E 2195
921974
mozart don giovanni: finch' han del vino; deh vieni alla finestra
021975 A 2223
021978
handel serse: ombra mai fu; giordani caro mio ben
021976 E 2234
021977

0782/28 april 1937/columbia sessions/**hans rosbaud**/walter gieseking, piano
grieg piano concerto in a minor
CRX 55 LWX 210/LX 647/american columbia 69087
56
57 LWX 211/LX 648/american columbia 69088
58
59 LWX 212/LX 649/american columbia 69089
60
61 LWX 213/LX 650/american columbia 69090
CRX 55 was remade on 18 october 1937 and 11 november 1937
also published by columbia in automatic coupling as LX 8339-8342

28 april 1937 / columbia sessions / hans rosbaud / walter gieseking / concluded
beethoven piano concerto no 1 in c op 15
CRX 62   LWX 229/LX 631/american columbia 69049
     63
     64   LWX 230/LX 632/american columbia 69050
     65
     66   LWX 231/LX 633/american columbia 69051
     67
     68   LWX 232/LX 634/american columbia 69052
     69
also published by columbia in automatic coupling as LX 8332-8335
cd issue of beethoven: classical collector FDC 2008

0783/19 june 1937/odeon session/**hermann abendroth**
liszt hungarian rhapsody no 1
XXB 8617   O-7734/parlophone E 11334
       8618
dohnanyi the veil of pierette: wedding waltz
BE 11723   O-4759
     11724
cd issue of both items: pristine PASC 258

0784/28 june 1937/grammophon session/**johannes schüler**/julius patzak, tenor
massenet werther: pourquoi me reveiller?
7191 ½ gr VIII   30031
cd issues: preiser 89075 and 89233 and pearl GEMMCD 9383
puccini tosca: e lucevan le stelle; recondita armonia
7192 ½ gr VIII   30035
7193 ½ gr VIII
cd issue of both arias: preiser 89233

0785/7 october 1937/grammophon session/**johannes schüler**/franz völker, tenor
verdi otello: tu indietro?
7320 ½ gr IX   62776
cd issue: preiser 89060

0786/18 october 1937/*see 28 april 1937*

0787/25 october 1937/grammophon session/**johannes schüler**/franz völker, tenor
wagner die walküre: wintersturme; ein schwert verhiess mir der vater
727 ½ gs   67142/95493
728 ½ gs
cd issue of both items: preiser 89070
verdi la forza del destino: o tu che in seno agli angeli
730gs I   unpublished recording
leoncavallo i pagliacci: no pagliaccio non son
731 ½ gs   67159/95494
cd issue: preiser 89070

0788/25 october 1937/grammophon session/**franz marszalek**/franz völker, tenor
wenn die liebe singt, operetta potpourri
732gs I 35079/27346
733 ½ gs

0789/october 1937/electrola session/**bruno seidler-winkler**
helge rosvaenge, tenor; gerhard hüsch, baritone
verdi la forza del destino: solenne in quest' ora; puccini la boheme: o mimi tu piu non tormi
2RA 2364 DB 4499
2366
cd issues of both items: preiser 89211 and pearl GEMMCD 9394

0790/november 1937/electrola sessions/**bruno seidler-winkler**
helge rosvaenge, tenor
kattnigg der prinz von thule: juble mein herz!; wille küss die hand schöne frau!
ORA 2460 EG 6200
2461
kattnigg balkanliebe: heimat mit der seele grüss ich dich; leise erklingen
ORA 2462 EG 6165
2463
cd issue of all items: preiser 89225

0791/november 1937/electrola sessio/**bruno seidler-winkler**/staatsopernchor
margherita perras, soprano; margarete klose, contralto
verdi aida: fu la sorte; puccini madama butterfly: scuoti della fronde
2RA 2464 DB 4500
2467
2465 DB 4501
2468
verdi il trovatore: stride la vampa; condotta ell' era in ceppe
2RA 2466 DB 4502
2469
cd issue of all items: preiser 89082

0792/9 november 1937/odeon session in konzertsaal des europahauses/
robert heger
tchaikovsky capriccio italien
XXB 8631 O-7769/parlophone E 11345
8632
8633 O-7770/parlophone E 11346
8634

0793/11 november 1937/*see 28 april 1937*

0794/1937-1938/telefunken sessions/**hans schmidt-isserstedt**/erna sack, soprano
bach ave maria; schubert ave maria
22030 A 2219
22031
vlies schlafe mein prinzchen; brahms wiegenlied
22032 A 2257
22033

0795/1938/grammophon session/**hermann weigert**/franz völker, tenor
verdi aida: celeste aida
754go I   67205

0796/8 february 1938/grammophon session/**franz alfred schmidt**/franz völker, tenor
mozart die zauberflöte: dies bildnis; wie stark ist nicht dein zauberton
788 ½ gr I   67161
789 ½ gr I
cd issue: preiser 89070

0797/1938/grammophon session/**gerhard steeger**/heinrich schlusnus, baritone
verdi rigoletto: cortigiani!
853gs   67253
cd issues: preiser 89006 and 89212

0798/1938/grammophon session/**gerhard steeger**/franz völker, tenor
weber der freischütz: nein länger trag' ich nicht die qualen
909gs VIII   67260
910gs VIII
cd issue: preiser 89070

0799/8 march 1938/electrola session in the philharmonie/**bruno seidler winkler**
erna berger, soprano
mozart die zauberflöte: o zittre nicht mein lieber sohn!
2RA 2549   DB 4645/DB 3468/DB 8478
recorded for insertion in complete hmv version of the opera conducted by beecham with berliner philharmonisches orchester

0800/march 1938/electrola session/**bruno seidler-winkler**/tiana lemnitz, soprano
mozart le nozze di figaro: porgi amor; dove sono
2RA 2697   DB 3462
    2698
cd issues of both arias: preiser 80902 and zyx music PD 50182

0801/17 march 1938/electrola session/**bruno seidler-winkler**/margarete teschemacher
soprano; helge rosvaenge, tenor; wilhelm strienz, bass
gounod faust: seigneur daignez permettre
2RA 2747   DB 4523
    2748
cd issue: pearl GEMMCD 9155
gounod faust: alerte! alerte!
2RA 2749   DB 4507
    2750
cd issues: preiser 89211 and hamburger archiv für gesangskunst HAG 1034

0802/april 1938/electrola session/**bruno seidler-winkler**/helge rosvaenge, tenor
bizet carmen: la fleur que tu m'avais jetee
2RA 2851   DB 4424
verdi il trovatore: ah si ben mio; di quella pira
2RA 2852   DB 4524
    2853
cd issues of all arias: preiser 89211 and 90328, pearl GEMMCD 9394 and nimbus NI 7899

0803/6 april 1938/odeon session/**robert heger**/staatsopernchor
wagner der fliegende holländer: sailors' chorus; tannhäuser: pilgrims' chorus
XXB 8643　　　　　　　　　　O-7779/parlophone E 11361
　　　8644
strauss der rosenkavalier, waltz sequence
XXB 8645　　　　　　　　　　O-7782/parlophone E 11364
　　　8646

0804/27 april 1938/odeon session/**alois melichar**
johann strauss an der schönen blauen donau
XXB 8647　　　　　　　　　　O-7785/parlophone E 11370
　　　8648

0805/4 may 1938/electrola session/**bruno seidler-winkler**/margarete teschemacher, soprano; marta fuchs, soprano; marcel wittrisch, tenor
verdi aida: o patria mia; ritorna vincitor
2RA 2893　　　　　　　　　　DB 4554
　　　2894
cd issue of both arias: preiser 90068
smetana the bartered bride: as my mother blessed me; what an obstinate girl!
2RA 2895　　　　　　　　　　DB 4538
　　　2896
cd issue of both duets: pearl GEMMCD 9256
wagner die walküre: war es so schmählich?
2RA 2898　　　　　　　　　　DB 4555
　　　2899

0806/may 1938/electrola session/**bruno seidler-winkler**
margarete klose, contralto
gluck orfeo ed euridice: objet de mon amour; che faro senza euridice?
2RA 2957　　　　　　　　　　DB 4531
　　　2956
gluck alceste: divinites du styx!; paride ed elena: o del mio dolce ardor
2RA 2958　　　　　　　　　　DB 4532
　　　2959
cd issue of all arias: preiser 89082

0807/16-18 may 1938/grammophon sessions/**alois melichar**/favres solistenvereinigung/maria riener, soprano; julius patzak, tenor
massenet elegie
7828 ½ gr VIII   unpublished recording
published on cd by the record collector
bach matthaus-passion: ich will bei meinem jesu wachen
7829 ½ gr VIII   62790/decca PO 5134
7830 ½ gr VIII
bach johannes-passion: ach mein sinn
7831gr VIII   62791/decca PO 5135
7832gr VIII
cd issue of all arias: preiser 89233
klänge aus dem unsterblichen wien, potpourri
7835 ½ gr VIII   47217
7836 ½ gr VIII
johann strauss der zigeunerbaron, potpourri
886 ½ gs VIII   15212
887 ½ gs VIII

0808/8 june 1938/electrola session/**joseph keilberth**
johann strauss an der schönen blauen donau
2RA 3033   EH 1204
    3034
cd issue: tahra TAH 358-361

0809/8 june 1938/electrola session/**bruno seidler-winkler**/max lorenz, tenor
wagner die walküre: ein schwert verhiess mir der vater; die meistersinger von nürnberg: am stillen herd
2RA 2987   DB 4547
    2988
wagner tannhäuser: inbrunst im herzen
2RA 2989   DB 4553
    2990
cd issue of all items: preiser 89232

0810/22 june 1938/odeon sessio/**robert heger**
flotow alessandro stradella overture
XXB 8663   O-7880/parlophone E 11408
    8664
gounod faust, ballet music
XXB 8665   O-7843/parlophone E 11378
    8666

0811/24 june 1938/odeon session/**alois melichar**
weber-berlioz aufforderung zum tanz
XXB 8667   O-7844/parlophone E 11379
    8668

0812/july 1938/electrola session/**bruno seidler-winkler**/lea piltti, soprano
johann strauss rosen aus dem süden, vocal version
ORA 3044   EG 6425/hmv B 8966
    3045

0813/9 september 1938/odeon session/**robert heger**/staatsopernchor
anny von stosch, soprano
verdi la forza del destino: madre pietosa vergine
XXB 8669 O-7879
8670
verdi la forza del destino: vergine degli angeli; pace pace mio dio!
XXB 8671 O-7881
8672

0814/15 september 1938/grammophon session/unnamed conductor/
franz völker, tenor
lehar das land des lächelns: dein ist mein ganzes herz; immer nur lächeln
7900gr VIII 62803/48498
7901gr VIII
cd issue: preiser 89221

0815/19-20 september 1938/electrola sessions/**bruno seidler-winkler**
marta fuchs, soprano; margarete klose, contralto; lauritz melchior, tenor;
hans hotter, bass-baritone
wagner die walküre: siegmund sieh' auf mich!
2RA 3256 DB 4606/DB 3726/victor 15513
    3257
    3258 DB 4607/DB 3727/victor 15514
    3259 mm
wagner die walküre: der alte sturm die alte müh'
2RA 3262 DB 4599/DB 3719/victor 15506
    3263
    3264 DB 4600/DB 3720/victor 15507
    3265
    3261 DB 4601/DB 3721/victor 15508
these scenes were recorded in order to complete the performance of act two
commenced by hmv in vienna under bruno walter
cd issue of all scenes: emi 764 2552

0816/november 1938/electrola sessions/**bruno seidler-winkler**
tiana lemnitz, soprano: helge rosvaenge, tenor
verdi otello: piangea cantando; ave maria
2RA 3321 DB 4595
    3322
cd issues of both arias: preiser 89025 and emi 566 7742
willer königsballade: ewig muss ich dein gedenken; euren könig will ich preisen
2RA 3426 DB 4623
    3427
cd issue of both arias: preiser 89211
strauss der rosenkavalier: di rigori armato
ORA 3428 DA 4465
cd issues: preiser 89211 and 90328

0817/9 december 1938/grammophon session/**herbert von karajan**
mozart die zauberflöte overture
825ge 67465/decca LY 6145
826ge
cd issues: deutsche grammophon 423 5312, 457 6892 and 477 6237

0818/1939/grammophon session/**hans pfitzner**
pfitzner das christelflein overture
327bi 66606
328bi
329bi 66607
329bi coupled with a 1927 recording by max von schillings (session no. 0238)

0819/1939/grammophon session/**erwin baltzer**
erna berger, soprano; gino sinimberghi, tenor
donizetti don pasquale: tornami a dir
1084 ½ gs 67536
cd issue: preiser 89092

0820/february 1939/grammophon session/**herbert von karajan**
verdi la forza del destino overture
5gz 67466
6gz
wagner die meistersinger von nürnberg overture
1020 ½ gs 67532
1021 ½ gs
cd issues of both items: deutsche grammophon 423 5262 and 477 6237

0821/march 1939/electrola session/**bruno seidler-winkler**/helge rosvaenge, tenor
massenet manon: en fermant les yeux; gounod faust: salut demeure
2RA 3775 DB 4655
    3776
cd issue of both arias: preiser 89211
cornelius der barbier von bagdad: ach das leid hab' ich getragen
2RA 3777 DA 4465
cd issue: preiser 89211

0822/april 1939/electrola session/**bruno seidler-winkler**
tiana lemnitz, soprano; torsten ralf, tenor
verdi otello: gia nella notte densa
2RA 3840 DB 4668
    3841
cd issues: preiser 89077 and emi 566 7742
wagner lohengrin: das süsse lied verhallt
2RA 3842 DB 4667
    3843
cd issues: preiser 89022, emi 566 7742 and pearl GEMMCD 9926

0823/april-may 1939/grammophon sessions/**herbert von karajan**
wagner die meistersinger von nürnberg, act three prelude
1115 ½ gs 67527
1116 ½ gs
cd issues: deutsche grammophon 423 5262 and 477 6237
cherubini anacreon overture
1117 ½ gs 67514
1119 ½ gs
cd issues: deutsche grammophon 423 5312 and 477 6237

0824/april-june 1939/grammophon sessions/**gerhard steeger**
gino sinimberghi, tenor
puccini tosca: e lucevan le stelle
8499 ½ gr   unpublished recording
donizetti l'elisir d'amore: una furtiva lagrima
1113 ½ gs   67543
cd issue of both arias: deutsche grammophon 459 0052

0825/may 1939/electrola session/**bruno seidler-winkler**
margarete teschemacher, soprano; irma beilke, soprano
mozart le nozze di figaro: che soave zeffiretto; venite inginocchiatevi
2RA 3909   DB 4690
    3910
strauss arabella: aber der richtige; das war sehr gut mandryka
2RA 3911   DB 4675
    3912
verdi don carlo: tu che la vanita
2RA 3913   DB 4691
    3914

0826/5 may 1939/odeon session/**robert heger**
tchaikovsky evgeny onegin: waltz and polonaise
XXB 9785   O-26270/parlophone E 11414
    9786

0827/24 october 1939/electrola session/**bruno seidler-winkler**
tiana lemnitz, soprano; helge rosvaenge, tenor
leoncavallo i pagliacci: un tal gioco; vesti la giubba
ORA 4336   DA 4472
    4337
cd issue of both arias: preiser 89211
weber der freischütz: leise leise
2RA 4338   DB 5549
    4339
cd issue: preiser 89025

0828/1940/grammophon session/**gerhard steeger**/walther ludwig, tenor
kienzl der kuhreigen: zu strassburg auf der schanz
1042 5/8 ge   57115
kienzl der evangelimann: selig sind die verfolgung leiden
1071 ½ ge   57115
cd issue of both items: preiser 89088

0829/30 january 1940/electrola session/**bruno seidler-winkler**
helge rosvaenge, tenor
leoncavallo i pagliacci: no pagliaccio non son!
2RA 4460   DB 5569
glinka ivan susanin: brothers follow me!
2RA 4461   DB 5568
cd issue of both arias: 89211

0830/march-april 1940/electrola sessions/**bruno seidler-winkler**
margarete teschemacher, soprano
verdi un ballo in maschera: ecco l'orrido campo!
2RA 4524   DB 5574
cd issue: hamburger archiv für gesangskunst HAG 1034
verdi la forza del destino: pace pace mio dio!
2RA 4525   DB 5574

0831/june 1940/electrola session/**bruno seidler-winkler**/marta fuchs, soprano; friedl beckmann, contralto; helge rosvaenge, tenor
wagner der fliegende holländer: traft ihr das schiff am meere an?
2RA 4584   DB 5592
verdi aida: celeste aida; tchaikovsky evgeny onegin: faint echo of my youth
2RA 4586   DB 5580
    4588
mussorgsky boris godunov: dimitri! zarewitsch!
2RA 4589   DB 5593
    4587
cd issue of verdi, tchaikovsky and mussorgsky arias: preiser 89211

0832/31 october 1940/odeon session/**fritz lehmann**
mozart le nozze di figaro overture
XXB 8748   O-7949
    8749
mozart die zauberflöte overture
XXB 8750   O-7944
    8751

0833/19 november 1940/grammophon session/**gerhard steeger**
franz völker, tenor
smetana dalibor: whose is the spell?
1517 ½ gs IX   67603
1518 ½ gs IX
d'albert tiefland: ich grüss' noch einmal; mein leben wagt' ich drum
1528 ½ gs IX   67685
1529 ¾ gs IX
cd issue of all items: preiser 89070

0834/december 1940/electrola session/**bruno seidler-winkler**/tiana lemnitz, soprano; gerhard hüsch, baritone
strauss arabella: mein elemer!; und du wirst mein gebieter sein
2RA 4765   DB 5606
    4766
cd issues of both items: preiser 89950, emi 566 7742 and zyx music PD 50182

0835/2 december 1940/odeon session/**robert heger**
johann strauss die fledermaus overture
XXB 9098   O-3616
    9099
smetana the bartered bride overture
XXB 9100   O-3661
    9101

0836/1941/grammophon session/**gerhard steeger**
irmgard langhammer, soprano; franz völker, tenor
wagner der fliegende holländer: auf hohem felsen; rienzi alllmächtiger vater!
1671 ½ ge IX   67799
1672 ½ ge
cd issue of both items: preiser 89070

0837/1941/reichsrundfunk recording of an abridged version for radio/
johannes schüler/staatsopernchor/hilde scheppan, soprano; margarete klose, contralto; max lorenz, tenor; gustav rödin, tenor; jaro prohaska, baritone; wilhelm hiller, bass
wagner rienzi
cd issue: preiser 90223
previously published on lp by preiser and historia

0838/6 january and 15 february 1941/odeon sessions/**arthur grüber**
wagner siegfried: forest murmurs
XXB 8770   O-7952
     8771
wagner parsifal: good friday music and transformation music
XXB 8776   O-7953
     8777
     8778   O-7954
     8779

0839/march 1941/electrola session/**hans udo müller**/torsten ralf, tenor
wagner die meistersinger von nürnberg: fanget an!; die walküre: winterstürme
ORA 4868   DA 4493
     4867
cd issue of both items: preiser 89981

0840/march 1941/electrola session/**erwin baltzer**/tiana lemnitz, soprano; helge rosvaenge, tenor
tchaikovsky the enchantress: my fate is strange
2RA 4871   DB 5624
     4872
cd issues: preiser 89211, cantus classics CACD 500024 and hamburger archiv für gesangskunst HAGLEM 2

0841/april 1941/electrola session/**reinhold merten**
margarethe teschemacher, soprano
verdi la forza del destino: la vergine degli angeli; un ballo in maschera: morro ma prima in grazia
2RA 4978   DB 5635
     4979

0842/8 and 10 may 1941/odeon sessions/**fritz lehmann**
mozart serenata notturna k239
XXB 8806	O-7965
8807	
8808	O-7966

beethoven two german dances
XXB 8811	O-7966

reger eine lustspiel-ouvertüre
XXB 8809	O-9121
8810	

0843/24 may 1941/french newsreel film of a concert encore in the paris opera during guest visit by the berlin staatsoper/**herbert von karajan**
wagner die meistersinger von nürnberg overture, concluding bars only
laserdisc issue (japan): TES 132/LSZS 009191

0844/june 1941/grammophon sessions/**herbert von karajan**
beethoven symphony no 7 in op 92
1492 5/8 ge	67643
1493 ¾ ge	
1494 ¾ ge	67644
1495 ¾ ge	
1485 ¾ ge	67645
1486 ¾ ge	
1487 5/8 ge	67646
1490 ¾ ge	
1491	67647
1488 ½ ge	
1489 ½ ge	67648

cd issues: deutsche grammophon 423 5262 and 477 6237

0845/27 june 1941/odeon session/**arthur grüber**
pfitzner das käthchen von heilbronn overture
XXB 8838	O-7967
8839	
8840	O-7968
8841	

0846/29 september and 4 october 1941/odeon sessions/**fritz lehmann**
corelli concerto grosso no 8 "christmas concerto"
XXB 8870	O-7985
8871	
8872	O-7986
8873	

rudi stephan musik für orchester in einem satz
XXB 8874	O-9132
8875	
8876	O-0133
8877	

0847/1942/grammophon session/**leopold ludwig**/helena braun, soprano
wagner tristan und isolde: mild und leise
1893ge   67964
1894ge
beethoven fidelio: abscheulicher wo eilst du hin?
1895 ½ ge   67929
1896 ½ ge
cd issue of both items: preiser 89953

0848/1942/grammophon session/**robert heger**/hans hotter, bass-baritone
wagner die meistersinger von nürnberg: wahn wahn überall wahn
2173ge   67972
2174ge
wagner die walküre: lebwohl du kühnes herrliches kind!
2175ge   67973
2176ge
cd issue of both items: preiser 90280

0849/1942/reichsrundfunk recording in haus des rundfunks/**artur rother**
margarete klose, contralto
gluck orfeo ed euridice: che faro senza euridice?
published by acanta on lp only

0850/january 1942/electrola session/**bruno seidler-winkler**
josef herrmann, bass-baritone
weber der freischütz: hier im ird'schen jammertal
ORA 5286   DA 4498
cd issues: preiser 89076 and hamburger archiv für gesangskunst
marschner hans heiling: an jenem tag
2RA 5287   DB 5678
cd issues: preiser 89076 and hamburger archiv für gesangskunst
bizet carmen: votre toast
2RA 5288   DB 5678
verdi la forza del destino: son pereda son ricco d'onore
ORA 5289   DA 4498

0851/12-15 january 1942/reichsrundfunk recording in haus des rundfunks/
hanns steinkopf/ staatsopernchor/maria cebotari, soprano;
helge rosvaenge, tenor; heinrich schlusnus, baritone
verdi la traviata, abridged version for radio
published on lp by urania and acanta
cd issue: preiser 90160

0852/5 february 1942/reichsrundfunk recording in haus des rundfunks/
artur rother/tiana lemnitz, soprano; maria cebotari, soprano;
lore hoffman, mezzo-soprano; willi domgraf-fassbaender, baritone;
eduard kandl, bass-baritone
mozart le nozze di figaro, act four from aprite un po quegli occhi to end
published on lp by melodiya 3241 0 3000

0853/19 march 1942/reichsrundfunk recording in haus des rundfunks/
artur rother/staatsopernchor/maria cebotari, soprano; elisabeth waldenau, contralto; helge rosvaenge, tenor; willi domgraf-fassbaender, baritone
verdi rigoletto, abridged version for radio
cd issue: preiser 90272

0854/april 1942/electrola session/**erich orthmann**/tiana lemnitz, soprano
verdi il trovatore: tacea la notte placida; d'amor sull' ali rosee
2RA 5538   DB 7656
    5539
cd issues of both arias: preiser 89167 and zyx music PD 50182

0855/may 1942/reichsrundfunk recording in haus des rundfunks/**artur rother**
staatsopernchor/hilde scheppan, soprano; marie luise schilp, contralto; helge rosvaenge, tenor; karl schmitt-walter, baritone; wilhelm lang, bass
verdi il trovatore
unpublished recording

0856/24 june 1942/reichsrundfunk recording in haus des rundfunks/**artur rother**
staatsopernchor/tiana lemnitz, soprano; margarete klose, contralto; georg hann, bass-baritone; matthieu ahlersmayer, bass
verdi don carlo: soccorso alla regina!; o don fatale
cd issues: preiser 90257 and hamburger srchiv für gesangskunt HAGLEM 2
also published on lp by acanta

0857/21 november 1942/reichsrundfunk recording in haus des rundfunks/**artur rother**
staatsopernchor/hilde scheppan, soprano; margarete klose, contralto; helge rosvaenge, tenor; hans hotter, bass-baritone; wilhelm schirp, bass; wilhelm lang, bass
verdi aida, abridged version for radio
cd issue: preiser 90219
also published on lp by acanta

0858/november-december 1942/electrola sessions/**hans udo müller**
maria reining, soprano
mozart le nozze di figaro: dove sono
ORA 5795   DA 4508
    5796
mozart le nozze di figaro: porgi amor; deh vieni non tardar
2RA 5797   DB 7665
    5798
cd issue of all arias: preiser 89065

0859/2 december 1942/odeon session/**robert heger**
johann strauss die fledermaus overture
XXB 9098   O-3616
    9099
smetana the bartered bride overture
XXB 9100   O-3661
    9101
bartered bride overture re-made on 9 march 1948 using same matrix numbers

0860/1942-1943/reichsrundfunk recording/**johannes schüler**/peter anders, tenor
nicolai die lustigen weiber von windsor: horch die lerche singt im hain
cd issues: acanta 43 268 and berlin classics BC 21682

0861/1943/electrola sessions/**bruno seidler-winkler**
margarete teschemacher, soprano; willy treffner, tenor
cornelius der barbier von bagdad: o holdes bild in engelsschöne!; flotow martha: blickt sein auge doch so ehrlich
2RA 5984   unpublished recordings
     5985
eine nacht mit rosita: die erste grosse liebe; lehar giuditta: schön wie die blaue sommernacht
2RA 5986   unpublished recordings
     5987
cd issue of all items: preiser 89545

0862/1943/grammophon sessions/**paul van kempen**/vasa prihoda, violin
dvorak violin concerto in a minor
2407 ge IX   68201
2408 ge IX
2409 ge IX   68202
2410 ge IX
2411 ge IX   68203
2412 ge IX
2413 ge IX   68204
2414 ge IX
2415 ge IX   68205
cd issue: arkadia CDHP 623

0863/1943/electrola session/**bruno seidler-winkler**
friedel beckmann, contralto; helge rosvaenge, tenor
verdi il trovatore: madre non dormi?
2RA 6010   unpublished recording
     6011
verdi aida: gia I sacerdoti adunansi!
2RA 6012   DB 7720
     6013
cd issue of both duets: preiser 89211

0864/1943/columbia session/**bruno seidler-winkler**
margarete teschemacher, soprano; helmut schweebs, bass
verdi la forza del destino: venite fidente alla croce
CRX 255   LWX 376
     256
cd issues: preiser 89980 and hamburger archiv für gesangskunst HAG 1034

0865/1943/reichsrundfunk recording in haus des rundfunks/**hanns steinkopf**
staatsopernchor/maria reining, soprano; elisabeth waldenau, contralto; helge rosvaenge, tenor; valentin haller, tenor; hans reinmar, baritone; reinhard dörr, bass-baritone
verdi otello, abridged version for radio
cd issue: preiser 90271

0866/1943/reichsrundfunk recordings/**robert heger**/staatsopernchor/maria müller, soprano; ludwig suthaus, tenor; ludwig hofmann, bass-baritone
wagner die meistersinger von nürnberg: guten abend meister; morgenlich leuchtend; verachtet mir die meister nicht
cd issues: music and arts CD 1068 and hamburger archiv für gesangskunst HAG 1063
wagner die walküre: eine waffe lass' mich dir weissen....der männer sippe
published on lp by acanta

0867/26 january 1943/reichsrundfunk recordings/**robert heger**/ staatsopernchor/tiana lemnitz, soprano; peter anders, tenor
orff carmina burana: in trutina
flotow martha: horch die lerche singt im hain
both are unpublished recordings

0868/4-5 february 1943/odeon sessions/**robert heger**
grieg peer gynt, first and second suites

XXB 9112	O-3623
9113	
9114	O-3624
9115	
9116	O-3625
9117	
9118	O-3626
9119	

0869/20 march 1943/reichsrundfunk recordings/**robert heger**
margarete klose, contralto
gluck orfeo ed euridice: che faro senza euridice; handel serse: ombra mai fu
cd issue of both arias: preiser 89583

0870/1 april 1943/reichsrundfunk recording of the premiere in the staatsoper unter den linden/**robert heger**/staatsopernchor/maria cebotari, soprano; marta fuchs, soprano; ruth berglund, contralto; peter anders, tenor; erich zimmermann, tenor; willi domgraf-fassbaender, baritone; eugen fuchs, bass-baritone; josef greindl, bass
schoeck das schloss durande
cd issue: jecklin JD 6922

0871/21-22 april 1943/odeon sessions/**arthur grüber**
verdi aida: ballet music

XXB 9152	unpublished recording
9153	

bizet carmen, suite

XXB 9154	O-3634
9155	

0872/22 april 1943/odeon session/**fritz lehmann**
johann strauss rosen aus dem süden

XXB 9156	O-3674
9157	

johann strauss wo die zitronen blüh'n

XXB 9158	unpublished recording
9159	

0873/14-19 may 1943/reichsrundfunk recording of a concert performance without audience on the rehearsal stage of the staatsoper unter den linden/**robert heger**
staatsopernchor/paula buchner, soprano; margarete klose, contralto; max lorenz, tenor; erich zimmermann, tenor; benno arnold, tenor; ludwig hofmann, bass-baritone; jaro prohaska, baritone; eugen fuchs, bass
wagner tristan und isolde
cd issues: preiser 90243 and grammofono AB 78840-78842

0874/20 may 1943/reichsrundfunk recording in haus des rundfunks/**robert heger**
peter anders, tenor
schillings 4 glockenlieder nach gedichten von carl spitteler
cd issues: acanta 43 275 and berlin classics BC 21682

0875/22 june 1943/odeon session/**arthur grüber**
busoni eine lustspiel-ouvertüre
XXB 9169	O-3652
9170	

0876/30 october 1943/reichsrundfunk recording in haus des rundfunks/**robert heger**/staatsopernchor/hilde scheppan, soprano; ruth berglund, contralto; willi domgraf-fassbaender, baritoe; josef greindl, bass
monteverdi-orff orfeo
unpublished recording

0877/30 october 1943/reichsrundfunk recording in haus des rundfunks/**robert heger**/margarete klose, contralto
monteverdi-orff lament of ariadne
cd issue: preiser 89583

0878/31 october 1943/reichsrundfunk recording of a concert performance without audience on the rehearsal stage of the staatsoper unter den linden/**robert heger**/staatsopernchor/maria müller, soprano; margarete klose, contralto; franz völker, tenor; ludwig hofmann, bass-baritone; jaro prohaska, baritone; walter grossmann, baritone
wagner lohengrin
cd issue: preiser 90043

0879/1943/reichsrundfunk recording for electrola/**heinz gerhard zilcher**
hermann zilcher, piano
mozart piano concerto no 27 in b flat k595
2RA 5448	DB 7641
5449	
5450	DB 7642
5451	
5452	DB 7643
5453	

0880/26 and 28 june 1944/magnetofonkonzert without audience in haus des rundfunks/**herbert von karajan**
bruckner symphony no 8 in c minor, second and third movements
cd issue: koch 3-1448-2

0881/7 july 1944/reichsrundfunk recording in haus des rundfunks/
robert heger/tiana lemnitz, soprano
wagner wesendonk-lieder
cd issue: acanta 43 275

0882/19 september 1944/magnetofonkonzert without audience in haus des rundfunks/**herbert von karajan**
bruckner symphony no 8 in c minor, fourth movement
cd issues: koch 3-1448-2 and arkadia CD 705
this was an experimental twin-channel recording

0883/17-19 october 1944/reichsrundfunk recording of a concert performance without audience on the rehearsal stage of the staatsoper unter den linden/
johannes schüler/staatsopernchor/erna berger, soprano; else tegethoff, contralto; peter anders, tenor; eugen fuchs, baritone; franz sauer, baritone; josef greindl, bass
flotow martha
cd issue: berlin classics BC 21632

0884/7 november 1944/reichsrundfunk recording of a concert performance without audience on the rehearsal stage of the staatsoper unter den linden/**robert heger**
staatsoperchor/hilde scheppan, soprano; irmgard langhammer, soprano; margarete klose, contralto; max lorenz, tenor; jaro prohaska, baritone; ludwig hofmann, bass-baritone
wagner götterdämmerung, act three as far as trauermusik
cd issue: preiser 90245

0885/20-22 november 1944/reichsrundfunk recording of a concert performance without audience on the rehearsal stage of the staatsoper unter den linden/
robert heger/staatsopernchor/erna berger, soprano; margarete klose, contralto; helge rosvaenge, tenor; heinrich schlusnus, baritone; josef greindl, bass
verdi rigoletto
cd issue: preiser 90036

0886/december 1944/magnetophonkonzert without audience in haus des rundfunks/
herbert von karajan
beethoven symphony no 3 in e flat op 55 "eroica"
cd issues: koch 3-1509-2 and grammofono AB 78670

0887/1 february 1945/reichsrundfunk recording in haus des rundfunks/**robert heger**
tiana lemnitz, soprano; peter anders, tenor
mozart le nozze di figaro: porgi amor
published only on lp by rococo
mozart die entführung aus dem serail: hier soll ich dich denn sehen?
cd issues: acanta 43 268 and berlin classics BC 21682
mozart die entführung aus dem serail: konstanze dich wiederzusehen?
cd issue: berlin classics BC 21682
mozart die entführung aus dem serail: wenn der freude tränen fliessen
cd issue: acanta 43 268

0888/28 july 1946/radio berlin-ost recording of a staatsoper performance in admiralspalast/**karl schmidt**/staatsopernchor/erna berger, soprano; rita streich, soprano; peter anders, tenor; paul schmidtmann, tenor; ludwig hofmann, bass
mozart die entführung aus dem serail
unpublished recording
the duet "welch ein geschick" from this recording publshed on acanta cd 43 268

0889/24 july 1947/electrola session in the zwölf-apostel-kirche/**artur rother**
rudolf schock, tenor
flotow martha: ach so fromm
2RA 6103   DB 11522
offenbach les contes d'hoffmann: dieu de quelle ivresse; legende de kleinzach
2RA 6104   DB 11500
     6105

0890/3 october 1947/radio berlin-ost recording of a staatsoper performance in admiralspalast/**wilhelm furtwängler**/staatsopernchor/erna schlüter, soprano; margarete klose, contralto; ludwig suthaus, tenor; gerhard witting. tenor; jaro prohaska, baritone; gottlob frick, bass
wagner tristan und isolde, acts two and three
cd issues: societe wilhelm furtwängler SWF 981-982, dante LYS 194-195 and radio years RY 103-104

0891/29 january 1948/electrola session in zwölf-apostel-kirche/**johannes schüler**
erna berger, soprano
verdi la traviata: e strano!....sempre libera
2RA 6106   unpublished recording
     6107

0892/29 january and 2 february 1948/electrola sessions in zwölf-apostel-kirche/
leopold ludwig /rudolf schock, tenor
rimsky-korsakov sadko: hindulied; tchaikovsky evgeny onegin: faint echo of my youth
2RA 6108   DB 11520
     6109
meyerbeer l'africaine: o paradis
2RA 6118   DB 11552

0893/30 january 1948/electrola session in zwölf-apostel-kirche/**leopold ludwig**
tiana lemnitz, soprano; margarete klose, contralto
wagner lohengrin: euch lüften die mein klagen
2RA 6110   unpublished recording
     6111
     6112
     6113
cd issues: preiser 89167 and hamburger archiv für gesangskunst HAGLEM 3

0894/31 january 1948/electrola session in zwölf-apostel-kirche/**johannes schüler**
erna berger, soprano
verdi rigoletto: caro nome (versions in italian and german)
2RA 6114   unpublished recordings
     6115
johann strauss frühlingsstimmen, vocal version
2RA 6116   unpublished recording
     6117

0895/2 february 1948/electrola session in the zwölf-apostel-kirche/**leopold ludwig**
tiana lemnitz, soprano
wagner tannhäuser: allmächtige jungfrau
2RA 6119   DB 6809
     6120
cd issues: preiser 89167 and hamburger archiv für gesangskunst HAGLEM 3

0896/3 february 1948/electrola session in the zwölf-apostel-kirche/**leopold ludwig**
erna berger, soprano
mozart zaide: ruhe sanft; le nozze di figaro: deh vieni non tardar
2RA 6121   unpublished recordings
     6122

0897/4 february 1948/electrola session in the zwölf-apostel-kirche/**leopold ludwig**
tiana lemnitz, soprano; margarete klose, contralto
gluck orfeo ed euridice: su e con me vieni!; che fieri momento!
2RA 6124   DB 6801
     6125
cd issue of both items: preiser 89167

0898/9 february 1948/electrola session in the zwölf-apostel-kirche/**johannes schüler**
erna berger, soprano
verdi la traviata: e strano!....sempre libera
2RA 6133   unpublished recording
     6134

0899/13 february 1948/electrola session in the zwölf-apostel-kirche/**leopold ludwig**
bizet carmen, acts one and four preludes
2RA 6142   DB 11510/C 3993
     6143

0900/15, 16 and 20 february 1948/electrola sessions in the zwölf-apostel-kirche/
leopold ludwig/tiana lemnitz, soprano
weber der freischütz: und ob die wolke
ORA 6093   DA 1881/DA 5509
     6094
cd issues: preiser 89167 and emi 566 7742
verdi aida: ritorna vincitor
2RA 6144   DB 6806
     6157
verdi aida: o patria mia
2RA 6158   DB 6803
     6159
cd issue of both verdi arias: preiser 89167

0901/17 and 19 february 1948/electrola sessions in the zwölf-apostel-kirche/
leopold ludwig
tchaikovsky evgeny onegin: waltz and polonaise
2RA 6145   C 4037
    6146
mendelssohn hebrides overture
2RA 6147   DB 11513
    6149
offenbach orfee aux enfers overture
2RA 6150   C 3801/DB 11511
    6151
verdi nabucco overture
2RA 6155   DB 11501
    6156
mascagni cavalleria rusticana intermezzo; leoncavallo i pagliacci interemezzo
2RA 6159   DB 11502
    6160
thomas mignon overture
2RA 6161   unpublished recording
    6162

0902/9-13 march 1948/odeon sessions/**robert heger**
weber peter schmoll overture
XXB 9541   unpublished recording
    9542
schubert symphony no 8 in b minor d759 "unfinished"
XXB 9543   O-3679
    9544
    9545   O-3680
    9546
    9547   O-3681
    9548
ponchielli la gioconda: dance of the hours
XXB 9551   O-3678
    9552
rossini-respighi la boutique fantasque
XXB 9553   unpublished recording
    9554
    9555
    9556
    9557
    9558
see also 2 december 1942

0903/ 13-15 april 1948/odeon sessions/**robert heger**
mendelssohn a midsummer night's dream: wedding march and scherzo
XXB 9549   O-3671
    9550
smetana ma vlast: the moldau
XXB 9559   O-3672
    9560
    9561   O-3673
    9562
mendelssohn meeresstille overture; a midsummer night's dream: nocturne
XXB 9563   unpublished recordings
    9564
    9565
    9566

0904/ 16 april 1948/odeon session/**otto dobrindt**
offenbach orfee aux enfers overture
XXB 9567   O-3675
    9568
rubinstein lichtertanz der bräute; toreador and andalouse
XXB 9569   unpublished recordigs
    9570

0905/ 23 june 1948/electrola session in the zwölf-apostel-kirche/
johannes schüler/ rudolf schock, tenor
verdi il trovatore: ah si ben mio; di quella pira
ORA 6167   DA 5513
    6168

0906/ 19 december 1948/radio berlin-ost recording of a staatsoper performance in admiralspalast/**joseph keilberth**/tiana lemnitz, soprano; ludwig suthaus, tenor; helmut krebs, tenor; jaro prohaska, bass-baritone
wagner die meisrtersinger von nürnberg: grüss gott mein evchen!
unpublished recording

0907/ 1949/soundtrack to a defa film/staatsopernchor/**artur rother**
tiana lemnitz, soprano; erna berger, soprano; annelies müller, contralto; margarete klose, contralto; willi domgraf-fassbaender, baritone; matthieu ahlersmayer, bass-baritone
mozart le nozze di figaro
vhs video: defa musikfilm 10071
music appears in a very truncated version; actors mime for some of the singers

0908/ 20 september 1950/radio berlin-ost recording of a staatsoper performance in admiralpalast/**joseph keilberth**/staatsopernchor/martha mödl, mezzo-soprano; hildegard lüdtke, soprano; alfred hulgert, tenor; josef metternich, baritone; theo hermann, bass-baritone
verdi macbeth
cd issue: myto MCD 974 166

0909/19 december 1950/radio berlin-ost recording of a staatsoper performance in admiralspalast/**joseph keilberth**/staatsopernchor/christel goltz, soprano; anny schlemm, soprano; irmgard armgart, soprano; erich witte, tenor; josef metternich, baritone; heinrich pflanzl, bass-baritone
strauss arabella
cd issue: walhall WLCD 0185

0910/11 january 1951/electrola session/**werner eisbrenner**/peter anders, tenor
lehar zarewitsch: wolgalied; kalman die zirkusprinzessin: zwei märchenaugen
2RA 6561   EH 1359
    6562
cd issue of both items: emi 769 6822
lehar das land des lächelns: immer nur lächeln; dein ist mein ganzes herz
2RA 6563   EH 1364
    6564

0911/8 october 1951/radio ddr recording of a concert in admiralspalast/**hermann scherchen**/staatsopernchor/rita meinl-wiese, soprano; sigrid ekkehard, soprano; annelies müller, contralto; gertraud prenzlow, contralto; herbert reinhold, tenor; kurt rehm, baritone; willi heyer-krämer, bass
mahler symphony no 8 "symphony of a thousand"
cd issues of part one: tahra TAH 112 and TAH 147

0912/28 february 1952/electrola session in berlin-zehlendorf/**artur rother**
anny schlemm, soprano; rudolf schock, tenor
bizet carmen: parle-moi de ma mere
2RA 6898   DB 11541
    6899
cd issue: emi 826 4342
orchestra described on this recording as berliner symphoniker

0913/30 march 1952/radio ddr recording of a staatsoper performance in admiralspalast/**hermann abendroth**/staatsopernchor/hedwig müller-bütow, soprano; ruth keplinger, soprano; helge rosvaenge, tenor; gerhard unger, tenor; heinrich pflanzl, bass-baritone; jaro prohaska, baritone; kurt rehm, baritone
beethoven fidelio
cd issue: walhall WLCD 0173

0914/28 june 1952/electrola session in rheingauschule/**wilhelm schüchter**
rudolf schock, tenor
mozart die zauberflöte: dies bildnis ist bezaubernd schön
2RA 7119   DB 11546
cd issue: emi 767 1832
johann strauss der zigeunerbaron: als flotter geist
2RA 7008   EH 1421
orchestra described on these recordings as berlner symphoniker

0915/9 august 1952/electrola session in rheingauschule/**wilhelm schüchter**
rudolf schock, tenor
johann strauss der zigeunerbaron: komm in die gondel
2RA 7009   EH 1421
cd issue: emi 585 2852
orchestra described on this recording as berliner symphoniker

0916/4 february 1953/electrola session in hotel esplanade/**wilhelm schüchter**
rudolf schock, tenor
mozart cosi fan tutte: un aura amorosa
2RA 6987   DB 11546
oscar straus ein walzertraum: da draussen im duftigen garten; kalman gräfin maritza: grüss mir mein wien
2RA 7117   EH 1435
    7118
cd issue of oscar straus item: emi 585 2852
orchestra described on these recordings as berliner symphoniker

0917/13 april 1953/electrola session in berlin-zehlendorf/**wilhelm schüchter**
gottlob frick, bass
verdi don carlo: ella giammai m'amo
2RA 7190   DB 11555
    7191
cd issues: emi 574 7142 and 767 1872
orchestra described on this recording as berliner symphoniker

0918/20 april 1953/electrola session in berlin-zehlendorf/**wilhelm schüchter**
anny schlemm, soprano; gertrud stilo, contralto; rudolf schock, tenor
johann strauss der zigeunerbaron: mein aug' bewacht; wer uns getraut
2RA 7154   EH 1437
    7155
cd issue of both items: emi 585 2852
orchestra described on this recording as berliner symphoniker

0919/5 may 1953/electrola session in grunewaldkirche/**wilhelm schüchter**
josef metternich, baritone
leoncavallo i pagliacci: si puo; bizet carmen: votre toast
2RA 7176   DB 11548
    7177
cd issue of bizet item: emi 574 2682
orchestra described on this recording as berliner symphoniker

0920/7 july 1953/electrola session in berlin-zehlendorf/**wilhelm schüchter**
rudolf schock, tenor
verdi rigoletto: questa o quella; la donna e mobile
2RA 7186   DA 5520
    7187
cd issue of both items: emi 574 2642
orchestra described on this recording as berliner symphoniker

0921/22-25 september 1953/electrola sessions in berlin-zehlendorf/
wilhelm schüchter/erna berger, soprano; rudolf schock, tenor;
gottlob frick, bass
lehar paganini: gern hab' ich die frau'n geküsst; tauber du bist die welt für mich
2RA 7212   EG 8010
      7213
cd issue of paganini item: emi 582 2862
nicolai die lustigen weiber von windsor: als büblein klein; lortzing der waffenschmied:
auch ich war ein jüngling
2RA 7214   EH 1444
      7215
cd issue of both items: emi 575 5502
mozart die entführung aus dem serail: wer ein liebchen hat gefunden; solche
hergelauf'ne laffen!
2RA 7217   EH 1443
      7218
cd issue of both items: emi 826 4352
mozart die entführung aus dem serail: wenn der freude tränen fliessen; hier soll
ich dich denn sehen?
2RA 7220   EH 1447
      7260
cd issue of both items: emi 826 4352
mozart die entführung aus dem serail: welch ein geschick!
2RA 7224   DB 11559
      7225
cd issue: emi 826 4352
lortzing zar und zimmermann: o sancta justitia; man glaubt's dass ich nie mich trüge
2RA 7228   EH 1445
      7229
lincke im reich der indra: wenn auch die jahre enteilen; millöcker gasparone:
dunkelrote rosen
cd issue of lincke and millöcker items: emi 585 2862
orchestra described on these recordings as berliner symphoniker

0922/21 november and 1 december 1953/electrola sessions/
wilhelm schüchter/rudolf schock, tenor
verdi aida: celeste aida; un ballo in maschera: forse la soglia attinse
2RA 7240   DB 11561
      7241
cd issue of both items: emi 574 2632
orchestra described on these recordings as berliner symphoniker

0923/17 december 1953/columbia session/**wilhelm schüchter**
hermann prey, baritone
lortzing der wildschütz: heiterkeit und fröhlichkeit; sonst spielt' ich mit zepter
CRX 1193   DWX 5091
       1194
cd issue of both items: emi 769 5072
orchestra decribed on this recording as berliner symphoniker

0924/3 march 1954/electrola session in berlin-zehlendorf/
wilhelm schüchter/gottlob frick, bass
mozart le nozze di figaro: la vendetta; rossini il barbiere di siviglia: la calunnia
2RA 7263　　　　　　　　DB 11563
　　 7264
tchaikovsky evgeny onegin: love is no respecter of age; halevy la juive: wenn ewiger hass
2RA 7267　　　　　　　　DB 11566
　　 7268
cd issue of tchaikovsky and halevy items: emi 767 1872
orchestra described on these recordings as berliner symphoniker

0925/27 march 1954/electrola session in berlin zehlendorf/
wilhelm schüchter/staatsopernchor/gottlob frick, bass
mozart die zauberflöte: o isis und osiria
2RA 7275　　　　　　　　DB 11567
cd issue: emi 767 1872
orchestra described on this recording as berliner symphoniker

0926/april 1954/electrola session in grunewaldkirche/**wilhelm schüchter**
sieglinde wagner, mezzo-soprano
bizet carmen: l'amour est un oiseau rebelle; en vain pour eviter
2RA 7281　　　　　　　　DB 11570
　　 7282
cd issue of both items: emi 826 4342
orchestra described on these recordings as berliner symphoniker

0927/28 april 1954/electrola session in berlin-zehlendorf
wilhelm schüchter/gottlob frick, bass
mozart die zauberflöte: in diesen heiligen hallen
2RA 7276　　　　　　　　DB 11567
cd issue: emi 767 1872
orchestra decribed on this recording as berliner symphoniker

0928/1 and 5 may 1954/electrola sessions/**wilhelm schüchter/**sieglinde wagner, mezzo-soprano; margarethe klose, contralto; josef metternich, baritone
offenbach les contes d'hoffmann: scintille diamant; barcarolle
2RA 7265　　　　　　　　DB 11564
　　 7266
cd issue of both items: emi 574 2692
orchestra described on these recordings as berliner symphoniker

0929/7 june 1954/electrola session in berlin-zehlendorf/**wilhelm schüchter**
erika köth, soprano: sieglinde wagner, mezzo-soprano; rudolf schock, tenor; josef metternich, baritone
verdi rigoletto: un di se ben rammentomi; bella figlia dell' amore
2RA 7271　　　　　　　　DB 11565
　　 7272
verdi rigoletto: giovanna ho dei rimorsi; caro nome
2RA 7277　　　　　　　　DB 11571
　　 7278
cd issue of all items: emi 574 2642
orchestra described on these recordings as berliner symphoniker

0930/7 september 1954/electrola session in berlin-zehlendorf/**wilhelm schüchter**/erna berger, soprano; rudolf schock, tenor; dietrich fischer-dieskau, baritone
puccini la boheme: che gelida manina; o mimi tu piu non torni
2RA 7606   DB 11575
     7607
puccini la boheme: si mi chiamano mimi; o soave fanciulla
2RA 7608   DB 11574
     7609
cd issue of all items: emi 574 2652
orchestra described on these recordings as berliner symphoniker

0931/29 november-5 december 1954/electrola sessions in jesus-christus-kirche/**wilhelm schüchter**/chor der städtischen oper/erna berger, soprano; sieglinde wagner, mezzo-soprano; rudolf schock, tenor; erich zimmermann, tenor
puccini madama butterfly: un bel di; ancora un passo
ORA 7612   DA 5523
     7613
puccini madama butterfly: dovunque al mondo; addio fiorito asil
2RA 7614   DB 11578
     7615
puccini madama butterfly: viene la sera
2RA 7616   DB 11577
     7617
puccini madama butterfly: con onor muore; scuoti quella fronda
2RA 7618   DB 11576
     7619
cd issue of all items: emi 574 2662
orchestra described on these recordings as berliner symphoniker

0931/ca.1955/eterna session/**karl schmidt**/staatsopernchor
beethoven fidelio: prisoners' chorus
                                      120 008

0932/ca.1955/eterna sessions/**meinhard von zallinger**
männerchor der komischen oper/jutta vulpius, soprano;
sonja schöner, soprano; manfred jungwirth, bass
mozart die zauberflöte: o isis und osiris
                                      120 173

weber der freischütz: wie nahte mir der schlummer....leise leise
20 6625   120 190
   6626
mozart die zauberflöte: ach ich fühl's; in diesen heil'gen hallen
                                  120 191

mozart die zauberflöte: o zittre nicht mein lieber sohn; der hölle rache
20 6629   120 192
   6630
weber der freischütz: schelm halt fest!; kommt ein schlanker bursch gegangen
20 6635   120 197
   6636
weber der freischütz: und ob die wolke
20 6637   120 196
   6638

0933/ca.1955/eterna session/**franz konwitschny**/
ingeborg wenglor, soprano; gerhard unger, tenor
mozart don giovanni: batti batti; vedrai carino
20 6631   120 193
   6632
mozart don giovanni: dalla sua pace; cosi fan tutte: un aura amorosa
20 6633   120 194
   6634

0934/ca.1955/eterna sessions/**meinhold von zallinger**
ingeborg wenglor, soprano; sigrid ekkehard, soprano;
gertraud prenzlow, contralto; karl paul, baritone
mozart die zauberflöte: der vogelfänger bin ich ja; ein mädchen oder weibchen
20 6675   120 220
   6676
mozart die zauberflöte: hm hm hm!; pa pa pa!
20 6679   320 233
   6680

0935/ca.1955/eterna sessions/**horst stein**/clara ebers, soprano; ruth keplinger, soprano; julius katona, tenor; gerhard niese, batitone; heinrich pflanzl, bass
mozart cosi fan tutte: come scoglio; le nozze di figaro: porgi amor
20 6685   320 236
   6686
haydn die schöpfung: auf starkem fittiche
20 6691   320 239
   6692
wagner-regeny der günstling, scenes from the opera
20 6661   120 186
   6662
   6689   120 238
   6690
   6701   320 246
   6702

0936/ca.1955/eterna session/**matthieu lange**
mozart deutsche tänze nos 1, 2, 5 and 6
20 6707   120 247
   6708
   6709   120 248
   6710

0937/ca.1955/eterna session/**meinhard von zallinger**/ingeborg wenglor, soprano; john van kesteren, tenor; gerhard frei, bass-baritone
mozart die entführung aus dem serail: o wie will ich triumphieren; wer ein liebchen hat gefunden
20 6705   120 244
   6706
mozart die entführung aus dem serail overture; hier soll ich dich denn sehen?
20 6711   320 245
   6712
mozart die entführung aus dem serail: welche wonne welche lust!; ich gehe doch rat' ich dir
20 6715   320 250
   6716

0938/ ca.1955/eterna sessions/**horst stein**/clara ebers, soprano; ingeborg wenglor, soprano; robert lauhöfer, baritone; heinrich pflanzl, bass-baritone
haydn die schöpfung; nun beut die flur; lortzing der wildschütz: so munter und fröhlich; lass er doch hören!; mozart le nozze di figaro: deh vieni non tardar; che soave zeffiretti; crudel perche finora?
these items appear to have been published on 45rpm discs only

0939/ca.1955/eterna session/**franz konwitschny**/hedwig müller-bütow, soprano; irmgard arnold, soprano; gerhard stolze, tenor; gerhard frei, bass-baritone
beethoven fidelio: abscheilicher wo eilst du hin?; mir ist so wunderbar
these items appear to have been published on 45 rpm discs only

0940 / ca.1955 / eterna session / **meinhard von zallinger**
john van kesteren, tenor
mozart cosi fan tutte overture; die zauberflöte: dies bildnis ist bezaubernd schön
these items appear to have been published on 45 rpm discs only

0941 / ca.1955 / eterna session / **franz konwitschny**
beethoven overtures: egmont, fidelio and leonore no 3
published on eterna lp 720 061

0942 / 28 january 1955 / radio ddr recording of a concert in admiralspalast / **erich kleiber**
handel berenice overture; hartmann symphony no 6; beethoven symphony no 5 in c minor op 67
handel and beethoven items published on lp by discocorp; hartmann unpublished

0943 / 13 april 1955 / electrola sessions in berlin-zehlendorf / **wilhelm schüchter**
annesliese rothenberger, soprano; erika köth, soprano; rudolf schock, tenor; dietrich fischer-dieskau, baritone; gottlob frick, bass
nicolai die lustigen weiber von windsor: in einem waschkorb?
2RA 7634   DB 11580
      7635
cd issues: emi 565 6212 and testament SBT 1103
johann strauss die fledermaus: mein herr marquis; spiel' ich die unschuld vom lande
2RA 7636   EH 1454
      7637
suppe boccaccio: hab' ich nur deine liebe; mia bella fiorentina
2RA 7638   EH 1453
      7639
cd issue of suppe item: emi 585 2852
nicolai die lustigen weiber von windsor: nun eilt herbei; rossini il barbiere di siviglia: una voce poco fa
2RA 7644   DB 11581
      7647
orchestra described on these recordings as berliner symphoniker

0944 / may 1955 / electrola sessions in grunewaldkirche / **wilhelm schüchter**
anneliese rothenberger, soprano; rudolf schock, tenor; hermann prey, baritone
puccini gianni schicchi: o mio babbino caro; leoncavallo i pagliacci: qual fiamma avea nel guardo
2RA 7652   EH 1459
      7655
flotow martha: letzte rose
2RA 7653   EH 1458
      7654
leoncavallo i pagliacci: nedda! silvio! a quest ora che imprudenza
2RA 7656   EH 1460
      7657
cd issues of pagliacci duet: emi 252 3482, 574 3492 and 918 4932
orchestra described on these recordings as berliner symphoniker

0945/ 15-16 may 1955/electrola sessions in berlin-zehlendorf/**wilhelm schüchter/**chor der städtischen oper/leonie rysanek, soprano; sieglinde wagner, mezzo-soprano; rudolf schock, tenor; josef metternich, baritone; peter roth-ehrang, bass
verdi aida: o patria mia; la forza del destino: pace pace
2RA 7660 DB 11584
7661
cd issue of both items: emi 565 2012
verdi aida: ciel mio padre!....pur ti riveggo...to end act three; la fatal pietra..to end act four
cd issue of both sequences: emi 574 2632
orchestra described on these recordings as berliner symphoniker

0946/ 26 may 1955/electrola session in grunewaldkirche/**wilhelm schüchter** chor der städtischen oper
kreutzer das nachtlager von granada: schon die abendglocken klangen; nicolai die lustigen weiber von windsor: o süsser mond!
2RA 7645 EH 1455
7646
cd issue of both items: emi 575 5502
orchestra described on these recordings as berliner symphoniker

0947/ 4 september 1955/radio ddr recording of re-opening performance in staatsoper unter den linden/**franz konwitschny**/staatsopernchor/ruth keplinger, soprano; annelies müller, contralto; erich witte, tenor; gerhard unger, tenor; josef herrmann, bass-baritone; heinrich pflanzl, bass; gerhard niese, baritone; theo adam, bass-baritone; walter grossmann, bass
wagner die meistersinger von nürnberg
cd issue: walhall WLCD 0234

0948/ 17 september 1955/radio ddr recording of concert in staatsoper unter den linden/**franz konwitschny**/david oistrakh, violin
mozart violin concerto no 5 in a k219; bach violin concerto in e bwv1042; brahms violin concerto in d op 77; beethoven violin romance no 2
cd issue: weitblick SSS 00172/SSS 00192

0949/ ca.1956/electrola session/**hans löwlein**/josef traxel, tenor
boieldieu la dame blanche: viens gentille dame!
2RA 7738 EH 1472
7739
orchestra described on this recording as berliner symphoniker

0950/ ca.1956/electrola lp sessions in grunewaldkirche/**wilhelm schüchter** rudolf schock, tenor
recital of orchestral songs by richard strauss
orchestra described on these recordings as berliner symphoniker

0951/4-11 march 1956/electrola sessions in berlin-zehlendorf/**wilhelm schüchter**
erika köth, soprano; josef traxel, tenor; marcel cordes, baritone
wagner tannhäuser: den bronnen den uns wolfram nannte; der fliegende holländer: mit gewitter und sturm
2RA 7709   EH 1469
    7730
verdi rigoletto: pari siamo; la traviata: di provenza al mar
2RA 7722   EH 1468
    7723
cd issue of verdi items: emi 574 2642
donizetti don pasquale: tornami a dir
2RA 7729   EH 1470
    7730
cd issue: emi 763 1382
mozart don giovanni: dalla sua pace; il mio tesoro
2RA 7731   EH 1471
    7732
orchestra described on these recordings as berliner symphoniker

0952/10-13 september 1956/electrola lp sessions in grunewaldkirche/**wilhelm schüchter**/chor der städtischen oper/josef traxel, tenor
recital of operatic arias by mozart, meyerbeer, verdi, ponchielli, leoncavallo, puccini and wagner
cd issue of pagliacci aria: emi 574 2682
orchestra described on these recordings as berliner symphoniker

0953/23-25 september 1956/electrola sessions in berlin-zehlendorf/
wilhelm schüchter/rudolf schock, tenor
kalman die zirkusprinzessin: zwei märchenaugen
2RA 7785   EH 1475
cd issue: emi 769 4752
künneke die lockende flamme: ich träumte mit offenen augen; die grosse sünderin: das lied vom leben des schrenk
cd issue of both items: emi 585 2862
operatic arias by puccini and giordano
cd issue: emi 769 1832
orchestra described on these recordings as berliner symphoniker

0954/october 1956/electrola lp session in rheingauschule/**wilhelm schüchter**
bizet carmen, four entr'actes
cd issue: emi 826 4342
orchestra described on these recordigs as berliner symphoniker

0955/9-10 november 1956/electrola lp sessions in berlin-zehlendorf/
wilhelm schüchter/chor der städtischen oper/lisa otto, soprano; anneliese rothenberger, soprano; josef traxel, tenor; manfred schmidt, baritone; hans pick, bass
zeller der vogelhändler, scenes from the operetta
cd issue: emi 575 1532
orchestra described on this recording as berliner symphoniker

0956/ca.1957/eterna lp session/**hans löwlein**/staatsopernchor/ hedwig müller-bütow, soprano; erna roscher, soprano; gertraud prenzlow, contralto; gerhard niese, baritone; günther gützloff, bass
gerster die hexe von passau, scenes from the opera
lp issue: 720 014

0957/ca.1957/eterna lp session/**wilhelm loibner**
mozart symphony no 39 in e flat k543
lp issue: 720 020

0958/30-31 january 1957/electrola lp sessions in grunewaldkirche/ **wilhelm schüchter**/chor der städtischen oper/erika köth, soprano; hertha töpper, contralto; rudolf schock, tenor; manfred schmidt, tenor; josef metternich, bass-baritone; gottlob frick, bass
donizetti lucia di lammermoor, scenes from the opera
cd issue: emi 826 4332
orchestra described on this recording as berliner symphoniker

0959/5 february 1957/electrola lp session in grunewaldkirche/**wilhelm schüchter**/erika köth, soprano; sieglinde wagner, contralto; marcel cordes, baritone; karl christian kohn, bass; walter stoll, bass
verdi rigoletto, scenes from the opera
cd issue: emi 574 2642
orchestra described on this recording as berliner symphoniker

0960/12 february 1957/electrola lp session in grunewaldkirche/ **wilhelm schüchter**/gottlob frick, bass
lortzing der wildschütz: fünftausend taler!; rossini il barbiere di siviglia: a un dottor della mia sorte
cd issues: emi 767 1872 (both arias) and testament SBT 1103 (rossini)
orchestra described on these recordings as berliner symphoniker

0961/14-15 february 1957/columbia lp sessions in grunewaldkirche/ **wilhelm schüchter**/chor der städtischen oper/helga hildebrand, soprano; hermann prey, baritone; karl christian kohn, bass
nessler der trompeter von säckingen, scenes from the singspiel; marschner hans heiling: an jenem tag
cd issue of all items: emi 918 4932
orchestra described on these recordings as berliner symphoniker

0962/2 march 1957/electrola lp session in grunewaldkirche/ **wilhelm schüchter**/rudolf schock, tenor
gounod faust: salut demeure; bizet les pecheurs de perles: je crois entendre encore
cd issue of bizet item: emi 767 1832
orchestra described on these recordings as berliner symphoniker

0963/3 march 1957/radio ddr recording of a performance in staatsoper unter den linden/**hans löwlein**/staatsopernchor/gisela behm, soprano; helge rosvaenge, tenor
puccini tosca, act three
cd issue: preiser 90103

0964/ 25-26 may 1957/electrola sessions in grunewaldkirche/**wilhelm schüchter/**chor der städtischen oper/erika köth, soprano; rudolf schock, tenor
lehar der zarewitsch and friederike, scenes from the operettas
cd issue: emi 575 1512
lehar der zarewitsch: wolgalied
2RA 7788   EH 1475
cd issue: emi 769 4752
orchestra described on these recordings as berliner symphoniker

0965/ 10-12 september 1957/electrola lp sessions in berlin-zehlendorf/ **wilhelm schüchter/**erika köth, soprano; helga hildebrand, soprano; rudolf schock, tenor; manfred schmidt, tenor
lehar das land des lächelns, scenes from the operetta
cd issue: emi 575 1512
orchestra described on this recording as berliner symphoniker

0966/ 3 october 1957/radio ddr recording of a performance in staatsoper unter den linden/**lovro von matacic**/sigrid ekkehard, soprano; hedwig müller-bütow, soprano; margarete klose, contralto; günther treptow, tenor; gerhard niese, baritone
strauss elektra   unpublished recording

0967/ 10 and 27 october 1957/electrola lp sessions in grunewaldkirche and berlin-zehlendorf respectively/**wilhelm schüchter/**erika köth, soprano; richard holm, tenor; hermann prey, baritone; gottlob frick, bass
rossini il barbiere di siviglia, scenes from the opera
cd issue: emi 826 4322
orchestra described on this recording as berliner symphoniker

0968/ 11 october 1957/electrola session in grunewaldkirche/ **wilhelm schüchter/**marcel cordes, baritone
giordano andrea chenier: nemico della patria?
cd issue: emi 574 2662
orchestra described on this recording as berliner symphoniker

0969/ 25-30 october 1957/columbia lp sessions in grunewaldkirche/ **leopold ludwig/**vladimir ashkenazy, piano
brahms piano concerto no 2 in b flat op 83
lp issues: columbia 33CX 1637 and angel 35649

0970/ 4 november 1957/columbia lp session in grunewaldkirche/ **martin mälzer/**hermann prey, baritone
kreutzer das nachtlager in granada: ein schütz bin ich; die nacht ist schön
cd issues: emi 575 5502 and 918 4932
orchestra described on these recordings as berliner symphoniker

0971/7-12 december 1957/electrola lp sessions/**werner schmidt-boelcke**
erika köth, soprano
donizetti don pasquale: son anchio la virtu magica
cd issue: emi 763 1382
orchestra described on this recording as berliner symphoniker

0972/ca.1958/electrola lp session/**wilhelm schüchter**
anneliese rothenberger, soprano
mozart die zauberflöte: ach ich fühl's
cd issue: emi 252 3492
orchestra described on this recording as berliner symphoniker

0973/26-27 february 1958/electrola lp sessions in grunewaldkirche/
wilhelm schüchter/ferdinand frantz, bass-baritone
borodin prince igor: no peace no rest; mussorgsky boris godunov: i have attained the highest power; wagner der fliegende holländer: die frist ist um
lp issue: E 70355

0974/march 1958/eterna lp session /**franz konwitschny**
igor oistrakh, violin
bach violin concerto in d minor bwv1052
cd issues: berlin classics BC 21302 and BC 02172

0975/4-8 march 1958/electrola lp sessions in grunewaldkirche/
wilhelm schüchter/staatsopernchor/melitta muszely, soprano; anneliese müller, contralto; rudolf schock, tenor; manfred schmidt, tenor; josef metternich, baritone; karl christian kohn, bass; wilhelm lang, bass
verdi la traviata, scenes from the opera
cd issue: emi 5/4 2672
orchestra described on this recording as berliner symphoniker

0976/13 march 1958/electrola lp session in grunewaldkirche/**arthur grüber**/erika köth, soprano; helga hildebrand, soprano; lore hoffmann, contralto
humperdinck hänsel und gretel, scenes from the opera
cd issue: emi 585 9802
orchestra described on this recording as berliner symphoniker

0977/19 september 1958/columbia lp session/**wilhelm schüchter**
hermann prey, baritone
gounod faust: avant de quitter ces lieux
cd issues: emi 769 5072 and 918 4932
orchestra described on this recording as berliner symphoniker

0978/23-26 september 1958/electrola lp sessions/**wilhelm schüchter/**
marcel cordes, baritone
offenbach les contes d'hoffmann: scintille diamant
cd issue: emi 574 2692
leoncavallo i pagliacci: si puo?
cd issue: emi 574 2662
orchestra described on these recordings as berliner symphoniker

0979/22 october 1958/electrola lp session in grunewaldkirche/
wilhelm schüchter/chor der städtischen oper
verdi aida: triumphal scene and ballet music
cd issues: emi 574 2632 and 574 7142
orchestra described on this recording as berliner symphoniker

0980/17 january 1959/electrola lp session in grunewaldkirche/**werner schmidt-boelcke/**chor der städtischen oper/erika köth, soprano; marcel cordes, baritone
verdi rigoletto: cortigiani!; chi e mai e qui in sua vece
cd issues: emi 574 2642 and 826 4312
orchestra described on these recordings as berliner symphoniker

0981/24-25 february 1959/electrola lp sessions in grunewaldkirche/
hans zanotelli/chor der städtischen oper/melitta muszely, soprano; sieglinde wagner, contralto; rudolf schock, tenor; manfred schmidt, tenor; josef metternich, baritone
verdi il trovatore, scenes from the opera
cd issue: emi 252 2182
orchestra described on this recording as berliner symphoniker

0982/27 february 1959/electrola lp session in grunewaldkirche/**berislav klobucar/**chor der städtischen oper/marlies siemeling, soprano; herbert henke, tenor; karl christian kohn, bass-baritone; gottlob frick, bass
verdi la forza del destino: il santo nome; la vergine degli angeli; don carlo: il grand' inquisitor!
cd issue of all items: emi 574 7142
orchestra described on these recordings as berliner symphoniker

0983/4-5 march 1959/electrola lp sessions in grunewaldkirche/
franz konwitschny /staatsopernchor; elisabeth grümmer, soprano; gottlob frick, bass
wagner tannhäuser: dich teure halle; entry of the guests; gar viel und schön; götterdämmerung: hier sitz' ich zur wacht; hoiho ihr gibichsmannen!
cd issues of götterdämmerung excerpts only: emi 565 2122 and testament SBT 1103

0984/ 10-11 march 1959/electrola lp sessions in grunewaldkirche/
rudolf kempe/ johanna blatter, mezzo-soprano; rut siewert, contralto; lisa otto, soprano; melitta muszely, soprano; sieglinde wagner, mezzo-soprano; rudolf schock, tenor; helmut melchert, tenor; ferdinand frantz, bass-baritone; josef metternich, baritone; benno kusche, bass-baritone
wagner das rheingold, scenes from the music drama
cd issues: emi 565 2122 and berlin classics 20352

0985/ 13 march 1959/electrola lp session/**berislav klobucar**
erika köth, soprano
mozart le nozze di figaro: deh vieni non tardar; voi che sapete
cd issue of both items: emi 763 1382
orchestra described on these recordings as berliner symphoniker

0986/ 17 april 1959/electrola lp session in grunewaldkirche/**berislav klobucar/** melitta muszely, soprano; rudolf schock, tenor
korngold die tote stadt: glück das mir verblieb; o freund ich werde sie nicht wiedersehen
cd issue of glück das mir verblieb: emi 767 1832
orchestra described on these recordings as berliner symphoniker

0987/ june 1959/electrola lp sessions in grunewaldkirche/**horst stein/** staatsopernchor/melitta muszely, soprano; rudolf schock, tenor; manfred schmidt, tenor; marcel cordes, baritone; josef metternich, bass-baritone
leoncavallo i pagliacci
cd issue: berlin classics BC 91022
orchestra described on this recording as berliner symphoniker

0988/ september 1959/columbia lp session/**berislav klobucar**
hermann prey, baritone
mozart le nozze di figaro: hai gia vinta la causa
cd issue: emi 918 4932
orchestra described on this recording as berliner symphoniker

0989/ 28-30 september 1959/electrola lp sessions in grunewaldkirche/**berislav klobucar/** chor der städtischen oper/lisa della casa, soprano; rudolf schock, tenor; josef metternich, bass-baritone; wilhelm strienz, bass
puccini tosca, scenes from the opera
cd issue: emi 252 3482
orchestra described on this recording as berliner symphoniker

0990/ 13-14 november 1959/electrola lp sessions in grunewaldkirche/**berislav klobucar/** chor der städtischen oper/helga hildebrand, soprano; fritz wunderlich, tenor; marcel cordes, baritone; ernst wiemann, bass-baritone; gottlob frick, bass
lortzing zar und zimmermann, scenes from the singspiel
cd issue: emi 252 2212
orchestra described on this recording as berliner symphoniker

0991/19 november 1959/radio ddr recording in haus des rundfunks/
hans knappertsbusch
wagner götterdämmerung: siegfried's rhine journey and funeral march;
tristan und isolde: prelude and liebestod; die meistersinger von nürnberg overture
cd issue: dynamic IDIS 6569

0992/1960/deutsche grammophon lp recording/**horst stein**/staatsopernchor/
kinderchor der komischen oper/stefania woytowicz, soprano; sandor konya,
tenor; kim borg, bass; günter leib, bass-baritone
puccini tosca
cd issue: berlin classics BC 91172

0993/1960/electrola lp sessions/**berislav klobucar/**josef traxel, tenor
recital of operatic arias by handel, weber, donizetti and wagner
orchestra decribed on this recording as berliner symphoniker

0994/27 january-17 february 1960/electrola lp sessions in grunewaldkirche/
karl forster/chor der hedwigs-kathedrale/elisabeth grümmer, soprano;
josef traxel, tenor; gottlob frick, bass
haydn die schöpfung
cd issue: emi 762 5952
orchestra described on this recording as berliner symphoniker

0995/1-3 february 1960/electrola lp sessions in grunewaldkirche/**hans
zanotelli/**chor der städtischen oper/elisabeth grümmer, soprano;
hildegard hillebrecht, soprano; erika köth, soprano; fritz wunderlich,
tenor; hermann prey, baritone; thomas stewart, baritone; ernst
wiemann, bass-baritone; karl christian kohn, bass
mozart don giovanni, scenes from the opera
cd issue: emi 252 2172
orchestra described on this recording as berliner symphoniker

0996/15-20 february 1960/electrola lp sessions in grunewaldkirche/
franz konwitschny/staatsopernchor/marianne schech, soprano;
sieglinde wagner, mezzo-soprano; rudolf schock, tenor; fritz wunderlich,
tenor; dietrich fischer-dieskau, baritone; gottlob frick, bass
wagner der fliegende holländer
cd issues: berlin classics BC 02322, BC 20972 and BC 32922

0997/15-16 may 1960/electrola sessions in grunewaldkirche/**berislav
klobucar/**chor der städtischen oper/anneliese rothenberger, soprano;
hetty plümacher, mezzo-soprano; fritz wunderlich, tenor;
gottlob frick, bass
flotow martha, scenes from the opera
cd issue: emi 252 2152
orchestra described on this recording as berliner symphoniker

0998/8-10 june 1960/electrola lp sessions/**karl forster**/chor der hedwigs-kathedrale/pilar lorengar, soprano; betty allen, mezzo-soprano; josef traxel, tenor; josef greindl, bass
rossini stabat mater
cd issue: emi 568 5532
orchestra described on this recording as berliner symphoniker

0999/13-14 september 1960/electrola lp sessions in grunewaldkirche/ **horst stein**/chor der städtischen oper/hildegard hillebrecht, soprano; pilar lorengar, soprano; betty allen, mezzo-soprano; rudolf schock, tenor; gottlob frick, bass
verdi aida: possente ftha....fu la sorte (temple scene)
cd issue: emi 574 7142
orchestra described on this recording as berliner symphoniker

1000/14 october 1960/radio ddr recording of a concert in staatsoper unter den linden/**franz konwitschny**/david oistrakh, violin
beethoven violin concerto in d op 61
cd issue: weitblick SSS 00182

1001/17-21 october 1960/electrola lp sessions in grunewaldkirche/ **franz konwitschny**/staatsopernchor/elisabeth grümmer, soprano; marianne schech, soprano; lisa otto, soprano; hans hopf, tenor; fritz wunderlich, tenor; gerhard unger, tenor; dietrich fischer-dieskau, bass-baritone; gottlob frick, bass
wagner tannhäuser
cd issues: emi 763 2142 and 096 5502

1002/28 october 1960/radio ddr recording of a concert in staatsoper unter den linden/**franz konwitschny**
brahms symphony no 4 in e minor op 98
cd issue: weitblick SSS 00092

1003/6-8 december 1960/electrola lp sessions in grunewaldkirche/ **horst stein**/chor der städtischen oper/marlies siemeling, soprano; lisa otto, soprano; rut siewert, contralto; rudolf schock, tenor; marcel cordes, baritone; peter roth-ehrang, bass
verdi un ballo in maschera, scenes from the opera
cd issue: emi 252 2162
orchestra described on this recording as berliner symphoniker

1004/24 march 1961/radio ddr recording of a concert in staatsoper unter den linden/**franz konwitschny**/ricardo odnoposoff, violin
paganini violin concerto no 1; tchaikovsky symphony no 4 in f minor op 36
cd issue: weitblick SSS 00082

1005/april 1961/electrola lp sessions in grunewaldkrche/**berislav klobucar**/chor der komischen oper/pilar lorengar, soprano; sieglinde wagner, mezzo-soprano; fritz wunderlich, tenor; georg baumgartner, tenor; hermann prey, baritone
puccini madama butterfly, scenes from the opera
cd issue: emi 575 5532
orchestra described on this recording as berliner symphoniker

1006/june 1961/electrola lp sessions in grunewaldkirche/**berislav klobucar**/chor der komischen oper/anneliese rothenberger, soprano; ruth-margret pütz, soprano; fritz wunderlich, tenor; georg völker, baritone; gottlob frick, bass
puccini la boheme, scenes from the opera
cd issue: emi 252 2132
orchestra described on this recording as berliner symphoniker

1007/june 1961/electrola lp sessions in grunewaldkirche/**berislav klobucar**/chor der städtischen oper/ruth-margret pütz, soprano; hildegard hillebrecht, soprano; pilar lorengar, soprano; sieglinde wagner, mezzo-soprano; rudolf schock, tenor; marcel cordes, baritone; karl-ernst mercker, bass-baritone
offenbach les contes d'hoffmann, scenes from the opera
cd issue: emi 252 2142
orchestra described on this recording as berliner symphoniker

1008/june 1961/electrola lp sessions in grunewaldkirche/**berislav klobucar**/chor der komischen oper/pilar lorengar, soprano; ruth-margret pütz, soprano; fritz wunderlich, tenor; gottlob frick, bass
thomas mignon, scenes from the opera
cd issue: emi 252 3832
orchestra described on this recording as berliner symphoniker

1009/june 1961/deutsche grammophon lp sessions/**alberto erede**
staatsopernchor/kinderchor der komischen oper/pilar lorengar, soprano; rita streich, soprano; sandor konya, tenor; horst günter, baritone; dietrich fischer-dieskau, baritone
puccini la boheme
cd issue: deutsche grammophon 447 8322

1010/june-september 1961/electrola lp sessions in grunewaldkirche/ **karl forster**/chor der hedwigs-kathedrale/elisabeth grümmer, soprano; lisa otto, soprano; christa ludwig, contralto; fritz wunderlich, tenor; josef traxel, tenor; dietrich fischer-dieskau, baritone; karl christian kohn, bass
bach johannes-passion bwv 245
cd issue: emi 764 2342
orchestra described on this recording as berliner symphoniker

1011/september 1961/columbia lp sessions in grunewaldkirche/ **horst stein**/chor der städtischen oper/christa ludwig, contralto; melitta muszely, soprano; rudolf schock, tenor; hermann prey, baritone; iwan rebroff, bass
bizet carmen
orchestra described on this recording as berliner symphoniker

1012/october-november 1961/columbia lp sessions/**horst stein** hermann prey, baritone
recital of german operatic arias by mozart, kreutzer, marschner, lortzing, wagner, nessler, humperdinck and korngold
cd issue: emi 918 4932
orchestra described on this recording as berliner symphoniker

1013/12 november 1961/electrola lp session in berlin-zehlendorf/ **karl forster**/chor der hedwigs-kathedrale/erika köth, soprano; annelies kupper, soprano; fritz wunderlich, tenor; dietrich fischer-dieskau, baritone
bach cantata no 208 "was mir behagt ist die muntere jagd"
cd issue: emi 565 7292
orchestra described on this recording as berliner symphoniker

1014/1962/electrola lp sessions/**karl forster**/chor der hedwigs-kathedrale/ pilar lorengar, soprano; christa ludwig, contralto; josef traxel, tenor; walter berry, bass-baritone
bruckner mass no 3 in f minor
orchestra described on this recording as berliner symphoniker

1015/1962/electrola lp sessions/**karl forster**/chor der hedwigs-kathedrale/ pilar lorengar, soprano; agnes giebel, soprano; marga höffgen, contralto; josef traxel, tenor; karl christian kohn, bass
mozart masses in c k317 "krönungsmesse" and in c k220 "spatzenmesse"
orchestra described on these recordings as berliner symphoniker

1016/1962/electrola lp sessions/**karl forster**/chor der hedwigs-kathedrale/ ruth-margret pütz, soprano; karl christian kohn, bass
handel judas maccabaeus and messiah, selections from the oratorios
orchestra described on these recordings as berliner symphoniker

1017/1962/electrola lp session/**karl forster**/chor der hedwigs-kathedrale
schubert deutsche messe in f d872
orchestra described on this recording as berliner symphoniker

1018/january-march 1962/columbia lp sessions in grunewaldkirche/
horst stein/christa ludwig, contralto; hermann prey, baritone
gluck orfeo ed euridice: che faro; handel giulio cesare: v'adoro pupille
cd issues: emi 764 0472 (ludwig) and 918 4932 (prey)
orchestra described on these recordings as berliner symphoniker

index of conductors
numbers refer to the recording sessions and are not page numbers

hermann abendroth/1883-1956
0766   0783   0913

erwin baltzer
0819   0840

carl besl
0055   0056   0057   0061   0064   0066

leo blech/1871-1958
0001   0004   0005   0013   0183   0205   0207   0209   0211   0212
0213   0215   0218   0228   0239   0240   0242   0245   0246   0260
0267   0268   0269   0270   0271   0272   0273   0274   0275   0277
0279   0281   0283   0285   0286   0288   0290   0295   0296   0297
0298   0299   0302   0305   0307   0314   0316   0322   0328   0341
0364   0369   0372   0377   0379   0380   0384   0386   0396   0403
0411   0413   0419   0420   0425   0431   0441   0445   0448   0455
0457   0458   0462   0467   0468   0472   0496   0511   0514   0517
0520   0523   0537   0544   0547   0548   0557   0560   0561   0576
0587   0615   0617   0618   0638   0640   0641   0642   0643   0662
0665   0666   0680   0700   0703   0704   0705   0706   0707   0708
0709   0714   0722   0726   0728   0737

artur bodanzky/1877-1939
0282   0373   0387   0389   0423   0426   0531   0532   0538

paul breisach/1896-1952
0112   0154

fritz busch/1890-1951
0434

albert coates/1882-1953
0574

otto dobrindt/1886-1963
0247   0539   0647   0677   0904

issay dobrowen/1891-1953
0516   0563   0567

werner eisbrenner/1908-1981
0910

alberto erede/1908-2001
1009

max fiedler/1859-1939
0602

dirk fock/1886-1973
0185

karl forster/1904-1963
0994   0998   1010   1013   1014   1015   1016   1017

oskar fried/1871-1941
0042   0051   0093   0102   0129   0170   0174   0184   0203   0232
0233   0318   0331   0475

wilhelm furtwängler/1886-1954
0890

paul graener/1872-1944
0735
see further entry in late addition section

index of conductors / continued

arthur grüber / born 1910
0838   0845   0871   0875   0976

manfred gurlitt / 1890-1972
0312   0324   0327   0336   0354   0357   0370   0478   0479   0487
0488   0521   0679

ernst hauke
0398   0405   0412   0435   0569

siegmund von hausegger / 1872-1948
0166

robert heger / 1886-1978
0724   0734   0746   0758   0760   0792   0803   0810   0813   0826
0835   0848   0859   0866   0867   0868   0869   0870   0873   0874
0876
see further entry in late addition section

johannes heidenreich
0049   0058   0065   0111   0147

georg hoeberg / 1872-1950
0137

willem van hoogstraten / 1884-1965
0674

armas järnefelt / 1869-1958
0555

herbert von karajan / 1908-1989
0817   0820   0823   0843   0844   0880   0882   0886

joseph keilberth / 1908-1968
0808   0906   0908   0909

rudolf kempe / 1910-1976
0984

paul van kempen / 1893-1955
0862
see further entry in late addition section

alexander kitschin
0489

erich kleiber / 1890-1956
0041   0060   0077   0103   0164   0175   0179   0186   0201   0202
0204   0213a   0231   0258a   0315   0338   0365a   0429   0477   0502
0513   0625   0942

otto klemperer / 1885-1973
0104   0125   0145   0189   0236   0276   0348   0399   0545   0551
0570   0650

berislav klobucar / born 1924
0982   0985   0986   0988   0989   0990   0993   0997   1005   1006
1007   1008

hans knappertsbusch / 1888-1965
0126   0355   0422   0583   0597   0699   0991

franz konwitschny / 1902-1962
0933   0939   0941   0947   0948   0974   0983   0996   1000   1001
1002   1004

index of conductors / continued

clemens krauss / 1893-1954
0691   0747   0748   0749   0760a

eduard künneke / 1885-1953
0727   0739

matthieu lange / 1905-1992
0936

franz lehar / 1870-1948
0584

fritz lehmann / 1904-1956
0832   0842   0846   0872

wilhelm loibner / 1909-1971
0957

hans löwlein / born 1909
0949   0956   0963

leopold ludwig / 1908-1979
0847   0892   0893   0895   0896   0897   0898   0899   0900   0901
0969
see further entry in late addition section

martin mälzer
0970

franz marszalek / 1900-1976
0788
see further entry in late addition section

wolfgang martin
0740   0743   0750   0761

pietro mascagni / 1863-1945
0292   0293
see further entry in late addition section

lovro von matacic / 1899-1985
0966

alois melichar / 1896-1976
0651   0652   0655   0669   0670   0683   0684   0686   0689   0710
0718   0720   0727   0732   0741   0742   0762   0804   0807   0811
see further entry in late addition section

reinhold merten / 1894-1943
0841

selmar meyrowitz / 1875-1941
0589   0610   0682

eduard mörike / 1877-1929
0006   0007   0008   0009   0010   0011   0012   0014   0015   0017
0019   0021   0022   0023   0025   0026   0028   0029   0030   0031
0032   0037   0039   0040   0067   0073   0074   0083   0092   0100
0109   0118   0136   0137   0151   0153   0178   0223   0229   0250
0265   0278   0335   0367   0424   0452

karl muck / 1859-1940
0321   0395   0440

index of conductors/continued

hans udo müller
0731 0774 0839 0858

edmund nick/1891-1974
0717

klaus nettstraeter/1887-1952
0347

erich orthmann
0646 0661 0664 0667 0678 0681 0775 0854

hansgeorg otto
0767

hans pfitzner/1869-1949
0079 0169 0194 0234 0337 0476 0601 0687 0818
see further entry in late addition section

julius prüwer/1874-1943
0332 0480 0490 0653

ernst röhmer/1893-1974
0492

hans rosbaud/1895-1962
0765 0782

joseph rosenstock/1895-1985
0529 0552

ludwig roth
0715

artur rother/1885-1972
0773 0781 0849 0852 0853 0855 0856 0857 0889 0907
0912

hugo rüdel/1868-1934
0220 0461

franz schalk/1863-1931
0343

hermann scherchen/1891-1966
0911

max von schillings/1868-1933
0016 0052 0078 0127 0235 0317 0323 0376 0437 0469
0522 0534 0546 0575 0585 0698

hans schindler/1889-1974
0769

clemens schmalstich/1880-1960
0409 0438 0504 0505 0524 0571 0581 0582 0592 0613
0618 0623 0626 0636 0639 0648 0663 0675 0693

franz alfred schmidt
0676 0685 0697 0745 0776 0796

karl schmidt
0888 0931

werner schmidt-boelcke/1903-1985
0971 0980

hans schmidt-isserstedt/1900-1973
0725 0768 0794

index of conductors/ continued

frederik schnedler-petersen/1867-1938
0138

fritz schönbaumsfeld
0721 0723 0730

franz schreker/1878-1934
0119 0191 0304

wilhelm schüchter/1911-1974
0914 0915 0916 0917 0918 0919 0920 0921 0922 0923
0924 0925 0926 0927 0928 0929 0930 0931 0943 0944
0945 0946 0950 0951 0952 0953 0954 0955 0958 0959
0960 0961 0962 0964 0965 0967 0968 0972 0973 0975
0977 0978 0979
see further entry in late addition section

johannes schüler/1894-1966
0690 0770 0771 0772 0784 0785 0787 0837 0860 0883
0891 0894 0898 0905
see further entry in late addition section

georg schumann/1866-1952
0418 0465

carl schuricht/1880-1967
0493

walter schütze
0711 0712

bruno seidler-winkler/1880-1960
0319 0733 0736 0738 0744 0751 0752 0753 0754 0755
0756 0757 0759 0763 0764 0777 0778 0779 0780 0789
0790 0791 0799 0800 0801 0802 0805 0806 0809 0812
0815 0816 0821 0822 0825 0827 0829 0830 0831 0834
0850 0861 0863 0864
see further entry in late addition section

joseph snaga/1871-1946
0339 0340

gerhard steeger
0797 0798 0824 0828 0833 0836
see further entry in late addition section

horst stein/1928-2008
0935 0938 0987 0992 0999 1003 1011 1012 1018

william steinberg/1899-1978
0474

hanns steinkopf
0851 0865

fritz stiedry/1883-1968
0034 0035 0473 0562 0594

richard strauss/1864-1949
0002 0192 0195 0214 0258 0333 0553 0634 0692

george szell/1897-1970
0091 0141 0142 0152 0182 0187 0199 0219 0221 0222
0224 0226 0230 0238 0243 0256

eugen szenkar/1891-1977
0410

index of conductors/concluded

michael taube/1890-1972
0198   0388

helmut thierfelder
0146

ernst viebig/1897-1959
0193	0206	0251	0254	0262	0362

siegfried wagner/1869-1930
0120a	0123	0139	0189	0208	0227	0244	0257

bruno walter/1876-1962
0128   0495

hermann weigert/1890-1955
0084	0085	0086	0087	0088	0095	0097	0106	0107	0108
0171	0173	0326	0397	0407	0414	0421	0481	0482	0483
0484	0485	0486	0599	0600	0603	0604	0605	0606	0607
0608	0609	0654	0657	0658	0659	0660	0688	0696	0795

see further entry in late addition section

frieder weissmann/1893-1984
0024	0027	0033	0036	0038	0043	0044	0045	0046	0047
0048	0053	0054	0062	0063	0068	0069	0071	0075	0076
0082	0090	0098	0099	0101	0105	0110	0115	0117	0121
0124	0130	0132	0133	0134	0143	0148	0149	0150	0156
0157	0158	0160	0163	0168	0176	0177	0180	0181	0190
0196	0200	0210	0216	0217	0225	0237	0241	0248	0252
0255	0263	0266	0280	0287	0289	0291	0294	0303	0306
0309	0311	0313	0320	0325	0329	0334	0344	0345	0349
0350	0351	0353	0358	0360	0361	0363	0366	0368	0371
0374	0375	0378	0381	0382	0383	0385	0390	0391	0392
0394	0400	0401	0404	0406	0408	0415	0416	0417	0427
0428	0430	0432	0433	0436	0439	0442	0443	0444	0447
0449	0450	0451	0453	0454	0456	0459	0460	0463	0464
0466	0470	0471	0491	0494	0497	0498	0499	0500	0501
0506	0507	0508	0509	0510	0512	0515	0518	0519	0525
0526	0527	0528	0530	0533	0535	0536	0541	0542	0543
0549	0554	0556	0559	0564	0565	0572	0573	0577	0578
0580	0586	0591	0593	0596	0598	0611	0612	0614	0616
0620	0621	0622	0624	0627	0628	0629	0630	0632	0633
0635	0645								

bruno weyersberg
0018	0096	0114	0122	0131

walter wohllebe/1899-1965
0059

meinhard von zallinger/1897-1990
0932	0934	0937	0940

hans zanotelli/1927-1993
0981   0995

fritz zaun/1893-1966
0673	0694	0695	0701	0702	0713	0716

heinz gerhard zilcher
0879

fritz zweig/born 1893
0249	0253	0261	0264	0308	0310	0346	0352	0356	0365
0649	0668	0671	0672						

late additions to the discography

these have not been allocated session numbers and are not included in the index of conductors

1931/grammophon session/**hans pfitzner**
pfitzner die rose vom liebesgarten: trauermarsch
325bi 66557
326 ½ bi
pfitzner palestrina, act one prelude
1148 ½ bi I 95459
1149 bi I
pfitzner palestrina, act three prelude
1150 ½ bi I 95461
1151 bi I
pfitzner palestrina, act two prelude
1152 bi I 95460
1153 bi I

undated grammophon sessions/**pietro mascagni**
mascagni cavalleria rusticana intermezzo; verdi aida ballet music
350 ½ bi 66584
539bg
mascagni iris: hymn to the sun; guglielmo ratcliff intermezzo
351 ½ bi 66580
352bi
353bi 66583
537bg
mascagni vision lyrique; amico fritz intermezzo
535bg 66585
536bg

undated grammophon session/**robert heger**
johann strauss morgenblätter waltz
538bm 15122
539bm

212

late additions/ continued

1932-1938/grammophon sessions/**alois melichar**

suppe leichte kavallerie overture
237 ½ br I   27179/10027/decca PO 5040
238br I
smetana the bartered bride overture
595 ½ gs VIII   15103/decca CA 8232
601gs VIII
reger ballettsuite op 130: valse d'amour
620 ½ be I   95396
this item was issued as fill-up to the richard strauss recording of bürger als edelmann (see 20-28 june 1930)
tchaikovsky capriccio italien; evgeny onegin polonaise
644go I   27221
645go I
646go I   27222
647go I
mussorgsky-ravel pictures from an exhibition
649 go I   15448
650 go I
651 go I   15449
652 go I
653 go I   15450
654 go I
655 go I   15451
mascagni cavalleria rusticana, potpourri
657 ½ gs I   57069
658 ½ gs I
johann strauss rosen aus dem süden; frühlingsstimmen
772 gs VIII   15177
773 gs VIII
suppe die schöne galathea overture
899gs VIII   15210/decca LY 6143
900gs VIII
josef strauss delirienwalzer
989bi I   27204
990 ½ bi I
verdi aida: triumphal march
1072 gs IX   68395/27234
1104 gs IX
tchaikovsky romeo and juliet
1125 ½ bi I   27251
1126 ½ bi I
1127 ½ bi I   27252
1156 ½ bi I
flotow martha overture
1133bi I   27244/decca LY 6068
1134bi I

213

late additions / melichar / continued

verdi il trovatore, potpourri
1136bi I   27245
1137bi I
liszt hungarian rhapsody no 2 in c sharp minor
1138ge IX   15364/decca LY 6005
1139ge IX
puccini madama butterfly, orchestral fantasy
1195bi I   27267/10002/decca LY 6015
1196 ½ bi I
popy suite orientale
1213bi I   27273
1214 ½ bi I
glazunov concert waltz
1220 ½ bi I   27279/decca LY 6002
1221 ½ bi I
potpourri from verdi operas
1228 ½ bi I   27281/decca LY 6034
1229 ½ bi I
rossini guilleaume tell overture
2654 ¾ bh I   10128/decca PO 5074
2611 ½ bh
2612 ½ bh I   10129/decca PO 5075
2613bh I
johann strauss der zigeunerbaron, potpourri
2656 ½ bh I   23912
2657 ½ bh I
suppe dichter und bauer overture
2704 bh I   24234/decca PO 5030
2705 bh I
waldteufel espana waltz
2773 bh I   24149/decca PO 5034
2774 bh I
glinka kamarinskaya
2859 bh I   10196/decca LY 6056
2860 bh I
verdi rigoletto, potpourri
2918 bh I   24270/41142
2919 bh I
thomas mignon, potpourri
2920 bh I   24443/decca PO 5049
2921 bh I
heuberger der opernball overture
2965 ½ gn VIII   47053/decca DE 7066
2966 ½ gn VIII

late additions/ melichar/ concluded
puccini la boheme, potpourri
3031 bh I   24441
3032 bh I
melichar had previously recorded the same selection with orchester der stadtischen oper
richard strauss zwei militärmärsche für grosses orchester
3065 bh I   25090
3066 bh I
suppe ein morgen ein mittag und ein abend in wien overture
3078 ½ bh I   24595/decca PO 5051
3079 bh I
puccini tosca, potpourri
3177 ½ bh I   24799
3178 ½ bh I
wagner tannhäuser, potpourri
5153 bd VIII   25101
5154 bd VIII
liszt hungarian rhapsody no 1 in f
6161 br   27253
6162 br
lubomirsky danse orientale
                                    10457

waldteufel estudianita waltz
                                    24148/decca PO 5006

grothe-melichar symphonic waltz
                                    decca PO 5090

die bajadere, potpourri
                                    25022

elgar pomp and circumstance, marches nos 1 and 2
                                    25070

zeller der vogelhändler, potpourri
                                    25160

berte das dreimädlerhaus, potpourri
                                    25187

sousa marches: stars and stripes; high school cadets
                                    25272

strauss der rosenkavalier: act three waltzes
                                    57065

meyerbeer les huguenots, selection
                                    decca LY 6027

late additions / continued

undated grammophon sessions / **franz marszalek**
künneke der vetter aus dingsda, potpourri
725 ½ gs I   57089
726 ½ gs I
lehar paganini, potpourri
764 ½ gs I   15164
765 ½ gs I
lehar das land des lächelns, potpourri
779 ¾ gs VIII   15172
780 ½ gs I
künneke glückliche reise, potpourri
812 ½ gs I   15178
813 ½ gs I

undated grammophon session / **hermann weigert**
bizet carmen: act two ballet and act four prelude
953 ½ bi   27191
954 bi I

1938 / grammophon sessions / **leopold ludwig**
johann strauss kaiserwalzer
699 go I   15199
700 go I
wagner rienzi overture; lohengrin act three prelude
723 go I   15192
724 go I
725 go I   15193
726 go I
wagner die meistersinger von nürnberg: dance of the apprentices and entry of the masters
831 gs I   15198
832 gs I
reznicek donna diana overture; weber abu hassan overture
858 gs I   15213
819 gs I

1939 / electrola session / **bruno seidler-winkler** / margherita perras, soprano
mozart die entführung aus dem serail: ach ich liebte
2RA 8684   DB 4439 / victor 12007
cd issue: nimbus NI 7848

late additions/continued

1940/grammophon sessions/**leopold ludwig**
d'albert tiefland, sinfonisches vorspiel
996 ge IX   15486/57149
997 ge IX
flotow alessandro stradella overture
998 ge IX   15485/57148
999 ge IX
puccini madama butterfly, intermezzo act three
1000 ge IX   15530
1001 ge IX
johann strauss czardas from ritter pasman; perpetuum mobile
1002 ge IX   15359
1003 ge IX

undated grammophon session/**wolfgang beutler**
ponchielli la gioconda, dance of the hours
1109 gs IX   15307
1110 gs IX
humperdinck hänsel und gretel overture
                     decca LY 6177

1943/grammophon sessions/**karl elmendorff**
wagner die walküre, walkürenritt und feuerzauber
1496 ge IX   67642
1497 ge IX
wagner götterdämmerung, siegfrieds rheinfahrt
1498 ge IX   67641
1499 ge IX
wagner siegfried, waldweben
1500 ge IX   67640
1501 ge IX
wagner das rheingold, einzug der götter in walhall
1502 ge IX   68430

1943/grammophon session/**paul van kempen**
nicolai die lustigen weiber von windsor, overture
1169 gs   15302
1170 gs
grieg symphonic dances
1505 ge IX   15491
1506 ge IX
1507 ge IX   15492
1508 ge IX

late additions/concluded

undated grammophon session/gerhard steeger
lortzing zar und zimmermann: holzschuhtanz
885 gr IX   26514

undated grammophon session/hans swarowsky
egk die zaubergeige, overture
                               26516

undated grammophon session/paul graener
graener schwedische tänze
8246 ½ gr IX   62811
8247 ½ gr IX

undated grammophon session/berthold lehmann
brahms hungarian dances no 1 in g minor and no 3 in f
10040 gd IX   62844
10041 gd IX

1948/electrola session/johannes schüler/josef greindl, bass
gounod faust: le veau d'or; vous qui faites l'endormie
ORA 6124   DA 5505
      6125

1950/electrola session/karl böhm
mozart eine kleine nachtmusik
2RA 6327   DB 11514
      6328
      6329   DB 11515
      6330

undated electrola lp session/wilhelm schüchter/gustav neidlinger, bass-baritone
wagner die walküre: leb wohl du kühnes herrliches kind
lp issue: electrola E 60053
orchestra described on this recording as berliner symphoniker

List of subscribers

This includes not only current subscribers but also those who have supported these discographies on an occasional basis over the past twenty-five years

Masakasu Abe
Stefano Angeloni
Yoshihiro Asada
Jack Atkinson
John Baker
Bruno Barthelme
Richard Benson
Reinier van Bevervoorde
J.M. Blyth
Michael Bral
Marc Bridle
J. Brookner
Roger Brown
Peter Buescher
Wes Burgar
George Burr
J. Camps-Ros
David Carroll
Javier Casellas
Eduardo Chibas
Robert Christoforides
A. Copeman
Brian Crowley
John Cutting
Dennis Davis
F. De Vilder
Erik Dervos
Robert Donaldson
Ronald Easdon
Hans-Peter Ebner
Shuntaro Enatsu
Bill Flowers
T. Foley
Gerhard Frenzel
Nobuo Fukumoto
Geoffrey Gammon
Guy Glenet
Jens Golumbus
Jean-Pierre Goossens
Gordon Grant
A. Greenburgh
Rev. Alan Haine
James Hansford
Tadashi Hasegawa
Christopher Herring
Naoya Hirabayashi
Martin Holland
John T. Hughes
Bodo Igesz
Kammersängerin Gundula Janowitz
Ernest Johnson

Richard Ames
Stathis Arfanis
Mike Ashman
Gary Bagnall
Andrew Barker
John Bartley
Derek Bevan
E.C. Blake
G.E. Bowen
Andreas Brandmair
Charles Brooke
Jonathan Brown
Stewart Brown
Gordon Buffard
Guy Burkill
J.A. Butler
Brian Capon
Ken Carter
J. Charrington
Siam Chowkwanyun
George Cobby
Prof. David Crighton
Richard Cumberland
Robert Dandois
Richard Dennis
Prof. John Derry
J. Dietz
Dr. Christopher Dowling
K. Eayrs
Dr Martin Elste
Gustav Fenyö
Henry Fogel
Andrew Fox
Peter Fu
Peter Fülop
James Giles
Brian Godfrey
Philip Goodman
N. Goulty
Johann Gratz
P. Hadoulis
Peter Hamann
Michael Harris
Hiromichi Hatta
Martin Hickley
Donald Hodgman
John Hughes
Chris Hunt
Richard Igler
T.M. Jensen
A.L. Jones

list of subscribers / continued

Dame Gwyneth Jones
Eugene Kaskey
Masahito Kawashima
Rodney Kempster
Koji Kinoshita
Eric Kobe
Waidi Kublawi
J-F. Lambert
John Larsen
Graham Lilley
Sylvia Loeb
Jean-Francois Longerstay
Norman MacDougall
Neil Mantle
Kevork Marouchian
Donald McIntosh
Donald Miller
Jean-Michel Molkhou
Philip Moores
William Moyle
Alessandro Nava
Coilin O'Broin
Ates Orga
Canon Gregory Page-Turner
Keith Parry
Laurence Pateman
John Pattrick
Brian Pearson
C. Pemberton
Johann Christian Petersen
Tully Potter
Peter Pogson
Phil Rees
Vivienne Rendall
Mavis Robinson
Valery Ryvkin
T. Scanes
Kammersängerin Elisabeth Schwarzkopf DBE
Tom Scragg
John Shackleton
Graham Silcock
Roger Smithson
Kazuhiko Soma
Rev, John Squire
Neville Sumpter
Ian Sutcliffe
Masashi Takenata
Arne Tingström
H.A. Van Dijk
Giovanna Visconti
Malcolm Walker
Dr Urs Weber
Hermann Wendel
Michael Wierer
Nigel Wood

Michael Jones
Shiro Kawai
Andrew Keener
Hisao Kimura
Detelf Kissmann
Kazuhiko Koma
Alan Lambert
Kathryn Lanford
Lanny Lewis
Tony Locantro
David Long
Ernst Lumpe
John Mallinson
Prof. Carlo Marinelli
Ryosuke Masuda
John Meriton
Finn Moeller Larsen
Jorge Monteiro Dos Santos
Bruce Morrison
Michael Naish
Alan Newcombe
Takaaki Omoto
Richard Osborne
Hugh Palmer
Jim Parsons
David Patmore
J.A. Payne
James Pearson
Linda Perkins
Sergi Petit
Donald Priddon
James Read
Gordon Reeves
Klaus Reuther
Patrick Russell
Yves Saillard
Ingo Schwarz
Robin Scott
David Selwyn
Clare Shepherd
Robert Simmons
Göran Söderwall
T. Spoors
Holger Steinhauff
Carl Suneson
Yoshihiko Suzuki
Dr Michael Tanner
Julian Tremayne
Dr Mario Vicentini
Hiromitsu Wada
Alan Warren
John Welson
Björn Westberg
John Willson
David Woodhead

list of subscribers/ concluded
Graeme Wright
Ken Wyman
T. Yamaguchi

Stephen Wright
Michiaki Yabuta
Ferenc Zemplenyi

Books published by Travis & Emery Music Bookshop:

Anon.: Hymnarium Sarisburiense, cum Rubricis et Notis Musicis.
Anon.: Säcularfeier des Geburtstages von Ludwig van Beethoven
Agricola, Johann Friedrich from Tosi: Anleitung zur Singkunst.
Allen, Percy: The Stage Life of Mrs. Stirling: With ... C19th Theatre
Bach, C.P.E.: edited W. Emery: Nekrolog or Obituary Notice of J.S. Bach.
Bateson, Naomi Judith: Alcock of Salisbury
Bathe, William: A Briefe Introduction to the Skill of Song
Berlioz, Hector: Autobiography of Hector Berlioz, (2 vols.)
Buckley, Robert John: Sir Edward Elgar
Burney, Charles: The Present State of Music in France and Italy
Burney, Charles: The Present State of Music in Germany, The Netherlands ...
Burney, Charles: Account of an Infant Musician
Burney, Charles: An Account of the Musical Performances ... Handel
Burney, Karl: Nachricht von Georg Friedrich Handel's Lebensumstanden.
Burns, Robert: The Caledonian Musical Museum .. Best Scotch Songs. (1810)
Cobbett, W.W.: Cobbett's Cyclopedic Survey of Chamber Music. (2 vols.)
Corrette, Michel: Le Maitre de Clavecin
Cox, John Edmund: Musical Recollections of the Last Half Century. (2 vols.)
Crimp, Bryan: Dear Mr. Rosenthal ... Dear Mr. Gaisberg ...
Crimp, Bryan: Solo: The Biography of Solomon
Crotch, William: Substance of Several Courses of Lectures on Music
d'Indy, Vincent: Beethoven: Biographie Critique
d'Indy, Vincent: Beethoven: A Critical Biography
d'Indy, Vincent: Cesar Franck (in English)
d'Indy, Vincent: César Franck (in French)
Dianna, B.A.: Benjamin Britten's Holy Theatre
Dolge, Alfred: Pianos and Their Makers. A Comprehensive History
Fischhof, Joseph: Versuch einer Geschichte des Clavierbaues. (Faksimile 1853).
Fuller-Maitland, J.A.: The Music of Parry and Stanford
Geminiani, Francesco: The Art of Playing the Violin.
Häuser: Musikalisches Lexikon. 2 vols in one.
Hawkins, John: A General History of the Science & Practice of Music (5 vols.)
Herbert-Caesari, Edgar: The Science and Sensations of Vocal Tone
Herbert-Caesari, Edgar: Vocal Truth
Holmes, Edward: A Ramble among the Musicians of Germany
Hopkins, Antony: The Concertgoer's Companion - Bach to Haydn.
Hopkins, Antony: The Concertgoer's Companion – Holst to Webern.
Hopkins, Antony: Music All Around Me
Hopkins, Antony: Sounds of Music / Sounds of the Orchestra
Hopkins, Antony: The Nine Symphonies of Beethoven
Hopkins, Antony: Understanding Music

Books published by Travis & Emery Music Bookshop:

Hopkins, Edward & Rimboult, Edward: The Organ. Its History & Construction.
Hunt, John: - see separate list of discographies at the end of these titles
Iliffe, Frederick: The Forty-Eight Preludes and Fugues of John Sebastian Bach
Isaacs, Lewis: Hänsel and Gretel. A Guide to Humperdinck's Opera.
Isaacs, Lewis: Königskinder (Royal Children). Guide to Humperdinck's Opera.
Kastner: Manuel Général de Musique Militaire
Kenney, Charles Lamb: A Memoir of Michael William Balfe
Klein, Hermann: Thirty years of musical Life in London, 1870-1900
Lacassagne, M. l'Abbé Joseph : Traité Général des élémens du Chant
Lascelles (née Catley), Anne: The Life of Miss Anne Catley.
McCormack, John: John McCormack: His Own Life Story.
Mainwaring, John: Memoirs of the Life of the Late George Frederic Handel
Malcolm, Alexander: A Treaty of Music: Speculative, Practical and Historical
Manshardt, Thomas: Aspects of Cortot
Marx, Adolph Bernhard: Die Kunst des Gesanges, Theoretisch-Practisch
May, Florence: The Life of Brahms
May, Florence: The Girlhood Of Clara Schumann: Clara Wieck And Her Time.
Mellers, Wilfrid: Angels of the Night: Popular Female Singers of Our Time
Mellers, Wilfrid: Bach and the Dance of God
Mellers, Wilfrid: Beethoven and the Voice of God
Mellers, Wilfrid: Caliban Reborn - Renewal in Twentieth Century Music
Mellers, Wilfrid: Darker Shade of Pale, A Backdrop to Bob Dylan
Mellers, Wilfrid: François Couperin and the French Classical Tradition
Mellers, Wilfrid: Harmonious Meeting
Mellers, Wilfrid: Le Jardin Retrouvé, The Music of Frederic Mompou
Mellers, Wilfrid: Music and Society, England and the European Tradition
Mellers, Wilfrid: Music in a New Found Land: ... ... American Music
Mellers, Wilfrid: Romanticism and the Twentieth Century (from 1800)
Mellers, Wilfrid: The Masks of Orpheus: ...... the Story of European Music.
Mellers, Wilfrid: The Sonata Principle (from c. 1750)
Mellers, Wilfrid: Vaughan Williams and the Vision of Albion
Newmarch, Rosa: Henry J. Wood
Newmarch, Rosa: Jean Sibelius
Newmarch, Rosa: Mary Wakefield, a Memoir
Newmarch, Rosa: The Concert-Goer's Library
Newmarch, Rosa: The Music of Czechoslovakia
Newmarch, Rosa: The Russian Opera.
Nicholas, Jeremy: Godowsky, the Pianists' Pianist
Niecks, Frederick: The Life oc Chopin. (2 vols.)
Panchianio, Cattuffio: Rutzvanscad Il Giovine

Books published by Travis & Emery Music Bookshop:

Pearce, Charles: Sims Reeves, Fifty Years of Music in England.
Pepusch, John Christopher: A Treatise on Harmony ...
Pettitt, Stephen: Philharmonia Orchestra: A Record of Achievement, 1948-1985
Pettitt, Stephen (ed. Hunt): Philharmonia Orchestra: Discography 1945-1987
Playford, John: An Introduction to the Skill of Musick.
Porte, John: Sir Charles Villiers Stanford.
Quantz, Johann: Versuch einer Anweisung die Flöte traversiere zu spielen.
Rameau, Jean-Philippe: Code de Musique Pratique, ou Methodes.
Rameau, Jean-Philippe: Erreurs sur La Musique dans l'Encyclopédie
Rastall, Richard: The Notation of Western Music.
Rimbault, Edward: The Pianoforte, Its Origins, Progress, and Construction.
Rousseau, Jean Jacques: Dictionnaire de Musique
Rubinstein, Anton : Guide to the proper use of the Pianoforte Pedals.
Sainsbury, John S.: Dictionary of Musicians. (1825). (2 vols.)
Schumann, Clara & Brahms, Johannes: Letters 1853-1896. (2 vols.)
Scott-Sutherland: Arnold Bax
Serré de Rieux, Jean de : Les dons des Enfans de Latone
Simpson, Christopher: A Compendium of Practical Musick in Five Parts
Smyth, Ethel: Impressions That Remained. (2 vols.)
Spohr, Louis: Autobiography
Spohr, Louis: Grand Violin School
Tans'ur, William: A New Musical Grammar; or The Harmonical Spectator
Terry, Charles Sanford: Bach's Chorals – Parts 1, 2 and 3.
Terry, Charles Sanford: John Christian Bach
Terry, Charles Sanford: J.S. Bach's Original Hymn-Tunes - Congregational Use.
Terry, Charles Sanford: Four-Part Chorals of J.S. Bach. (German & English)
Terry, Charles Sanford: Joh. Seb. Bach, Cantata Texts, Sacred and Secular.
Terry, Charles Sanford: The Origins of the Family of Bach Musicians.
Tosi, Pierfrancesco: Opinioni de' Cantori Antichi, e Moderni
Tosi, Pierfrancesco: Observations on the Florid Song.
Tovey, Donald Francis: A Musician Talks, The Integrity of Music
Tovey, Donald Francis: A Musician Talks, Musical Textures
Tovey, Donald Francis: A Companion to "The Art of the Fugue" J.S. Bach
Tovey, Donald Francis: A Companion to Beethoven's Pianoforte Sonatas
Tovey, Donald Francis: Beethoven
Tovey, Donald Francis: Essays in Musical Analysis. (6 vols.).
Tovey, Donald Francis: The integrity of music
Tovey, Donald Francis: Musical Textures

Books published by Travis & Emery Music Bookshop:

Tovey, Donald Francis: Some English Symphonists
Tovey, Donald Francis: The Main Stream of Music.
Van der Straeten, Edmund: History of the Violoncello, The Viol da Gamba ...
Van der Straeten, Edmund: History of the Violin, Its Ancestors... (2 vols.)
Walther, J. G. [Waltern]: Musicalisches Lexikon [Musikalisches Lexicon]
Wagner, Richard: Beethoven (Leipzig 1870)
Wagner, Richard: Lebens-Bericht (Leipzig 1884)
Wagner, Richard: The Musaic of the Future (Translated by E. Dannreuther).
Wyndham, Henry Saxe: The Annals of Covent Garden Theatre. (2 vols.)
Zwirn, Gerald: Stranded Stories From The Operas

Books Distributed by Travis & Emery Music Bookshop:

Herbert-Caesari, Edgar: The Alchemy of Voice

Music published by Travis & Emery Music Bookshop:

Bach, Johann Sebastian: Sacred Songs for SCTB, arranged by Franz Wullner.
Bax, Arnold: Symphony #5, Arranged for Piano Four Hands by Walter Emery
Beranger, Pierre Jean de: Musique Des Chansons de Beranger: Airs Notes ...
Bizet, Georges: Djamileh. Vocal Score.
Donizetti, Gaetano: Betly. Dramma Giocoso in Due Atti. Vocal Score.
Frescobaldi, Girolamo: D'Arie Musicali per Cantarsi. Primo & Secondo Libro.
Handel, Purcell, Boyce, Greene ... Calliope or English Harmony: Volume First.
Hopkins, Antony: Sonatine
Purcell, Henry et al: Harmonia Sacra ... The First Book, (1726)
Purcell, Henry et al: Harmonia Sacra ... Book II (1726)
Sullivan, Arthur Seymour: Ivanhoe. Vocal score.
Sullivan, Arthur Seymour: The Rose of Persia. Vocal Score.
Weckerlin, Jean-Baptiste: Chansons Populaires du Pays de France

Other Books, not on Music:

Anon: A Collection of Testimonies Concerning Several Ministers of the Gospel Amongst People called Quakers, Deceased. [Facsimile of 1760 edn.].
Sandeman-Allen, Arthur: Bee-keeping with Twenty hives.

Available from: Travis & Emery at 17 Cecil Court, London, UK.
(+44) (0) 20 7 240 2129. email on sales@travis-and-emery.com .

Discographies by John Hunt.

3 Italian Conductors and 7 Viennese Sopranos: 10 Discographies: Arturo Toscanini, Guido Cantelli, Carlo Maria Giulini, Elisabeth Schwarzkopf, Irmgard Seefried, Elisabeth Gruemmer, Sena Jurinac, Hilde Gueden, Lisa Della Casa, Rita Streich.

A Gallic Trio: 3 Discographies: Charles Muench, Paul Paray, Pierre Monteux.

A Notable Quartet: 4 Discographies: Gundula Janowitz, Christa Ludwig, Nicolai Gedda, Dietrich Fischer-Dieskau.

American Classics: The Discographies of Leonard Bernstein & Eugene Ormand

Antal Dorati 1906-1988: Discography and Concert Register.

Back From The Shadows: 4 Discographies: Willem Mengelberg, Dimitri Mitropoulos, Hermann Abendroth, Eduard Van Beinum.

Carlo Maria Giulini: Discography and Concert Register.

Columbia 33CX Label Discography.

Concert Hall Discography: Concert Hall Society and Concert Hall Record Club

Conductors On The Yellow Label: 8 Discographies: Fritz Lehmann, Ferdinand Leitner, Ferenc Fricsay, Eugen Jochum, Leopold Ludwig, Artur Rother, Franz Konwitschny, Igor Markevitch.

Dirigenten der DDR: Conductors of the German Democratic Republic

From Adam to Webern: the Recordings of von Karajan.

Frosh: Discography of the Richard Strauss Opera Die Frau ohne Schatten

Giants of the Keyboard: 6 Discographies: Wilhelm Kempff, Walter Gieseking, Edwin Fischer, Clara Haskil, Wilhelm Backhaus, Artur Schnabel.

Gramophone Stalwarts: 3 Separate Discographies: Bruno Walter, Erich Leinsdorf, Georg Solti.

Great Violinists: 3 Discographies: David Oistrakh, Wolfgang Schneiderhan, Arthur Grumiaux.

Hans Knappertsbusch: Kna: Concert Register and Discography of Hans Knappertsbusch, 1888 1965. Second Edition.

Her Master's Voice: Concert Register and Discography of Dame Elisabeth Schwarzkopf [Third Edition].

Hungarians in Exile: 3 Discographies: Fritz Reiner, Antal Dorati, George Szell.

Leopold Stokowski (1882-1977): Discography and Concert Register

Leopold Stokowski: Discography and Concert Listing.

Leopold Stokowski: Second Edition of the Discography.

Makers of the Philharmonia: 11 Discographies Alceo Galliera, Walter Susskind, Paul Kletzki, Nicolai Malko, Issay Dobrowen, Lovro Von Matacic, Efrem Kurtz, Otto Ackermann, Anatole Fistoulari, George Weldon, Robert Irving.

Metropolitan Sopranos: 4 Discographies: Rosa Ponselle, Eleanor Steber, Zinka Milanov, Leontyne Price.

Mezzo and Contraltos: 5 Discographies: Janet Baker, Margarete Klose, Kathleen Ferrier, Giulietta Simionato, Elisabeth Hoengen.

Mid-Century Conductors and More Viennese Singers: 10 Discographies: Karl Boehm, Victor De Sabata, Hans Knappertsbusch, Tullio Serafin, Clemens Krauss, Anton Dermota, Leonie Rysanek, Eberhard Waechter, Maria Reining, Erich Kunz.

More 20th Century Conductors: 7 Discographies: Eugen Jochum, Ferenc Fricsay, Carl Schuricht, Felix Weingartner, Josef Krips, Otto Klemperer, Erich Kleiber.

More Giants of the Keyboard: 5 Discographies: Claudio Arrau, Gyorgy Cziffra, Vladimir Horowitz, Dinu Lipatti, Artur Rubinstein.

More Musical Knights: 4 Discographies: Hamilton Harty, Charles Mackerras, Simon Rattle, John Pritchard.

Musical Knights: 6 Discographies: Henry Wood, Thomas Beecham, Adrian Boult, John Barbirolli, Reginald Goodall, Malcolm Sargent.

Philharmonic Autocrat 1: Discography of: Herbert Von Karajan [Third Edition]

Philharmonic Autocrat 2: Concert Register of Herbert Von Karajan Second Ed.

Philips Minigroove: Second Extended Version of the European Discography.

Pianists For The Connoisseur: 6 Discographies: Arturo Benedetti Michelangeli, Alfred Cortot, Alexis Weissenberg, Clifford Curzon, Solomon, Elly Ney.

Sächsische Staatskapelle Dresden: Complete Discography.

Singers of the Third Reich: 5 Discographies: Helge Roswaenge, Tiana Lemnitz, Franz Voelker, Maria Mueller, Max Lorenz.

Singers on the Yellow Label: 7 Discographies: Maria Stader, Elfriede Troetschel, Annelies Kupper, Wolfgang Windgassen, Ernst Haefliger, Josef Greindl, Kim Borg

Six Wagnerian Sopranos: 6 Discographies: Frieda Leider, Kirsten Flagstad, Astrid Varnay, Martha Moedl, Birgit Nilsson, Gwyneth Jones.

Staatskapelle Berlin. The shellac era 1916-1962.

Sviatoslav Richter: Pianist of the Century: Discography.

Teachers and Pupils: 7 Discographies: Elisabeth Schwarzkopf, Maria Ivoguen, Maria Cebotari, Meta Seinemeyer, Ljuba Welitsch, Rita Streich, Erna Berger

Tenors in a Lyric Tradition: 3 Discographies: Peter Anders, Walther Ludwig, Fritz Wunderlich.

The Art of the Diva: 3 Discographies: Claudia Muzio, Maria Callas, Magda Olivero.

The Furtwaengler Sound Sixth Edition: Discography and Concert Listing.

The Great Dictators: 3 Discographies: Evgeny Mravinsky, Artur Rodzinski, Sergiu Celibidache.

The Lyric Baritone: 5 Discographies: Hans Reinmar, Gerhard Huesch, Josef Metternich, Hermann Uhde, Eberhard Waechter.

The Post-War German Tradition: 5 Discographies: Rudolf Kempe, Joseph Keilberth, Wolfgang Sawallisch, Rafael Kubelik, Andre Cluytens.

Wagner Im Festspielhaus: Discography of the Bayreuth Festival.

Wiener Philharmoniker 1 - Vienna Philharmonic and Vienna State Opera Orchestras: Discography Part 1 1905-1954.

Wiener Philharmoniker 2 - Vienna Philharmonic and Vienna State Opera Orchestras: Discography Part 2 1954-1989.

Available from: Travis & Emery at 17 Cecil Court, London, UK.
(+44) (0) 20 7 240 2129. email on sales@travis-and-emery.com .

www.ingramcontent.com/pod-product-compliance
Lightning Source LLC
Chambersburg PA
CBHW071840230426
43671CB00012B/2020